W9-ADM-059

CHARLES LEE

RIVERGATE REGIONALS

Rivergate Regionals is a collection of books published by Rutgers University Press focusing on New Jersey and the surrounding area. Since its founding in 1936, Rutgers University Press has been devoted to serving the people of New Jersey, and this collection solidifies that tradition. The books in the Rivergate Regionals Collection explore history, politics, nature and the environment, recreation, sports, health and medicine, and the arts. By incorporating the collection within the larger Rutgers University Press editorial program, the Rivergate Regionals Collection enhances our commitment to publishing the best books about our great state and the surrounding region.

CHARLES LEE

Self Before Country

DOMINICK MAZZAGETTI

RUTGERS UNIVERSITY PRESS

NEW BRUNSWICK, NEW JERSEY, AND LONDON

Library of Congress Cataloging-in-Publication Data

Mazzagetti, Dominick A.

  Charles Lee : self before country / Dominick Mazzagetti.

    pages cm. — (Rivergate regionals)

  Includes bibliographical references and index.

  ISBN 978–0–8135–6237–7 (hardcover : alk. paper) — ISBN 978–0–8135–6238–4
(e-book)

  1. Lee, Charles, 1731–1782. 2. Generals—United States—Biography. 3. United
States—History—Revolution, 1775–1783—Biography. 4. United States—History—
Revolution, 1775–1783—Campaigns. I. Title.

  E207.L47M39 2013

  355.0092—dc23

  [B]

                                                            2013000421

A British Cataloging-in-Publication record for this book is available from the British
Library.

Visit our website: http://rutgerspress.rutgers.edu

Manufactured in the United States of America

For my Father

CONTENTS

PREFACE

In Greek mythology, references to the goddess Athena often identify her as "Pallas Athena," in recognition of her victory over the Titan Pallas in Zeus's battle for supremacy over the Titans. According to the tale, Athena stripped the skin from the dead Pallas and used it as a shield in the continuing fight. Images of Pallas Athena thereafter were displayed as talismatic guardians or shields, particularly the wooden image that stood before the walls of Troy, known as the "Palladium," which was believed to have been thrown down from the heavens by Zeus. Only after this statue was captured by Odysseus and Diomedes were the walls of Troy breached. In the eighteenth century, several British newspaper editors used the term to refer to Major General Charles Lee, especially after he was seized by British grenadiers at Basking Ridge, New Jersey, in 1776. This use of the word implied that Charles Lee represented a champion for a just cause and, perhaps, suggested that the capture of Charles Lee, who had taken up the cause of the thirteen American colonies in the fight against the strongest nation in the world, would signal a favorable outcome for Great Britain.

Charles Lee accepted this characterization. We know this because he refers to himself late in his life as the "American Palladium." This self-reference also reveals his singular personal trait, an ego that knew no bounds and countenanced no rivals. Even though few contemporaries in Europe shared Lee's own opinion of his merits, the Americans who met him after his arrival in New York City in 1773 accepted his personal history without question. As a result, Lee reached heights that might otherwise have been improbable, only to fall just as quickly from those heights. History has not been kind to Charles Lee, and for good reasons.

Lee was a man with "a waywardness of temper, a rashness of resolution, a license of speech, an eager ambition, and an eccentricity of manners," according to biographer Jared Sparks. All of Lee's early biographers felt the need to acknowledge his irascible nature before discussing his virtues and contributions to the American Revolution. The unfavorable court-martial verdict after the Battle of Monmouth in 1778 and Lee's tirades thereafter also made it difficult for these writers to praise Lee too loudly. Lee vilified George Washington in the years between his court-martial and his death in 1782. Washington loomed large on the American scene when Edward Langworthy wrote Lee's first biography in 1787, so much so that an effort to print Lee's papers in 1785 had received a cool reception. This effort would have to wait almost one hundred years and be completed under an even more damning view of Lee's life. Langworthy advanced the theory that Lee came to New York City in 1773 imbued with the essence of the American cause and ready to add his military experience in the fight. Lee's second biographer, Sir Henry Bunbury, provided a favorable view of his father's cousin, but added little to the facts of Lee's life not already covered by Langworthy. Indeed, some of the commentary must be viewed with suspicion, such as the baronet's discussion of Lee's capture at Basking Ridge in 1776: "[I]n his anxiety to procure intelligence he went out in person with a small reconnoitering party [and on] his return towards his camp, he halted for refreshment at a farm-house, and he was there surprised by Colonel Harcourt." A decade later, Jared Sparks added a workmanlike biography of Charles Lee as part of his *Library of American Biography* (1846). For the most part, the narrative remained the same.

The history surrounding Charles Lee changed dramatically in 1858. In that year, George Moore, librarian of the New-York Historical Society, delivered a lecture before the society that was printed as *The Treason of Charles Lee*. The lecture and book followed the discovery of a manuscript in Lee's hand, written eighty-one years earlier, "Mr. Lee's Plan," a detailed strategy for the defeat of the American colonies. Apparently, Lee had authored the plan and delivered it to the British during his captivity in New York City in 1777. Everything written after 1858 has had to contend with Moore's treatise and his vituperative assessment of Charles Lee as a man who deliberately betrayed the American cause. In the one hundred years that followed, only John Fiske attempted to deal with the enigma that was Charles Lee. He wrote a short and reasoned biography in 1902 that synthesized the previous works and dealt just briefly with Lee's newly acknowledged betrayal.

Modern biographies offer alternative views and explanations in an attempt to rehabilitate Charles Lee. Samuel White Patterson's 1958 biography, *Knight Errant of Liberty: The Triumph and Tragedy of General Charles Lee*, tries vainly to emphasize Lee's brilliance and courage and to explain away his shortcomings and failures. As a result, this work adds little to the historical record. John Alden's thorough biography in 1951 does a fine job of describing Lee's life and retelling his story, but Alden, like Patterson, refused to accept some of the truth about Lee. Add to these works Theodore Thayer's 1976 discussion of the Battle of Monmouth, *The Making of a Scapegoat: Washington and Lee at Monmouth*, which argues that Lee saved the day on June 28, 1778, preventing the loss of the entire Continental Army and the war in what was a foolish attempt by Washington to find a telling victory. I knew Professor Thayer as a student at Rutgers University in the late 1960s. He shared an office—the former living room of a brownstone on a side street in Newark, New Jersey—with Hubert G. Schmidt, another American history professor whom I assisted for four years as a work-study student. Professor Thayer could have been working on his book at the time, but I had no knowledge of Charles Lee then and could not have known that I would so disagree with his thesis so many years later.

All of the research on Charles Lee today begins with *The Lee Papers*, a four-volume collection of Lee's letters and writings compiled from 1871 to 1874 by the New-York Historical Society. Although not the entirety of Lee's letters, it contains a vast number collated from the originals, which were last known to be in the hands of William Goddard of Maryland in the early 1800s and have since been lost. Most of Lee's quotations in this volume come directly from this work. Lee's extensive references, Latin quotations, and colorful prose resonate throughout each volume as thoroughly as his self-conceit.

Charles Lee deserves a full modern review of his contributions to the American Revolution and his fall from grace. Did he sail to New York City in 1773 to personally assist the Americans in their struggle for liberty against the tyranny of George III? I do not think so. Although an outspoken critic of the Crown and an early supporter of American causes, it appears more likely that Charles Lee stumbled into the American cause in 1773 at the tail end of his meaningless travels throughout Europe and quickly realized that it could serve his ambition and ego. Unfortunately, he lacked the moral strength necessary for a commitment to any cause other than his own, or to any person who did not share his opinion of his own worth. Charles Lee deserves credit for his contributions to the American cause, both politically and militarily, but he served it for only a brief time and for only so long as his vanity allowed him.

ACKNOWLEDGMENTS

This work started many years ago, with my curiosity about the name of a town on the Palisades of New Jersey, Fort Lee. This curiosity blossomed into a full-fledged preoccupation with its namesake, Charles Lee, and his extraordinary life. My research and writing would have remained a hobby except for the good fortune to have time to pursue it further and for the assistance of many diligent librarians, including those at Rutgers University, Princeton University, the New Jersey State Library, the New York Historical Society, and the Clements Library, University of Michigan. The project moved from a personal manuscript to a possible book owing to the willingness of Marlie Wasserman of Rutgers University Press to talk to a new author/historian, review his work, and offer encouragement. That encouragement eventually led to an offer to publish. The accuracy and evenness of the final draft reflects the assistance of copy editor Beth Gianfanga.

CHARLES LEE

Major General Charles Lee, etching and engraving by Alexander Hay Ritchie after
B. Rushbrooke, 1840–1895.
Metropolitan Museum of Art, Bequest of Charles Allen Munn, 1924, 24.90.387.
Reproduced with permission from the Metropolitan Museum of Art, New York.

CHAPTER 1

THE FATEFUL CHOICE

George Washington's physical presence alone gave him the aura of command. At six feet two inches tall, he towered over many of the other delegates in Philadelphia, just as he had at the House of Burgesses in Williamsburg, Virginia. He stood erect and carried himself with confidence. John Adams, who dominated the debates in and outside of the chamber in which the Continental Congress was meeting, stood at only five feet seven inches tall. He discovered early in his work that Washington did not need to dominate the debates to gain the respect of his peers. Sure knowledge on those subjects he chose to discuss, quiet determination in his dedication to the cause, and a bearing that demanded attention served Washington's purpose.

No one appeared surprised, then, when Washington arrived in Philadelphia in full military uniform for the crucial deliberations in June 1775. The Boston men threatening the British troops garrisoned in their city needed a leader. Even Artemas Ward, the churchwarden who served that role for the Boston rebels, knew that someone with more military knowledge and leadership skills needed to relieve him soon from the difficult command he now held. Men on both sides lay dead. The "army" of rebels faced thousands of British regulars, with guns pointed nervously at one another in close quarters. The delegates arguing in Philadelphia would need another thirteen months to make the philosophical break with Great Britain. Military decisions would not wait that long. If the Continental Congress was to get the time it needed to bring itself to the breaking point, it had to appoint a commander in chief immediately to hold the British Army at bay. Washington knew that he was the leading contender for the position, and he would not let the moment slip past him for lack of boldness. His uniformed presence in the hall said so.

John Adams rose in the chamber. As always, he had shrewdly calculated the politics of his choice. He knew the strengths and weaknesses of each of the men who could be commander in chief. He also knew the importance of making the right choice. One man would hold command over an army of American colonials representing a weak and bickering authority. This would be the most fateful choice for this Congress. Adams glanced at John Hancock, presiding at the head of the assembled delegates. Hancock—of Massachusetts—saw himself as the man to lead those Boston rebels. And there were others. But Adams could see only one man, and he held the floor for that man.

George Washington.

THE ALTERNATIVES

The selection of George Washington in June 1775 as commander in chief of the American forces may appear today as the only logical choice. Washington had the military skills, he commanded the respect of the men he worked with, and he had demonstrated his zeal for the American cause over the past ten years of political strife. In John Adams's political calculations, Washington offered one more advantage. He was a southerner acceptable to the New England firebrands who were driving the political resistance into a military contest. Washington's appointment would broaden the fight and help solidify the fragile association of the colonies with representatives in Philadelphia. In fact, the choices available to the delegates were few. Not many men identified with the revolutionary cause had command military experience. And aside from the broad political considerations paramount to John Adams, who struggled to keep the colonies united, the commander needed practical political abilities to deal with the Continental Congress, the men seeking places in the military command, and the farmers and merchants on the front lines.

Washington presented an intimidating choice, and his unanimous selection by the Continental Congress chills discussion. He had served in the military; he was a member of the landed gentry who came to the cause of liberty early and remained strong in its defense; he appeared to have the personal virtues that would enhance military leadership. But, in fact, the clarity of the choice has become clouded by Washington's place in American history. Only with difficulty can we ignore the gift he bestowed on the country at the end of the Revolutionary War by walking away from the army that had followed him for eight years. And few can overlook the adoration of the vast majority of his countrymen for his public service or the decades of historians rushing to his praises after 1797. This personal grandeur casts a shadow over all the other officers who served in the Continental Army and also on the few men who presented themselves as alternatives to Washington in 1775.

The Continental Congress appointed George Washington commander in chief on June 15, 1775. The next day, the Congress officially informed Washington of his appointment and recorded his remarks on accepting the office:

Mr. President,

Tho' I am truly sensible of the high Honour done me, in this Appointment, yet I feel great distress, from a consciousness that my abilities and military experience may not be equal to the extensive and important Trust: However, as the Congress desire it, I will enter upon the momentous duty, and exert every power I possess in their service, and for support of the glorious cause. I beg they will accept my most cordial thanks for this distinguished testimony of their approbation.

But, lest some unlucky event should happen, unfavourable to my reputation, I beg it may be remembered, by every Gentleman in the room, that I, this day, declare with the utmost sincerity, I do not think myself equal to the Command I am honored with.

As to pay, Sir, I beg leave to assure the Congress, that, as no pecuniary consideration could have tempted me to have accepted this arduous employment, at the expence of my domestic ease and happiness, I do not wish to make any proffit from it. I will keep an exact Account of my expences. Those, I doubt not, they will discharge, and that is all I desire.

On June 17, Congress appointed two major generals, specifically ranked in order: Artemas Ward and Charles Lee. Horatio Gates was named adjutant general with the rank of brigadier. Several days later, Congress appointed two additional major generals, Philip Schuyler and Israel Putnam.

John Adams suggested later that John Hancock harbored pretensions as the first in command. But Hancock's claim appears to have been purely personal political ambition. Political considerations may have placed him in the running for the top post, but his lack of military experience precluded any consideration for a field command, and he never received one.[1]

The man in command of the Americans at Boston was Artemas Ward. Like Washington, Ward traced his military experience back to the French and Indian War. As a major, he marched several companies of Massachusetts militia to Lake George in northern New York in the summer of 1758 to assist Major General James Abercromby. Despite superior numbers, the campaign proved a disaster for the British. Nevertheless, Ward carried himself well throughout the campaign and rose to colonel of the Middlesex and Worcester County Regiments shortly after his return to Massachusetts. The rigors of the campaign, however, impacted his health from that time forward, so much so that he was thought of as being much older than his forty-eight years in 1775. The Bostonians, and others, saw Ward as a formidable commander. He had worked actively with the revolutionary conventions in the colony in the years leading up to the colonists' siege of Boston, and in October 1774, he was named by the Massachusetts Committee of Safety as one of three generals, the second in command to Jedediah Preble (sixty-seven years old), to defy the British Army. Ward was a deeply religious man, a judge, well groomed and stern. Even among the Massachusetts candidates, Ward may not have had the most extensive military experience, but like Washington, he had demonstrated a political ability that persuaded his contemporaries that he could deal with the many other issues confronting a commander.

John Adams claimed that Ward had the "greatest number" of votes in the Congress for commander in chief, but subsequent events proved that the choice of Washington to replace Ward was a wise one. Artemas Ward could not have survived the test. The life of an active soldier proved too much for his fragile constitution, and he tendered his resignation as first major general of the American forces as soon as the British evacuated Boston. Old infirmities hampered his movement. At first, Washington asked him to oversee the fortification of Boston, which he did. In short order, however, Washington forwarded Ward's resignation to Congress, and it was accepted in May 1777. Although not the man to command the Continental Army, Ward offered a life of service to the United States until his death in 1800, with stints in the Continental Congress and the United States Congress.

In the months after Ward's departure, however, events in the field led many to doubt Washington's selection and to seek another, more capable, general to lead the Continental Army. Years would pass in the field before Washington could rest easy as commander in chief. Even today, few consider Washington a military genius, and most agree that he was not the best American commander in the field. Detractors have suggested that Washington survived the war by a unique combination of luck and British blundering; that he was blessed by the ignorance and incompetence of British politicians and generals; that he may have been the chief beneficiary of the political needs of France, Spain, and Holland to check the influence of Great Britain in Europe and the Americas; that freedom in the British colonies in North America may have been an inevitable outcome at the end of the eighteenth century. Nevertheless, Washington emerged from his command successful. He survived devastating military defeats, several political intrigues among his officers, second-guessing by members of Congress, military blunders, and personal risk taking. By 1781, after the surrender of the British forces at Yorktown, the delegates who served in the Continental Congress in June 1775 could take satisfaction with the choice they had made six years earlier.

The question, perhaps, should not be whether George Washington justified his selection, but whether the delegates in Philadelphia in June 1775 could or
should have selected someone else, given the information and the choices available at the time. It is this question that calls for an examination of the life of the
third-ranking man appointed by the Continental Congress in June: Charles Lee.

THE CASE FOR CHARLES LEE

Of the viable alternatives to George Washington, Charles Lee presented the
strongest credentials in 1775. Politics may have placed Ward above him in
rank, but most observers at the time understood that Lee, not Ward, was the
best alternative to Washington. A fair assessment of this choice, however, has
also been made difficult by subsequent events. Lee has fallen by the wayside in
American history. Like many other generals in the Continental Army, he ran
afoul of George Washington during his service and continued to battle the
aura of Washington thereafter. Lee's actions at the Battle of Monmouth in
1778 were bitterly debated by officers and politicians alike, and his court-
martial after that battle led to his early departure from the army and the war.

Many observers in 1778, especially those who did not like the rise of
Washington's personal and political stature, thought Lee had been railroaded
by the Monmouth court-martial. Lee himself could not remain silent. He
directly challenged Washington at that point in Washington's military career
when Washington was growing in strength as a commander and a leader.
Lee's intemperate approach brought on much of the opprobrium he received.
Even friends found it difficult to abide his relentless public attacks on
Washington and his demand for vindication. Dissipated financially and physically, Lee died an inglorious death alone at the age of fifty-one in 1782, before
the war ended. Many of those who served with him or were caught up in the
fury of his view of events were content to leave the controversy behind with
his death. In subsequent years, few rose to remember him or defend his name
while Washington was alive. Many years after his death, historians discovered
even more about his life and actions during the war that made it easier to pass
over his service to the Continental Army.

All of the controversy that became Charles Lee after June 28, 1778, however, did not cloud the thinking of those faced with the choice of commander
in chief in June 1775. The reputation that preceded Lee at that moment in
history was decidedly different from the one assigned to him since. Lee
demanded attention in 1775 and received it from every corner. His military
exploits were well known. He had fought and was wounded on American soil
in the French and Indian War. Like Artemas Ward, he suffered Abercromby's

defeat at Fort Carillon in 1758, leaving the field with a chest wound. He had led a daring raid on Spanish forces in Portugal in 1762 and was honored by the king of Portugal as a major general for his complete success. He had advised the king of Poland on military matters. His political bravura—or foolishness—was even more immediately evident. He challenged his own king, George III, in the press while still in the king's military service. He answered Loyalists in America who called the fight for the rights of man unnecessary. He corresponded with the leading thinkers in England and the colonies. He traveled throughout the colonies, north and south, from 1773 to 1775, talking with political leaders, urging them on in opposition to the king, assuring them they could win a fight, and reviewing defenses.

Charles Lee's personal history added even more color. As a lieutenant in 1755, he married a Seneca woman, the daughter of a chief, and become a member of the tribe. He escaped assassination at the hands of a disgruntled subordinate. He defied certain death crossing the frozen Carpathian Mountains after traveling with the Russian cavalry on a trek to Constantinople. He killed a man in a duel of honor in Italy and had to flee the country to avoid arrest.

Charles Lee returned to North America in 1773 a well-known critic of King George III and his government. The newspapers covered his movements from the first day, and within weeks of his arrival, he took up the colonists' cause in the press and in extensive conversations throughout the colonies. He did not discourage anyone from suggesting him as the one man with the demonstrated skills necessary to lead American farmers and merchants against British regulars. Indeed, Lee was his own best press agent. He made the rounds of the Revolutionary leaders, including particularly Washington and John Adams, and he appeared in Philadelphia during the sessions of both the First and Second Continental Congresses. He was mentioned often in Philadelphia as a dinner guest of Benjamin Rush, Richard Henry Lee, John Adams, and others.

Charles Lee possessed a gift. Influential men were drawn to him. He had traveled extensively in Europe, spoke several languages, and had the apparent confidence of kings. He was a unique acquaintance for many provincials, including the leaders of the rebellion. Some today might call Lee's gift "charm," but Lee was anything but a charming person. He was opinionated, often unkempt, and was always accompanied by his dogs. He was not grounded with family. His only close relative was a spinster sister still in England. He came from a family that held stature in England, but he was not a man of unlimited means. He did not entertain lavishly, if at all. And yet he could call upon influential men to listen to him and respond to his needs.

The answer may lie in the combination of his colorful history and his ability as a correspondent. His letters demand attention. Interspersed with the stilted language of the day are brilliant passages on the rights of man, literary and historical allusions, and wit.[2] If his conversations mirrored his writing, the mystery of his allure can be understood. Lee did not command respect by quiet grace. On the contrary, he did not hold back and would have been exciting company for the patriots in the backwater of America yearning for freedom.

By June 1775, Charles Lee considered himself the leading contender for commander in chief of the American forces. Many of his friends did as well. No lesser position would do him the honor he deserved. He considered George Washington with the polite respect that most British officers gave to officers of colonials. Charles Lee and George Washington were the same age, and both had served in the French and Indian War. But Washington's service was with the provincial forces of Virginia. Lee had served as a junior officer, but with the British regulars, having spent his life in the military from the age of eleven, when his father had enlisted him in his regiment. In Lee's mind, as in others in the colonies in 1775, the choice was not difficult.

Men on both sides of the Atlantic could also picture Lee at the front of the army defying King George. In December 1774, Lee wrote to Edmund Burke, the English politician and orator, continuing a correspondence on the state of American affairs. He assures Burke that the colonists will stand firm, that the British military is ill-informed and ill-prepared for the fight ahead, and that "the first estated gentlemen and the poorest planters . . . are determined to sacrifice everything, their property, their wives, children and blood, rather than cede a tittle of what they conceive to be their rights."[3] More telling, however, is that Lee brings up the subject of his own ambitions in America and his qualifications for the military command soon to be awarded, in a half-hearted effort denying his claim:

> I shall now trouble you with a few words respecting myself. I find it inserted in a paragraph of an English paper, that a certain officer (meaning me) had been busy in dissuading the people of Boston from submitting to the acts. It is giving me great importance to suppose that I have influence sufficient to urge or restrain so vast a community, in affairs of the dearest moment. The same paragraph adds, that I had offered to put myself at their head; but I hope it will not be believed that I was capable of so much temerity and vanity. To think myself qualified for the most important charge that ever was committed to mortal man, is the last stage of presumption. Nor do I think the Americans would, or ought to confide in a man (let his qualifications be ever so great) who has no property amongst them. It is true I most devoutly wish them success in the glorious struggle; that I have expressed both in writing and *viva voce:* but my errand to Boston was mere

curiosity, to see a people in so singular circumstances; and I had likewise an ambition of being acquainted with some of their leading men; — with them only I associated during my stay at Boston. Our ingenious gentlemen in the camp, therefore, very naturally concluded my design was to put myself at their head.[4]

Lee's less than modest denial notwithstanding, he moved almost immediately after revealing his one deficiency—the lack of landed property—to cure it. He made arrangements in 1775 to purchase an estate in Virginia and become a man of property in America.

John Adams, who rose at the Continental Congress to propose George Washington, agreed with Lee that his qualifications were "ever so great." Adams considered Lee the most astute military man in the Americas. Years later, in a comment in his *Autobiography* (that reveals his own vanity) Adams declared that by studying the art of war to better perform his duties as a member of Congress, he was inferior only to Charles Lee in military knowledge among all of the generals in the field for the Americans.[5] But Adams understood that appearances and political considerations shared equal position with military skills in the choice of a commander in chief.

George Washington received the honor of commander in chief. Although he may not have been thought to have the broadest military experience or skill, he was born in North America and could help unite the disparate colonies. Artemas Ward received the second position in honor of his current service under fire and, perhaps, in recognition that he would not be in the fight for long. Lee had to satisfy himself with being the third in command, behind Washington and Ward. Lee's vanity could not remain checked for long, however, and his true thoughts came out in an appeal to General John Thomas, just months later. Thomas had threatened to quit the service because of the insult that he perceived in the ranking that he had been assigned within the military command. Lee used his pen to convince him otherwise, arguing that Thomas was not the only officer slighted by the Continental Congress and that such affronts needed to be suffered for the greater good: "I am quite of the same opinion, but is this a time Sir, when the liberties of your country, the fate of posterity, the rights of mankind are at stake, to indulge our resentments for any ill treatment we may have received as individuals?" Here, early in the conflict, Lee reveals his ire at being placed third in command:

> I have myself, Sir, full as great, perhaps greater reason to complain than yourself. I have passed through the highest ranks, in some of the most respectable services in Europe. According to the modern etiquette notions

of a soldier's honor and delicacy, I ought to consider at least the preferment given to General Ward over me as the highest indignity, but I thought it my duty as a citizen and asserter of liberty, to waive every consideration. On this principle, although a Major General of five years standing, and not a native of America, I consented to serve under General Ward, because I was taught to think that the concession would be grateful to his countrymen, and flatter myself that the concession has done me credit in the eye of the world; and can You, Sir, born in this very country, which a band of banditti ministerial assassins are now attempting utterly to destroy with sword, fire and famine, abandon the defense of her, because you have been personally ill used?[6]

Most telling, of course, is the phrase "I ought to consider at least the preferment given to General Ward over me as the highest indignity." Only Washington ranked above Lee and Ward. Several months later, on Ward's retirement, Lee described Ward's preferment with more rancor: "Did I not consent to serve under an old church-warden, of whom you had conceived a most extravagant and ridiculous opinion? Your eyes were at length opened, and deacon Ward returned to his proper occupation."[7]

Indeed, much would happen in the coming months, and Lee knew that his time could still come.

CHAPTER 2

LEE'S "AMERICAN EXPEDITION"

Great Britain's on again, off again war with France heated up in 1753 when the French in North America moved into the Ohio River Valley and began constructing forts. This disputed territory separated the French settlers in Canada and the British settlers in the colonies. The extending French military presence unnerved not only the British settlers on the adjacent frontiers in Pennsylvania and Virginia, but throughout the colonies. Fighting erupted almost immediately between French and British colonials, even though the two European governments preferred to posture for some time. Once Great Britain declared war in 1756, land and sea forces were engaged in Europe and the West Indies as well as the North American frontier.

THE FRENCH AND INDIAN WAR

In Europe, this period of warfare is known as the Seven Years' War; in North America, it is known as the French and Indian War. The North American theater mixed colorful locations, native warriors on both sides, and many acts of savagery. The decisive political and military battles in this conflict were fought in Europe, however, and the North American fighting contributed little to the outcome of the war. The impact of the peace in North America was dramatic, nevertheless. The 1763 Treaty of Paris confirmed the French loss of all its North American territory east of the Mississippi River, excepting only New Orleans, and secured British control of its West Indies islands. Britain gained unrestricted navigation rights on the Mississippi River, Montreal and Quebec, the fort at Duquesne (Pittsburgh), and control of the Ohio Valley. This shift in the North American political and military landscape had a profound effect on the British colonists and the future of the British colonies. At the start of the hostilities, the British subjects in North America harbored no thoughts of independence. Quite to the contrary, the farmers and merchants building societies in the American colonies depended on their government in London to provide men and munitions for protection from French incursions and Indian raids. The developing economy of the thirteen colonies also depended on trade with Great Britain and the sea power that enabled and protected that trade. The ports of Boston, New York, Philadelphia, and Charleston brought necessities to those in the cities as well as those on the frontier and provided a market for the exported goods that paid for those necessities.

Throughout the first half of the eighteenth century, the British settlers experienced alternating periods of calm and distress. A foreign power maintained troops to the north and west and, even though the colonists lived thousands of miles and weeks by sea from London, the political and military tensions in the Old World could easily shatter the complacency of these British citizens. They especially felt the pressure and repercussions when these tensions escalated to open warfare. Early in the century, Great Britain tangled with France from 1702 to 1713 in Queen Anne's War (also known as the War of Spanish Succession). The Peace of Utrecht after Queen Anne's War led to thirty years of peace for the colonists, but in midcentury, King George's War (1744–1748), and the Seven Years' War (1756–1763), renewed hostilities.

During this period, it did not take much to frighten the settlers. Especially disturbing was the idea that the French were encouraging Indians to take to the warpath. Tales of scalping and other savage deeds spread through the colonies with the wind. Newspapers circulating in the colonies in the 1750s detailed these horrors and warned of more atrocities if action was not taken to stop the French and the Indians. Security on the frontier was a main concern to settlers scattered over thousands of miles from Massachusetts to Georgia. Even those close to the coastal seaports knew that security on the frontier helped to support their livelihoods. British regulars provided that security.

For many historians, the French and Indian War, and the results of its outcome, led directly to the American Revolution twenty years later. The defeat of the French and the gain of Canada as a British province secured the northern border of the thirteen colonies, providing more than ten years without fear of French soldiers nearby or French encouragement of Indian uprisings. Great Britain saw an opportunity to reduce its forces stationed in the colonies, and the garrisoning of British regulars in American cities disappeared along with the reliance on them for protection. From the end of hostilities in 1763, the colonies developed without significant interference from the French, the Indians, or the British. Roads improved, newspapers flourished, correspondence became more regular, and goods moved easily within the colonies and across the Atlantic Ocean. The British regulars, whose constant presence was once a welcome sight, were now just an occasional nuisance.

Another by-product of the last of these conflicts was the development of a military capacity within the colonies. Between 1754 and 1763, thousands of "provincials" fought alongside the 24,000 regulars the British government sent to North America. Every one of the thirteen colonies was required by the Crown to send a unit of militia to assist in the fight. Some of the colonies most impacted by the French—New York, Connecticut, Massachusetts, and New Jersey—sent several units. Militia units fought in every major battle, sometimes performing better than the regulars, who were unfamiliar with the frontier. Many of the men who would rise for independence in 1776 served in the provincial units, including George Washington, Artemas Ward, Israel Putnam, Henry Laurens, and Hugh Mercer. The British ministry and some British officers may have valued these units as little more than fodder for the fight, but many men and many units served with distinction and courage. And British opinion may be less important than the impact that raising and employing these units had on the colonists themselves. For many, this exercise demonstrated the ability of the settlers to stand with the regulars in a fight, and for many more it demonstrated that the settlers had the ability to stand on their own if need be.

Perhaps the most important outcome of the French and Indian War was the creation of an American consciousness. The fear on the frontier produced calls throughout the colonies for organization and unity. Benjamin Franklin's woodcut "Join or Die" showed a snake cut up into pieces, each labeled as one of the several colonies. This drawing and others like it appeared in many of the newspapers that were growing in circulation as hostilities commenced. George Washington's accounts, as a young militia colonel, of the intentions of the French and the fighting on the Virginia frontier, including the loss of Fort Necessity in 1754, captivated readers of colonial newspapers. Calls went out for meetings and congresses among the colonies to discuss and organize a united resistance. French victories at Fort Oswego, Fort William Henry, and Monongahela in 1755, where colonials were present and fighting, continued to alarm the population.

The French and Indian War, created in part by the fears of the English colonists on the North American frontier, became a defining moment for the British North American colonists. The fight gave them self-confidence and encouraged a unity that previously did not exist; the outcome gave them a sustained period of prosperity and limited interference from the mother country. The French and Indian War also brought to the forefront young men who would find their destinies in the war to come twenty years later for political independence. These young men served together to defeat the French. In the Revolutionary War, they would serve on both sides. One of those men was Charles Lee.

LIFE AMONG THE MOHAWKS

Charles Lee first saw North America in 1755 at the age of twenty-four, as a captain in the Forty-fourth Foot. This regiment was called from its garrison in Ireland and joined General Edward Braddock's force in an expedition against Fort Duquesne. For Lee, the fighting in America provided adventure. Far from the serenity of life in the English countryside and relieved of the boredom of Irish garrison duty, a young Lee saw landscapes, people, and life-threatening action he could have scarcely imagined. He gloried in his American experience, and he left North America six years later imbued with self-confidence and an incisive appreciation of what these colonies meant to England.

Lee shared the experience of the French and Indian War with the colonists and joined in the growth of self-confidence that developed in the colonies at its conclusion. Nevertheless, he viewed his sojourn in America from a different perspective—politically, his was an English worldview. He saw the Crown's North American possessions as a valuable asset to be carefully guarded and nurtured to provide full benefits to the British Empire. Lee served with the British regulars, and his view of the military engagements reflected the bias of the British forces. The Indians he met were allies of the British and treated as such. He marveled at these colorful figures and became intimate with them. Lee's personal perspective was just that—personal. Once he gained his footing, he set about to utilize his experience in North America to forward his standing with persons of influence who could advance him in the army. Charles soaked it all in with the energy of a young man eager to make his way in the world. The majesty of the land he traversed awed him; the movements of men and materiel, interposed with the dangers of combat, enlightened him, confirmed his personal courage; the curiosities of the native peoples fascinated him; the chance to move up within the military as a general officer captivated him. Charles Lee took note of every aspect of North America save one: the colonials who peopled the cities, the villages, the farms, and the frontiers. Lee simply failed to see them.

Lee faced the immediacy of life and death as a British regular who charged fortified positions, but not the pressures of living year to year with foreign troops within reach of a farmstead; he witnessed and understood the savagery of Indians on the warpath, but not the day-to-day fear that families living on the frontier had to contend with; he could observe the movement of troops and the fatal consequences of tactical errors on the field of battle, but it does not appear that he observed or understood the struggle of the colonists to organize a united resistance; he served side by side with units of provincials, but failed to notice their contributions to the war effort or to care about their passion for the fight.

Lee had been associated with the Forty-fourth Foot Regiment from the age of eleven, when his father, John Lee, added Charles to the muster. John Lee at about that time had become colonel of the regiment, and it was not uncommon for young sons to be added to the rolls in this manner to guide them to a future military career. In preparation for that career, young Charles was sent to the Continent to receive an education. He spoke French fluently and learned enough Spanish, Italian, and German to be competent in those languages throughout his life. In private schools he read the classics and developed a quick wit and a sharp tongue. He enjoyed politics and political thinking and became a follower of the rising political philosophy of the time that emphasized the rights of man and freedom from hereditary kings.

Returning to England, Charles Lee purchased a lieutenancy in the Forty-fourth Foot, and the military became his life. In eighteenth-century Great Britain, social stature and political favor were the clearest routes to military rank. Lee's family, especially through the Bunburys on his mother's side, had sufficient standing to expect that Charles would rise in the service. His mother's father was Sir Henry Bunbury of Stanney in Cheshire; her uncle, Sir Thomas Hanmer, had served as speaker of the House of Commons. Charles was one of three sons and the only one to reach maturity. He maintained a correspondence with his sister, Sidney, and members and friends of his extended family for his entire life, and it is from these letters that we can see Lee travel the world and take up his political and military contests.[1]

This correspondence starts with Lee's American adventures in the French and Indian War, and from the first, Charles Lee establishes himself as a master storyteller. The letters exhibit self-confidence, a delight in commentary, a flair for hyperbole, and an ingrained disdain for authority. These traits characterize Lee's letters to the very end of his life, whether writing to his sister, his peers, or his superiors. A reader of the early correspondence has to ask whether at least some of the stories result from a young man's need to embellish his exploits. Is Charles Lee simply trying to shock or entertain his sister? The lore of Lee's early life comes straight out of these letters. The stories border on the fantastic, but their essentials have been corroborated by third-party accounts. If they are true, even in part, Charles Lee's first American experiences provided a colorful beginning to his military and personal life.

Lee's regiment arrived in Virginia in 1754 and participated in an ill-fated campaign under General Edward Braddock that demonstrated the lack of understanding that British commanders had for the style of fighting that would prove successful on the American frontier. General Braddock marched the Forty-fourth (Lee's unit) and the Forty-eighth Regiments through the woods from Frederick, Maryland, toward his objective, the French Fort Duquesne at the confluence of the Monongahela and Allegheny Rivers. Braddock had accepted on his staff a young, but well-respected, colonial officer, George Washington, who was familiar with the territory and several Native Americans—Mingo warriors, along with the "Half King" Scarouady. But the campaign proceeded as a typical European assault. The British regulars crossed the Monongahela River and began their approach to the fort in tight units. (British officers crossing the river with their units included Lieutenant Colonel Thomas Gage and Captain Horatio Gates, both of whom would become prominent players in the American Revolution, albeit on opposite sides.) A body of French and Indians hidden in the woods well beyond the fort ambushed the regulars and proceeded to decimate their well formed ranks with fire from elevated positions behind trees and brush. The result was a devastating defeat for the British as they scrambled back across the river. Braddock died shortly thereafter of wounds from the battle, leaving Washington effectively in command. Lee's Forty-fourth Regiment eventually retreated to Philadelphia, moved to New York City, and then went into winter quarters in upstate New York.[2]

Lee's first letter from North America is a missive to his sister, Sidney, from "Schenectada (New York)" in June 1756.[3] It is not clear if Lee crossed the Monongahela with his unit, but his letter duly describes the terror that confronted the men who did: "There is one horrid circumstance attending this sort of service which is, that if you, happen to be left disabled in the Field, the highest blessing that you can wish for is, that some friends will immediately Knock you on the head, for it is great odds that you suffer some terrible lingering death from these savages; such I'm afraid was the fate of our poor wounded friends at the Monongahela; but the Indians may indeed be excus'd more than the French, for they are bred up in these bloody notions." Lee then weaves these horrors of war with a travelogue and personal delicacies for his sister:

It is an uncomfortable situation enough we are in here; we cannot stir out to take a walk unless we are twenty together in number well arm'd, for the French and Indians are continually skulking about us, and carry off every day a great many scalps—the place itself is very pleasant (not from any Society) but from the finess of the Situation and the delightful sky, which

must put ev'ry thing animate into spirits, indeed there is a magnificence
and greatness through the immense extent (which we have seen of this
Continent) not equal'd in any part of Europe; our Rivers and Lakes (even
the greatest) are to these rivulets and brooks; indeed Nature in every Article
seems to be in great here, what on your side of the Waters, she is in small.
Some of the Towns are very good; Philadelphia is charming, and really very
sociable people; the women there are extremely pretty and most passionately fond of red coats, which is for us a most fortunate piece of absurdity. [1]

All of this is prologue for a detailed description of the "Mohocks" and Lee's
acceptance into their "Councils."

Apparently sometime after his arrival in North America, Lee made the
acquaintance of William Johnson, the British Indian agent; accompanied
Johnson in conferences with the Six Nations, which included the Mohawks
and the Senecas; and so became deeply acquainted with these tribes. Johnson
played an important role in the French and Indian War as both an intermediary with the Six Nations and as a commander of British forces. One of Lee's
biographers suggests that Lee assisted in the recruiting of Native Americans
into the Forty-fourth Regiment to restore its depleted ranks. [5] In any event,
Lee had the chance to live "a great deal among" these natives and spoke of
them glowingly. They were "hospitable, friendly, and civil to an immense
degree"; they "infinitely surpass the French" in "good breeding"; "in their
persons they are generally tall, slender and delicate shapes" and carry themselves with "an ease and gracefulness in their walk and air which is not to be
met with elsewhere."

Lee provides Sidney with a surprisingly close description of the physical
features of the "Mohocks": their "Complexion is deep olive, their eyes and
teeth very fine, but their skins are most inexpressibly soft and silky." The
"men are in general handsomer than their women, but I have seen some of
them very pretty." He had been "adopted by the Mohocks into the Tribe of
the bear under the name of Ounewaterika, which signifies boiling water, or
one whose spirits are never asleep, by which I am entitled to a Seat and the
privilege of Smoking a pipe in their Councils." All of this came about, apparently, owing to his marriage to a chieftain's daughter: "My Wife is daughter to
the famous White Thunder who is Belt of Wampum to the Senekas which is
in fact their Lord Treasurer. She is a very great beauty and is more like your
friend Mrs. Griffith than anybody I know. I shall say nothing of her accom-
plishments for you must be certain that a Woman of her fashion cannot be
without many." One has to wonder at the reaction of Lee's spinster sister,
Sidney Lee, reading this letter in her native Chester, North Wales, from where

she barely wandered during her life. Lee expects that she will question his veracity, if not his judgment, and twice in this long letter gives "my word and honour" that his accounts are, in fact, truthful. Whatever her reaction, Charles Lee never mentioned this "very great beauty" to Sidney again.[6] It must have been through his association with William Johnson that Lee attained such an intimate relationship with the Indians supporting the British. Johnson is reputed to have bedded numerous Native American women during his lifetime and fathered more than a few children by these women.[7] And, apparently, Lee was not the only British officer to take an Indian wife.

This tale was immediately followed by another. Apparently a young brave named Joseph, to show his devotion to Lee, surprised him with a "handsome present," a scalp obtained specifically for the purpose of the gift: "[H]e lay skulking for two or three days before he had an opportunity of knocking on the head a French Sergeant, and taking off his scalp, with which he hurried away to me and presented it to me elegantly dress'd up with ribbons." Again, Lee acknowledges that Sidney may wonder at the truth of such a tale: "You may think that I am endeavouring to make my letter Romantic but I give you my word and honour that it is every syllable facts."[8]

Stories of personal danger continued. In late 1758, he sent a short letter to Sidney describing an attempt on his life by "a little Cowardly Surgeon" in the camp whom Lee had "thrashed" for spreading a "stupid libel" about him. The vignette of this encounter still remains fresh in it details to the reader: ". . . the scoundrel had not the spirit to resent [the thrashing] properly, but waited for me on a road which he knew I was to pass, seiz'd my horse by the bridle, presented a pistol at my heart, (so close that the muzzle almost touc'd me) and fir'd. My horse fortunately at that instant started to the right, which sav'd me; but the shock was very violent, and the contusion very great, exactly under my heart; He wou'd have dispatched me with a second pistol, but Capt. Dunbar (who was with me) struck it out of his hand."[9] Lee completes the story more than a full year later.[10] He was convinced to allow "the little Villain" to make a public apology in order to avoid the court-martial that would have broken him, but Lee soon regretted his kindness. It seems that the whole affair was the work of Major John Beckwith, also in the Forty-fourth Regiment, a "Yorkshire man" and "petty Caligula," who hated Lee and his friends and put the surgeon up to the assassination, even to the point of supplying the pistols. Lee vows to run this major out of the regiment or, failing to do so, to himself resign once the campaign against the French ends.

Lee took the time to drink in the wonders of North America as he traveled from place to place and passed accounts of their beauty on to his correspondents.

In an early letter he talks about "blue and yellow Nightingales, Mockingbirds and spotted squirrels," which he describes as "the most beautiful creatures in the world,"[11] and in another he tells Sidney of the "Deer, Bear, Turkeys, Raccoons" that can be found in this country along with salmon in the Niagara River. Niagara Falls is "the most stupendous Cataract in the known World," and he despairs that even if he had "a throat of Brass & a thousand tongues" he could not adequately describe it. Lee sums up his view of the wilderness by saying that "it is such a Paradise & such an acquisition to our Nation, that I wou'd not sacrifice it to redeem the dominions of any one Electoral Prince in Germany from the hands of the Enemy."[12]

FIRST ACTION

Captain Charles Lee of the Forty-fourth Regiment of the His Majesty's Grenadiers most likely saw his first action at Monongahela in 1755. As mentioned above, he refers to the horrors of the battle in a letter to his sister, but he does not mention whether he came under fire. Two-thirds of the 2,200 British regulars engaged were killed or wounded in this fight on the road to Fort Duquesne.

We next hear from Lee after the siege of Fort Carillon in July 1758 under Major General James Abercromby. Lee was one of 9,000 regulars and 6,000 provincials amassed outside of this rustic military outpost near the border of New York and the Canadian provinces. The fort sits on a plateau at the western edge of Lake Champlain and northern outlet of Lake George. It was built by the French in the 1750s and stood as their southernmost military presence in the British New World. As a garrison, a storehouse for artillery, and a location that commanded the northern end of an inland waterway to the ocean, Fort Carillon (renamed "Fort Ticonderoga" by the British in 1759) became a prime military objective for every army operating in New York from its construction through the end of the Revolutionary War. The French currently had control of the fort, with only 3,200 French, Indians, and Canadians under the command of the Marquis de Montcalm.

Notwithstanding the superiority of his numbers, Abercromby bungled the attack by not learning the lay of the land and not bringing his artillery into the fight in a meaningful way. He sent wave after wave of his precious regulars against heavily defended barricades in an attempt to take the fort at the point of a bayonet. The provincials were held back in support of the regulars on either side under the cover of the trees. The regulars rushed from the trees only to be cut down by the French as they became entangled in the thicket and the fallen trees in front of the barricades. Late in the fight the provincials joined in support of the regulars, but the French could not be moved from their defenses. Abercromby finally stopped the offensive as the daylight began to wane. The slaughter was tremendous: more than 1,900 men killed and wounded, including a full 25 percent of the regulars. Lee took a bullet in the chest that shattered two ribs. That night Abercromby ordered the troops to their boats and rushed back to the encampment at the south end of Lake George where the campaign began.[13]

Among the provincials backing up the British regulars at Fort Carillon was Major Artemas Ward, with four companies of Massachusetts militiamen, the same man who would be ranked above Charles Lee by the Continental Congress seventeen years later in June 1775. Ward witnessed this disaster along with Lee. Although Ward was not wounded in the fighting, his exertions in this campaign took a physical toll that plagued him for years thereafter and eventually led to his early resignation from the Continental Army.[14]

Charles Lee recuperated from his wound in Albany. He wrote as soon as he could to his sister, Sidney, to assure her of his recovery, because he surmised that she had heard of his wounds through earlier letters home from others. He passed over his injury quickly, however, to get to a more urgent point, the incompetence of General Abercromby: "As to a detail of our affairs, or rather the blunders of this damn'd beastly poltroon (who to the scourge and dishonour of the Nation, is unhappily at the head of our Army, an instrument of divine vengeance to bring about national losses and national dishonour) I refer you to the Narrative here inclos'd, a coppy of which I desire you will transmit to Coll. Armiger. I shall not be asham'd should it be communicated to others, as I think silence or even patience is some disgrace to a man who has been an eye witness to such superlative blundering, pusillanimity, and infamy."[15] He goes on to describe General Abercromby as "our Booby in Chief" and relates that the Indians refuse to fight under his command because he is "an old Squah." The Indians have told Abercromby that "he should wear a petticoat, go home and make sugar, and not by pretending to a task which he was not equal to, blunder so many braver men than himself into destruction."

Lee's "Narrative" provides a colorful and readable story of the assault, beginning with the landing of the troops and an early skirmish with "French Scouts" in the woods leading to the fort. Lee effusively praises Lord George Howe, the eldest of the three brothers who all served in North America as part of the British military. Howe served as second in command of the British troops, and Lee poetically mourns Howe's death in the skirmish. According to Lee, Howe had created the conditions for a successful assault on the barricades and made the troops on the field understand the superiority of the British position. The troops were ready for the victory that was then denied them by the incompetence of Abercromby:

> What a glorious Situation was this! In short everything had so charming an aspect, that without being much elated I shou'd have look'd upon any man as a desponding bastard who could entertain a doubt of our success; little did we dream that it was still in the power of one blunderer to render all these favorable promising circumstances abortive, but our noble Leader soon convinc'd us that there can be no situation so disadvantageous, no success & victory so certain, altho' it is absolutely in your hand & only waits until you grasp it, but that a miscarriage may be brought about by the incapacity of a single person. I really did not think that so great a share of stupidity and absurdity could be in the possession of any man. Fortune and the pusillanimity of the French had cram'd victory into his mouth, but he contrived to spit it out again.

As Lee continues, his blood runs higher and his pen hotter. He further condemns Abercromby and, even in this more public statement of the affair, cannot avoid brutal sarcasm and personal assault. Abercromby's foolish mistake to not utilize cannon from an eminence that gave the British command of the field drove Lee to distraction: "[B]ut notwithstanding some of our Cannon was brought up & in readiness, this never was thought of, which (one wou'd imagine must have occurr'd to any blockhead who was not absolutely so far sunk in Idiotism as to be oblig'd to wear a bib and bells. So far, his behaviour cou'd only be call'd stupid, ridiculous and absurd; but the subsequent part was dishonorable and infamous, & had some strong symptoms of cowardice." Lee refers in this last comment to the precipitous British retreat and abandonment of the field. He accuses Abercromby of being the first to leave the field: "He threw himself into one of the first boats, row'd off, and was almost the earliest Messenger of the Public loss and his own infamy." Even counting their heavy losses, the British still outnumbered the French two to one.

Lee was not alone in his praise for the fallen Lord Howe or his condemnation of General Abercromby. Both contemporary and historical consensus confirm his conclusions. But this first instance of Lee's willingness to publicly attack his superior officer is telling in its ferocity. Lee balances his criticism of General Abercromby by his profuse praise for Lord Howe, but we will see that Lee's lifelong habit is to save most of his praise for dead superiors. And it appears that Lee did not limit his criticism to firsthand encounters. In an undated letter, perhaps written before the defeat at Fort Carillon, Lee railed against the loss of Fort William Henry in August 1757. He admitted that although "almost on the spot" he has "very imperfect Ideas of the causes of this misfortune." This did not prevent him, however, from dredging up every malicious rumor about the commanding officers circulating at the time and referring to "Coll. Monroe" as a "very worthy gentlewoman" who was "terribly afflicted with a paraletic disorder of which She is since dead."[16] Lee suggested that "it wou'd be much better to make a present at once of all of our possession in America to the French" than to continue to rely on blunderers whose incompetence is glossed over.

Lee returned to the Forty-fourth Foot in time to participate in the siege of Niagara. He provided a brief description of this victory to Sidney and noted that "I myself escap'd unhurt, but two musket balls at the same instant grazed my hair,"[17] In a detailed description of the siege for his uncle, Sir William Bunbury, Lee failed to mention his close encounter with death this second time but did not fail to comment on the actions of his commanding officers. The British artillery was "trifling & bad," and the engineers "(as usual) execrably ignorant." Lee reported that Brigadier General John Prideaux and his second in command, were "both worthy and brave men," but unfortunately were killed in the action. The next in line was Sir William Johnson, the British Indian superintendent, who Lee reported as a "very good and valuable man, but utterly a stranger to military affairs."

Nevertheless, 2,000 British regulars and 1,000 "Indians of the Six Nations" (including the Senecas, "wavering and irresolute, ready to desert us on the first prospect of unsuccess") reduced the fort's garrison of 620 despite the appearance of 1,000 French and Indian reinforcements. Over nineteen days, the British dug trenches closer and closer to the fort, but the French did not surrender until their reinforcements attempted but were unable to break through the British lines. After the battle, Lee reported, the British had to restrain the "Mohocks and Oneida from sacrificing" the French officers, even though it would have been "justice for they had a few hours before surpris'd a party of our Light Infantry, cut off their heads & arms, and fix'd them upon poles."

Lee understood the strategic value of Fort Niagara and the military and economic impact of this victory: "[T]his important Fort of Niagara . . . is to the English Nation a most glorious and solidly advantageous acquisition, by its strength most formidable, & by its situation absolute Empress of the Inland parts of North America, commanding the two great Lakes, Erie, Ontario; the River Ohio, all the upper nations of Indians, and consequently engrossing the whole Fur trade, cutting off communication between Canada & Misasipi, & thus defeating their favourite and long projected scheme of forming a chain round our Colonies, so as in time to have justled us into the Sea."[18] The victory led quickly to an adventure of three months for Lee.

Along with one other officer and fourteen men, Charles Lee was sent to follow the remnants of the French Army that eluded the British after the surrender of Fort Niagara. He seems to have reveled in the chance to see so much country: "[W]e had the satisfaction of being the first English who ever cross'd the vast Lake of Erie; we pass'd through the French Forts of Presq' Isle and Vinango descended down the Rivers of Buffalo and Ohio and in 14 days arriv'd safe (tho' naked & almost starv'd) at Fort Duquesne; . . . from Fort Duquesne, I took a little jaunt of 700 miles to Gen. Amherst at Crown Point, from thence another of five hundred and fifty to Oswego, and from Oswego another trifling of 600 to this place [Philadelphia] where I am now recruiting."[19] This delightful travelogue served as the opening of a long letter to sister Sidney and a response to her "heavy accusations" that he had not written to her regularly. He discussed friends and relatives, the attempt on his life by a subordinate (described above), and gifts he was preparing to send her, including "a pair of fine shoes," a "Child's cradle, in case of marriage," and a few furs. He ends with this odd couplet: "My mother you must assure of my Most dutifull respects and Mr Mather—send me Thucidides."

AN AMERICAN EXPEDITION

Charles Lee's "American Expedition" from 1754 to 1761 had a profound effect on him and the later direction of his life. He had the opportunity to see much of the British New World, more than most of the colonists in North America. He traveled through the wilderness to Fort Duquesne, fought at Monongahela, passed through the seaport cities of New York and Philadelphia, traveled to Nova Scotia, was wounded near the Canadian border at Fort Carillon, participated in the siege of Niagara, crossed Lake Erie into the Ohio Valley, and witnessed the fall of Montreal.

The North American landscape, the natives, and the wildlife clearly impressed him, and he described each in detail in the several surviving letters from those early years. His commentary on the native peoples captured both their savagery and their gentility, and his intimate experience of their culture would have been lost on many of the settlers who feared even the friendliest Indians. He came to understand the vastness of the continent, its abundance, and its importance to the British Empire. It may be that his letters reflect the exuberance of his youth and the passion of being, literally, in the trenches for the fight on the North American continent, but Lee had already visited Europe and had some basis on which to make adequate comparisons. The New World offered wonders.

Charles Lee's "American Expedition" also introduced him to the realities of war.[20] Acquaintance with military life from an early age and garrison duty in Ireland probably did not prepare Lee for the hardships of camp life in a wilderness, the rigors of forced marches through dense forests, the drudgery of trenching, or the terror of enemy fire in the assault on fortified barricades. Lee learned the life of a soldier in North America and witnessed firsthand how battles should and should not be waged to obtain victory. He was not one to defer to the opinion of superiors on how to proceed, but despite his tendency to second-guess all opinions other than his own, he surely learned valuable lessons on the field. He exhibited courage, suffered a serious battle wound, and returned to the front for more.

It appears, however, that Charles Lee failed to take away one important lesson from his "American Expedition"—an understanding of the people living in British North America. One would think that interspersed among the descriptions of the rivers, the lakes, and the natural wonders, weaved into the narratives about the culture of the natives, and sprinkled among the colors of the wildlife, a reader would find in Lee's letters some words about the farmers, the villagers, the city people, the tradesmen, the frontiersmen, and the artisans who were about the business of civilizing this wilderness. There are none. Other than the pretty women in Philadelphia who were "most passionately fond of red coats," Americans are absent from his observation and his letters.

Only about a dozen letters survive from Lee during this time, some long narratives and some short notes, and it can be argued that Lee just did not get around to describing the people building the societies he visited. Does this excuse the complete lack of description of the people that his regiment was sent to North America to protect from the French? He fought alongside provincials; he lived in their cities and passed through their towns. He takes time to describe the colorful natives, providing details on their customs and their persons. It may be that Lee did not have enough contact with these people to include observations in his letters. He was a British officer assigned to a military unit and was perhaps too busy, or discouraged from, close contact with the local population. At least one story associated with Charles Lee during this time, however, suggests otherwise. Lee's wounds from the Battle of Fort Carillon took some time to heal, and he spent several months at a farmhouse outside of Albany being nursed back to health by a "Madame Schuyler." As the story goes, this same woman suffered depredations by Lee's men foraging for food and supplies when they had passed through her property earlier in the year.[21] If indeed this story is true, should not "Madame Schuyler" merit mention? Alas, like all other colonials, she did not find her way into Lee's writings.

Lee made sure that his sister understood the threat of scalping that followed British soldiers on the frontiers of North America, but he never discussed the fears of scalping that pervaded the psyche of settlers living on those
frontiers. Would those people have agreed with Lee's observation that the
Indians possessed a "gentillity" and were "hospitable and friendly"? British
citizens living in North America at the time, especially those making a living
in the seaport towns, might agree with Lee's observations about the impact of
the capture of Fort Niagara for the fur trade and the economy of Great
Britain, but certainly they were much more concerned with the impact the
fort had on the security of the villages at or near the frontiers when it was in
the hands of the French. And surely, the Americans would, as Lee, despair in
the defeats of the British forces and hail their victories, but the colonists
would be quick to add words of praise for the thousands of locals who filled
the ranks of the provincial forces for the role they played in those losses and
victories. The result is a blind spot in Charles Lee's "American Expedition."

Lee also at this time was developing his concepts of political thought,
which would lead him to extol the rights of man and rail against the tyranny
of corrupt governments over the next twenty years. So, too, the leading
political thinkers living in North American would undertake such a strong
belief in the rights of man that they would call eventually for the overthrow of
the government of King George III in the colonies. But in the 1750s, the
colonists were not thinking about human rights. On the contrary, they were
struggling with the process of building governmental organizations. They
recognized the need for the unification of the colonies and called for
conventions and correspondent societies that are the budding examples of a
government to rule territory and men. If Charles Lee saw this movement,
he did not recognize it, or, if he did recognize it, he did not chronicle it—
perhaps because he did not understand the need for it.

CHAPTER 3

LEE'S EUROPEAN EXPERIENCE

Charles Lee did not linger on the memories of his "American Expedition." He left North America sometime in 1760, no doubt with the hope and expectation that he could secure advancement in the British military. His uncle, Sir William Bunbury, suggested in a 1759 letter that the prospect existed. "We wish you to come again amongst your friends, and probably some change might be procured as well as advance on this side of the water if you desire it."[1] Filled with a knowledge of North America and tested as a soldier in the field, Charles Lee returned home with expectations.

RETURN TO ENGLAND

For all young officers in the British service, advancement depended on connections with the king and his councilors, and this was especially so in 1761, as the war in North America, Europe, and India was winding down. Great Britain had defeated France and Spain militarily and was in the process of negotiating terms for peace. The prospect of several years of relative peace ahead had government ministers already anticipating the financial savings that would come by dismantling some of the military apparatus and curtailing some of its forces. Advancement in the ranks of a dwindling military force would depend even more on the favor of the king. The optimism of Lee's uncle two years earlier at the height of the war would need to be tempered. In such an atmosphere, patience and tact were virtues to be rewarded. Lee found himself among many young officers vying for position, getting promises from the right politicians but not much more.

Charles Lee began this test of patience and tact with modest, not overwhelming, political clout. He was the only surviving son of Isabella Bunbury Lee and John Lee of Dernall, a baronet from Stanney, both in the County of

Cheshire in North Wales. His father had served as a captain of dragoons and as a lieutenant colonel of grenadiers but died in 1750, before Lee's departure for North America to fight in the French and Indian War. Colonel John Lee, albeit a military man of distinction, was not of noble parentage, and his early death caused young Charles to look to his mother's family, the Bunburys of Cheshire, for support. Their station was comfortable, but their status was not such that royal prerogative would come easily. In addition, the Bunburys were Tories, the political party out of favor and out of power in Great Britain for most of the 1750s and 1760s.

Charles Lee was not a Tory. Despite his mother's family connections, he developed a personal belief in the principles expressed by Whig thinkers and politicians in England and their counterparts on the Continent. The Whigs called for fewer royal prerogatives and greater rights for the individual citizen. The Whig philosophers of the time embraced the emerging political concepts of the Enlightenment—the "rights of man," the tyranny of hereditary kings, and societies as compacts between the governed and their rulers. The writings of Voltaire and John Locke struck a chord with the Whigs but received cold reception among Tories. Whig ministers formed all of the governments under King George II, during his reign from 1727 to 1760. In the rising disputes with the colonies, the Whigs sympathized with the Americans and sought a tolerant policy that would acknowledge their grievances and encourage their feelings for England. So it would seem that Lee was properly aligned until timing betrayed him. The British political scene shifted just as he was returning to England from North America. George III succeeded his grandfather on the throne in 1760, and shortly thereafter the Whigs lost power for several years. A Tory, and the first Scottish prime minister, John Stuart, the third Earl of Bute, took office in May 1762. Lord Bute inherited the responsibility to negotiate the Treaty of Paris ending the Seven Years' War. Another obstacle to Lee, apparently, was John Ligonier, the French-born British commander in chief during the Seven Years' War. Ligonier, for reasons not readily apparent today, was antagonistic to Lee. Friends and relatives hoped that the old man (he was eighty in 1760) would step down or die so that Lee could advance.[2]

Compounding his poor timing were Lee's personal quirks. Patience and tact were not among his virtues. As with his opinions on matters military, Charles Lee did not shy away from expressing political views at any time in his life, and it may have been criticisms of Ligonier's friends that created that stumbling block. As Lee's temper mixed with his politics, he resorted to polemics against individuals rather than reasoned arguments for a just cause. He attacked anyone and anybody who opposed him or his political views.

Lee was a volatile mixture of pride and inflated self-worth, a man who needed to let the world know his value. He expressed this arrogance in speech with a sharp tongue and in letters with a blistering pen. As we have seen, his intemperance with a fellow soldier in New York led to an attempt on his life, and over the course of the next twenty years, he fought several duels (and narrowly escaped the pacing for others) to answer for his uncensored remarks. His attacks on superiors received the most attention, but Lee lashed out at equals and subordinates as well. A close reading of his letters demonstrates that he could not pass up an opportunity to criticize anyone who disagreed with his opinions, failed to provide him his perceived due, or stood in his way, even when he recognized or should have recognized the ill effects of his remarks.

On his return to England, Lee's targets shifted from incompetent military commanders to politicians, the same people whose support he needed if he was to get the advancement he was seeking. Lee fancied himself an expert on American affairs as a result of his military service during the French and Indian War and injected himself into the public debate on American issues on at least two occasions between 1760 and 1764. Naturally, he sided with the Whig thinkers who saw the policies of the government as bungling and heavy-handed, and when his opinions made it to print, Lee, assuredly, was thrilled. The government's ministers, on the other hand, were not. Surely, their friends and informants must also have heard Lee verbally expressing his opinions in the London taverns and public houses.

One of the issues that aroused Lee was the fate of Canada. In 1762, diplomats were hammering out the details of the peace with France and Spain. In its final form, the Treaty of Paris would cover possessions of the several powers in North America, the Caribbean, South America, India, and even the Philippines. The issue most pertinent to the America colonies, of course, was possession of Canada. The treaty granted Britain sole possession of Canada. But the fate of Canada was not a foregone conclusion when Lee arrived back in England, despite the military successes in North America. European territorial issues dominated the negotiations, and the fate of India, as well as the islands in the West Indies, with their advantageous positions for trade, competed with the need to provide security on the North American continent. Lee, who had witnessed the fall of Montreal, felt strongly that Canada should belong to Great Britain and not be ceded in the negotiations for other territories.

Contemporaries referred to a pamphlet that Lee authored at about this time offering his views on the subject, notably ones that may not have been shared by the ministers in power. While no definitive writing can be traced directly to Lee, a pamphlet published in 1761 titled "The Importance of Canada Considered in Two Letters to a Noble Lord" is often referred to as this effort. Significantly, the letters are written in counterpoint, a style favored by Lee, wherein he starts with an assertion by an opponent and demonstrates its absurdity. This first letter examines the claim "*that the simple possession of Canada with the westward of the great lakes can be of no consequence to France.*" The writer sees it differently. If France retains any portion of Canada, the security of Britain and its colonies will be at risk: "He [who will only cast his eye on the map of that country] will there see that whoever possesses the dominion of Lake Ontario and the pass at Niagara, must engross the whole furr trade." Not only that, the Indians will play one side against the other if both Britain and France remain in this territory. Supplied by the French, the Indians can move swiftly with little equipment, will subsist off of the land, and cross the rivers with ease. The forts on the south of Lakes Ontario and Erie (Oswego, Niagara, Presque Isle, the Ohio and La Beuf Rivers) will be vulnerable, and once they fall, "the French will re-establish themselves firmly in the dominion of the lakes, pour daily fresh troops into Canada, and by strengthening and populating the communication betwixt the River St. Laurence and Mississippi surround our colonies, which must end in our total expulsion from America."

The writer goes further in a second letter. The hatred of the Indians for the English is so great, he lectures, that the Indians will join together to drive the English out of Canada, forming a "general confederacy betwixt the Ohion Indians and the upper Five Nations." Others that would join include the Hurons, Wyandots, "Puttawatamies," "Uttawas," "Chippewawas," and "Messasagas." The writer's prediction appeared to be on the verge of coming to pass in April 1762, when Chief Pontiac built a coalition of Ottawas, Chippewas, Hurons, Potawatomi, and other Lake tribes and attacked numerous forts in the Ohio Valley. The French may have been neutered by the conclusion of the war, but the Indians were not completely subdued. Pontiac arose as a strong native leader who understood that the expanding territorial demands of the settlers would not abate and who also believed that the Native Americans could defeat the settlers and their armies if they banded together. Pontiac himself held siege to Detroit. The impact on the settlers, who had hoped that the war had resolved this threat, was matched by the dismay of the British government, then in the process of concluding its treaty with France. Neither country wanted to revive the North American hostilities.

Charles Lee's first biographer, writing in 1792, suggests that Lee took the opportunity in London to let the government know how important he thought the resolution of this affair was to the Americans and, therefore, to

Great Britain.[3] Whether the historian is referring to the two letters referenced above from 1761 or to later letters is unclear, but the impact remains the same. Another biographer dismisses one letter attributed to Lee because it was written in 1759, but ascribes another as "more probable," in part because the style—"a severe and pungent philippic"—sounds more like Lee.[4] Lee could not hold his pen or his tongue even if his views could be detrimental to his efforts for military advancement. Did he expect that his diatribes would go unnoticed? No, indeed! The point was to catch the attention of the government's ministers so as to set England's policies right. Lee was also touting the benefits of establishing British settlements on the Ohio and Illinois Rivers at this time, a proposal not without merit but diametrically opposite to the desires of the king's ministers, who prohibited settlements beyond the Alleghenies.[5]

His opinions were noted among supporters of the American cause as well. At the time, Lee may not have realized that his Whig philosophies and his strong opinions on the value of North America to the British Empire would be seen by some in England and North America as support for the developing political movement toward independence. Like most Whigs, Lee saw Americans as British subjects entitled to the rights of British subjects but not as citizens of a sovereign and independent nation. As he observed in his letters from the American frontier, the lands captured and controlled by British forces added to the luster and glory of the empire. Most Whig politicians at the time (and throughout the years of the American Revolution) criticized the British government's handling of the American crisis and called for acceding to reasonable demands, but would not concede independence for the colonies. Tories perhaps understood that the political movement in North America would necessarily lead to independence if concessions were made.

At least one man in London at the time understood that the difficulties between the colonies and the mother country would not quickly fade and that America needed to develop supporters. Benjamin Franklin was in London for much of the 1750s and 1760s as an agent for Pennsylvania. He took notice of Lee's writings and included Lee in a dinner party in March 1768 at his London quarters, along with others whom Franklin saw as friends of America.[6] Horatio Gates, another British officer seeking promotion without too much success, and Benjamin Rush, a Pennsylvanian studying medicine at Edinburgh, were also at the gathering. Both of these men would serve the American cause along with Charles Lee. Gates returned to America, settled in Virginia, and joined the Continental Army as soon as hostilities began. Rush would serve in the Continental Congress and as a surgeon general during the war. Both Gates and Rush remembered and befriended Lee when he arrived in America in 1773. Franklin understood well the task he assigned himself in 1768.[7]

Charles Lee may have relished the attention, but he did not think of himself as an American and may not have yet understood where the agitation in America would lead. Gates left England in 1772 to make his future in Virginia as an American landowner. Rush had every intention of returning home upon completion of his studies to begin his medical practice. It is possible that Lee's views as a British military officer and nationalist were challenged and changed by the conversation in Franklin's London quarters. Thereafter, Lee continued to speak in favor of the American cause, and his voice grew louder as the revolutionary fervor grew. But his actions tell a different story. Lee left London shortly after the dinner party for the courts and resorts of Europe, not the frontier of Virginia as Gates did, and not for the provincial city life of Philadelphia as did Rush. It would take Lee another five years of traveling purposelessly in Europe before he would see how his political ideas could intersect with the political and military needs of America. Perhaps Benjamin Franklin could foresee this intersection of political expediency in 1768; Charles Lee needed time to understand that his future could be tied to the call for American independence.

Petitioning the King

When Lee returned to England in 1760, he did not rush home to visit his mother and sister. His relationship with his mother was cool, at best. His surviving correspondence does not include a single letter to her, even though he maintained a continuous albeit sporadic correspondence with his sister. Letters to Sidney, up until their mother's death in 1766, always included a curt remembrance to "my Mother" along with a list of other relatives and friends. After his mother's death, Lee would confide in Sidney that his relationship with their mother was not a warm one: "I have this instant rec'd yours with the melancholy account of my Mothers death; had it happen'd some years before, I shou'd not have been so shocked as I now really find myself; so I confess that in the latter part of her life my affection for her was much stronger than in the former."[8]

Some historians suggest that Isabella Lee was not easy to love. Perhaps Charles had inherited his acerbic wit and sharp tongue from his mother and had often felt the sting of both. The issue may also have centered on money. Charles Lee knew, and was not afraid to mention during her lifetime, that his mother's death would provide him financial freedom.[9] His mother was not without resources, and upon her death Charles would inherit her estate as the surviving son. In the interim he was without a steady income and had to rely on his own resources, perhaps not much more than his officer's salary, to sustain himself. Lee enjoyed the good life—trips to resorts, escapes to country estates, the theater—and the lack of a sufficient income to pursue these pleasures disturbed him. Throughout his lifetime, he demonstrated a concern with finances, almost to a public fault. He saw himself in a light that required status. Status required financial freedom.

So Lee threw himself into activities that would achieve personal and finan cial advancement, calling on friends and relatives to make connections that would lead to the king's preference. He intended to rely on his knowledge of America as an introduction and assistance in these efforts. In one of his first letters to Sidney after his return, Lee reports from London that "some of my friends here have promis'd to procure me" an audience with "Mr. Pitt," a Whig who eventually rose to prime minister as the Earl of Chatham in 1766. Lee continues: "I am inclin'd to flatter myself that it may be of service to me as I can inform him of many circumstances in regard to some parts of N. America which he may perhaps be glad to hear and which he can alone have from me."[10] Whether this introduction took place or not, it was just the beginning of Lee's London networking.

On February 18, 1761, Lee presented a petition to King George III and expected Lord Bute, a Tory, to "speak in my favor."[11] Lord Bute would become prime minister in 1762. Lee expected an answer to his petition quickly, but in July he was still waiting, relying now on his friend Lord Thanet to get an answer from or through "Mr. Townsend," the secretary of war under Lord Bute. When the answer still did not come, one of these lords approached the king in Lee's behalf, and the king "promis'd to promote me the first vacancy." Could Lee ask for more than this, a promise from the lips of the regent himself? He did not think so at the time: "Is not this friendship? By my soul I think so; and in the reflection of the Friendship of such men con sists the greatest happiness of my life."[12] This royal promise may have been the ultimate undoing of Charles Lee, because it was never fulfilled to his satisfaction.

Perhaps Lee (and the king) understood the king's promise to be fulfilled in May 1762 when Lee received a temporary commission as a lieutenant colonel in the 103rd Regiment and was sent to Portugal. The government had sent Brigadier General John Burgoyne to help the Portuguese turn back an inva sion by the Spanish that threatened the existence of the kingdom. Although this engagement did not last long, it gave Charles Lee the opportunity to demonstrate personal courage and military prowess. In October, the Spanish forces left a small detachment close to the British rear near the Moorish castle of Vila Velha. Burgoyne sent Lee on a daring nighttime raid to eradicate this threat. Lee led 250 grenadiers and 50 light horsemen across the Tagus River and through mountain passes and fell on the unsuspecting Spaniards from behind after midnight. The action proved a complete surprise and complete success. Lee was right in the midst of the fight, leading the charge fought mostly with bayonets. The Spanish lost a substantial number of men, their magazines, and a brigadier general. Lee's troops suffered few casualties and walked away with booty as well.

Lee's service in this engagement contributed to its success and did not go unnoticed by the British military or the Portuguese. Unfortunately, Lee's surviving correspondence contains a three-year gap, from July 1761 to July 1764, that hides his own perceptions and his feelings on his return to England as an honorary major general in the Portuguese service. Even if Lee understood his preferment as a colonel when he left for the Portuguese theater in 1762 as fulfillment of the king's promise, he may have returned with a different point of view. Whatever his feelings in 1762, Lee clearly saw himself further up the ladder after his return from Portugal, a decorated hero praised by the Portuguese king and recommended for advancement by the commander of the Portuguese forces, Count La Lippe.

To Poland

One would expect that Colonel Charles Lee, on his return from Portugal in 1763 with recommendations in hand and an honorary title in the Portuguese Service, would soon find himself moving up in the ranks of the British military. It did not happen. Instead, in November 1763, he was placed on half pay as a colonel, a military officer not presently needed, who could only wait to heed the call of his majesty, if the call would come. He had left England for the military theater in Portugal, newly commissioned a lieutenant colonel, with the promise of the king to spur him on. He served bravely and honorably yet came home to find the doors shut to advancement. How did it happen that Lee, not without family and political connections, returning home triumphant from his tour of duty on the Continent, found himself without possibilities in England?

Lee could not avoid politics, and he could not hold his tongue even when discussing family and business matters. As we have seen, on at least two occasions, he publicly raised his voice to lecture the British government on its American policy. The king and his ministers did not appreciate critics. If Lee, perhaps, did not understand the connection between keeping his criticisms to himself and his advancement in the army, that connection was not lost on the king, his ministers, and his generals. One biographer suggests that a letter published at about this time that can be attributed to Lee "attacked the military character of General Townshend and Lord George Sackville on such tender points, and with such polished keenness of sarcasm, as to render it impossible that he should be forgiven by the friends of those officers, or their supporters in the government."[13] This could explain the failure of Lee to move up. No royal preferment came Lee's way in 1763 and 1764.

One might think that the more experienced men pressing Lee's cause at court would have advised him to temper his views, or at least to stay out of print with his criticisms of the government. Apparently they did, but to no avail. One correspondent, several years later, alludes to Lee's inability to measure his remarks:

> I should have been heartily glad to have heard, my dear Colonel, that His Majesty's recommendation had been more successful in procuring you an establishment equal to your merits and wishes, but am not at all surprised that you find the door shut against you by the person who has such unbounded Credit, as you have ever too freely indulged a liberty of declaiming, which many infamous & invidious people have not failed to inform him of. The Principle on which you thus openly speak your mind is honest and patriotic, but not politic & as it will not succeed in changing men or times, common prudence should teach us to hold our tongues rather than to risque our fortunes without any prospect of advantage to ourselves or neighbors. Excuse this scrap of advice, my dear Colonel, & place it to the vent of a heart entirely devoted to your Interest.[14]

Relatives and friends might at first overlook or tolerate errors in judgment in an ambitious young man, especially one who could recount experiences and sights that most of them could only imagine. But the failure of that young man to listen to those friends and relatives explain the realities of politics after many months and setbacks must have been difficult for them. Continuing to make the case for advancement for Charles Lee in the court of King George III in 1764 must have been an arduous task.

It is not surprising then that Lee took his leave from England in disgust at his failure to achieve the rank that he saw as deserved and necessary for him to continue his state in life. His relatives and friends, privately, may not have been disappointed when Lee announced his intention to seek employment with the court of King Stanislaus in Poland. Indeed, the suggestion to pursue this post may have come from some of these people, and they may have felt considerable relief on his departure. We have only a fragment of a letter to

describe Lee's state of mind in December 1764 as he is about to depart for
Poland. Lee writes to his cousin, Sir Charles Bunbury:

> My present scheme is this, to go into the Polish service, to which I am so
> strongly recommended that I can scarcely fail. What can I do better? I see
> no chance of being provided for at home; my income is miserably scanty;
> my inclinations greater than those who are ignorant of my circumstances
> suppose. It is wretchedness itself not to be able to herd with the class of men
> we have been accustomed to from our infancy; it is dishonest to strain
> above our faculties, and it is mortifying to avail ourselves of shifts which I
> have found necessary. My resolutions are therefore to live in any part of the
> world where I can find respectable employment, at least 'till my mother's
> death.[15]

Considering Lee's difficulty in containing his ego during peacetime, the swift
shift of his fortunes in 1763 and 1764 must have severely impacted him. His
view of his king, his country, and his future changed. In July 1761, he proclaimed that the friendship of the king was the "greatest happiness of my life."
In December 1764, after risking his life on the battlefield, he left his country in
disgust and some apparent despair. His comments on the king thereafter fail
to reflect any shred of the respect and admiration he expressed in 1761.
The gap in Lee's surviving correspondence during this period, however,
denies us the opportunity to see this transition through his eyes.[16]

Lee spent the better part of the eight years from 1765 to 1773 on the
European continent. He returned to England for an extended stay between
December 1766 and December 1768 that included some time at French and
English seacoast resorts. He then went back to Poland and traveled throughout Europe. He returned to England only once again, in 1771, before his
departure for America in late 1773. He understood that his quest for appropriate advancement in the British military had run into serious difficulties,
especially by the end of 1768, and his efforts after this point were limited.
During these eight years, Lee's mother died, his political views hardened, he
grew increasingly uneasy about his future, and his connection with Great
Britain frayed. Lee undertook a search for an identity and a purpose that led
him to an American destiny.

It was not unusual in the second half of the eighteenth century for a
military man, especially an officer without a purpose in his own country,
to look elsewhere for suitable employment. Indeed, the outbreak of the
American war in 1776 occasioned a flood of foreign officers seeking commissions to fight on the side of the rebels. Nor was it unusual for a gentleman
with a comfortable income to vamp around the civilized world looking for

fun and adventure, owing to a restless spirit or disappointments at home. Charles Lee's European pursuits between 1765 and 1773, therefore, do not appear extraordinary and were apparently perceived, at the time, as an appropriate response to his circumstances. Lee describes his activities during this period first as a "courtier" and then as a "vagabond." What strikes a reader of his letters, however, are his self-centered world and his unceasing criticism of the British government. Almost everything else is superfluous. In the beginning he acknowledges his need to serve as a "courtier" to sustain a living; by the end of this peregrination, long after his financial standing had stabilized, he characterizes himself as a British citizen abandoned by a wrongful government.

Isabella Lee died in Chester in 1766 while her son was still on his first extended tour of the Continent. Lee had left England in late 1764 knowing that his mother's death would benefit him financially but that during her lifetime he would have to fend for himself. Immediately upon receiving the news of his mother's death, in a letter from his sister in May, Lee began to make his way home. By December 1766, he was in London. His letters leave little doubt that his concern was not to comfort his sister on his mother's death,[17] but to consolidate the financial benefits that resulted from it and to make another attempt to pursue his petitions to the king.[18]

Lee must have reconsidered his Continental adventure at this time. He dallied for some time before returning to Poland, and thoughts of remaining in England crossed his mind or, at least, were thrust upon him. He answered casually, from the resort town of Barton where he was taking the air to aid his health, Sidney's suggestions to settle down: "What you say is I think upon the whole just. When we are arriv'd at a certain time of life, a home is absolutely necessary. I must think of it seriously. Yourself, my Aunts and Cousins without any compliments w'd make Chester very agreeable to me if I could have at the same time, two or three or even one good man acquaintance—but except that poor invalid the eldest Fawkner, perhaps thro' my own caprice and self-sufficiency there is not one whose conversation is tolerable. I wish Mrs Manwarring wou'd fancy herself a man, and go to the Tavern, my objection wou'd be removed in a few days—."[19] Clearly, Lee is having fun here at his sister's expense, but his newly acquired financial freedom gave him alternatives that were not available in 1764. The letter suggests that he will off to bathe in the sea at "Harwich or Bologn in France which last I prefer as the wine and rides are better" before returning to Chester. The serenity of Chester and the life of a country gentleman held little appeal for him, but the life of a gentleman about the world did hold some sway.[20] Lee apparently found the time to visit the French towns of Calais and Lyons on his return to England in late 1766. The letter quoted above was written in April 1768, and he was back to France in 1772, complaining to a friend, "I am so tired with Tennis that I can scarcely hold up my head."[21] Lee could not be found at the beach before his mother's death, and his newly inherited income, even on the weak excuse of restoring ill health, clearly had been put to use in the service of pleasure-seeking.

Notwithstanding the side trips to beach resorts for his health, Lee's stay in England from December 1766 to December 1768 was for business purposes: to secure his financial position and to exhort the king yet again for advancement. On December 3, 1766, Lee received a royal grant of 20,000 acres of land in East Florida.[22] The grant came at about the time Lee returned, and his friends at court must have been maneuvering in his favor during his absence. Despite this display of regal beneficence, Lee did not rush off to secure his lands, which required that he personally undertake the settlements to keep them. It does not appear that Lee ever thought of the East Florida grant as a valuable asset. In the next months he learned that his attempt to secure land in New York had fallen through, but he negotiated the purchase of an estate in the Canada, on the island of St. John.[23] By November 1768, Lee had settled his "money affairs" to his "satisfaction and advantage." He was so pleased with himself that he wrote to Sidney boasting that had arranged everything "so well, that I think I can have no trouble for at least four years."[24] He then left England in early 1769 for the Continent and did not return until the summer of 1771.

Lee may have left England in 1765 for financial reasons, but his second departure appears to have been of a different nature. The tone of his letters and his meanderings on the Continent suggest that he returned there more as a man of leisure than a man seeking a career path. He spent less time as the fawning attaché and more as the gentleman about town, finding his way to European adventures or resorts. As soon as he made his way back to Warsaw in April 1769, Lee began angling for permission to leave to watch the Russian Army fight the Turks. He finally got his chance in the fall, and he did not return to Warsaw. Instead, he found his way to Moldavia with the Russian Army; and then to Buda in Hungary (in an effort to "try the waters"); and on to Vienna, Florence, Leghorn, Calabria, Sicily, and Malta. Venice, Minorca, and Gibraltar may also have been on the itinerary. He returned to England in June 1771 but did not stay long before hopping to France—to Dijon in January 1772 and then on to Lyons. By early 1773, he had found his way back to England. Clearly, a lack of finances no longer drove his wandering. On the contrary, a secure income from his inheritance made the wandering enjoyable and affordable.

Lee learned the life of the comfortable wastrel, but political disappointment and resentment continued to plague him. He could persuade King George III to grant him questionable East Florida acreage three thousand miles away, but he could not get what he wanted so dearly—an active commission. Charles Lee could see the writing on the wall, even if Sidney could not. In late 1768, before Lee left England for the second time, Sidney apparently argued that he should remain to see if Lord Rockingham would come to power. His chances for advancement would be better. Lee must have doubted his sister's take on British politics. He dismissed her arguments by insisting that his time away from England in the employ of a Continental king at war would "enhance my pretensions." But, in fact, he understood by this time that his political temperament stood in his way. The continual rejections over a number of years, obviously a result of his political diatribes against the king's policies, only served to make him bitter and his voice louder.

Patience and political tact were not virtues that Lee possessed in any abundance. His reasons for leaving England in 1765 may have been a mix of financial need and political disappointment, but by 1768, he had sufficient means to be successful in British society. His desultory travels in the spring of 1769 demonstrate his lack of need and his financial independence. He returned to Warsaw not as the needy supplicant of 1765, seeking both employment and political acceptance, but as an English gentleman dissatisfied with his government and unwilling to accommodate those in power who disagreed with him.

The coming of the American Revolution offered relief—and a cause.

CHAPTER 4

PERSONALITY AND
POLITICAL PHILOSOPHY

Without question, Charles Lee's personal and political opinions and his overwhelming desire to express his opinions cut short any chance he had of advancement in the British military after 1764, a time when officers were many and positions few. Lee's apologists could maintain that he chose principle over advancement if, indeed, his writings and his opinions demonstrate a principle that is proved worthy. But what great tenets did he espouse or defend in England other than simply "the rights of man" and the obligation to oppose tyrants? And could Charles Lee distinguish a just king from a tyrant?

In fact, Lee's letters contain more political invective than political philosophy. His chosen approach to political discourse was to attack opponents more than to lay out coherent principles. His best writing was rhetorical counterpoint, skewering the bold or broad statements of an opponent. Most often such an effort was accompanied with caustic flourishes to amuse compatriots or cutting personal attacks to disdain enemies. Some other writings attributed to Lee make the case that he possessed a fertile mind and a boldness of opinion. But, unfortunately, the totality of the work adds little to the enlightened theories of political philosophy that dominated his era. It appears that Lee was a rather mundane independent thinker, inconsistent in his judgment of men and more comfortable with broad principles than practical policies. Disturbingly, some of his writings demonstrate a fawning respect for those several royals who occasionally befriended him and an arrogant disregard for the common man.

Throughout his life, Lee tried to outline the essentials for the establishment of a "military colony," and he left a detailed essay on the subject. This could be read as Lee's view of a "societal compact," one of the favorite topics of Enlightenment thinkers like Rousseau and Locke. Actually, it reads like the rule of law according to Charles Lee. Lee's utopia is established with an authoritative tone and maintained by imposed religiosity. In practice, such a utopia would need to be peopled with cultlike followers to have any hope of success. Another essay describes the need for a commander in the field to possess the "coup d'oeil," as Lee phrases it, to see at a glance the entire field of battle and know how to use it to achieve victory. Lee believed that this is a skill to be learned, not an inherent gift available to only a chosen few. Some suggested years later that Lee himself lacked this talent, especially at the Battle of Monmouth in 1778. And a long essay describing a political exchange among officers of the British Army portrays a clear picture of Lee's opinion of himself.

Another writer in England captured the imagination of political activists and held their attention for a short period from 1769 to 1772, the anonymous "Junius." This prolific letter writer published a series of epistles that challenged the thinking and the actions of the English ruling class, with sharp invective and tireless responses. The publication in 1803 of a 1773 conversation in Maryland between Charles Lee and Thomas Rodney began a historical controversy that rages to today. Could Charles Lee have been the notorious Junius, scold of King George and his ministers?

EUROPEAN SOCIETY AND ROYALTY

In May 1769, shortly after leaving England to travel about the European continent, Lee confessed to one of his aristocratic friends in England, Lord Thanet: "I have greater reason every day to congratulate my prudence in having left England; I am persuaded, had I stayed, I should have brought myself into some cursed scrape; even here, at so great a distance, I am thrown into strange agitations of passion on the sight of every newspaper."[1] In a lucid political moment several years later, Lee embellished on his state of mind to his sister and put his European wanderings in context. He could see, if only for a moment, that his caustic political views and his personal disappointments ignited his fiery temper and scorched not only his own ambitions and standing but all of those who stood with him and around him. Even in this moment of lucidity, however, Lee brought the blame around to the king and his tyrannical policies:

> I begin in my cooler and candid moments to be sensible that my temper is alter'd for the worse, whether it is to disappointed ambition, too high an opinion of my own merit I cannot tell; but sometimes I am apt to flatter myself that the alteration which I am conscious of, may be attributed to a good principle, viz—the declension of publick virtue, and the giant strides

which Tyranny is taking towards the annihilation of every thing that ought
to be held dear by the sensible and manly part of human kind. But whatever
the causes may be, I feel the effects, and wish I only felt 'em myself, but I am
afraid that those who by accident are much connected with me must feel
'em still more sensibly. I have just merit enough to condemn and detest
myself, and to wish to throw myself at the feet of those whom my deport-
ment must disgust and shock. . . . When I shall be in England, Heaven
alone can tell. I have long explain'd to you the accurs'd feelings which flow
upon my spirits from those corrupted sources of St Stephens and St
James's. The consolation I might have received from the conversation of
my Chester relations and Friends, I dare not yet avail myself of. I must
continue therefore to play the Vagabond to dissipate and distract.[2]

His political bitterness toward England's ruling government affected Lee so
deeply that he claimed that he could not return in good conscience. His continued political writings sealed his fate: "My chief amusement is disgorging
part of my spleen on paper." But what had he written or said publicly that
brought, if not the wrath, then at least the indifference of those in power?
Was it a threatening political philosophy or his personal attacks?

Not all of Lee's writing survives from this period, but he never failed to
denigrate those in authority, military or government, whose views or actions
he opposed. Was he so politically naive that he did not understand that public lambasting of those in high positions or criticism of government policies
could hinder his personal ambitions, or was he so arrogant that he believed
he should be advanced in spite of, or indeed because of, his opinions? The
answer to this question is not clear. What becomes evident, however, with
each passing month and each letter back home, are his growing resentments.
Biographies of Lee are replete with the names of political figures or their
friends whom it appears that Lee may have called out at one time or another,
burning bridges without regret or regard to the consequences. Lee's temper
so clouds his reasoning that it becomes difficult to ascertain any clear
political statement that he embraces, other than opposition. He does not
establish himself as an articulate proponent of any philosophy—other than
an opponent of "tyranny."

Early in his wanderings, he decries those who support monarchs, especially his favorite target, historian David Hume: "On my journey [from
Warsaw to Constantinople] I cou'd not help reflecting upon the vast obligations our Country has to Mr. David Hume and other Monarchical Writers
who wou'd entail upon us their favourite absolute Government [and] weaken
our jealousy which is the preservative of liberty, and lessen the horrors of
despotism."[3] He decries the wretched state of the "Inhabitants" of continental

Europe and the tyranny of their monarchical rulers. He rails against the miseries that will befall posterity by those who support such princes in ravaging "the finest provinces of Europe upon which Nature has pour'd a profusion of her gifts." This tirade leads to one of Lee's most famous lines about England's American problem: "May God prosper the Americans in their resolutions, *that there may be one Asylum at least on the earth for men,* who prefer their natural rights to the fantastical prerogative of a foolish perverted head because It wears a Crown" (emphasis added). This reference to America as the "one Asylum" for men who prefer "natural rights" predates the similar language of Thomas Paine in *Common Sense* in 1776. Such powerful rhetoric, as early as 1766—no doubt expressed publicly as well as written privately to his sister—would establish Lee as a firebrand in the discourse of the day.

It would appear that Lee despised hereditary rulers in his zeal for the rights of humankind. On the contrary, he seemed to find all of the princes he met, other than King George III, delightful and intelligent. His first letter home, in April 1765, describes meeting with the Hereditary Prince of Brunswick and his wife Augusta, his introduction to the king of Prussia, and a conversation with the king's nephew and heir to the throne, the "Prince Hereditary of Prussia." All of them were interested to talk to Lee about "American affairs." Lee describes the king as "totally unceremonious and familiar"; expresses his adoration for Lady Augusta of Brunswick, "Her person, Her manner, but above all her excellent temper"; and declares the Prince Hereditary of Prussia "really an uncommon fine figure." Now here was royalty that a loyal subject could respect![4] Similarly, when Lee met the royal family of Austria several years later, he overcame his prejudice against monarchs and declared himself "smitten with the reigning one of this country."[5] Of course, as Lee pointed out, they were smart enough to seek out his views on the recent Turkish war and "what has passed in America."

Lee could not say enough about his patron, King Stanislaus Poniatowski of Poland. Lee arrived in Poland in 1765 with a letter of recommendation from Count La Lippe of Portugal, and within six weeks the king "declared me his Aid de Camp." First impressions enumerated many "good qualities" including a fine character, fluency in English, and familiarity with English writers. Within several months, Lee could be more precise: "The longer I am acquainted with this man, the more I like him, the more I admire his talents; a retentive memory, solid judgment, and quickness, are seldom united in the same person, yet they are so superlatively in him. To be master of several languages [like Lee himself], and possess likewise an extensive knowledge of things, is miraculous, yet he is possessed of one and the other. It is a pity that he has not a better theatre to act on."[6] Perhaps the greatest test of this king was his willingness to engage Charles Lee on politics, to hear Lee "converse on these subjects" and "advance [his] doctrines, not the most favourable to monarchy." And certainly the king was "as warm an advocate for the natural rights of mankind, as was Algernon Sydney himself." The king's only vice: "he passes too much time with the women." Lee had the sword of Cromwell, a family heirloom, sent to him in Warsaw as a present for the king. Soon after, Lee was cajoling Lord Thanet in England to send the king a horse as a present.

He did his best to solicit the support of these royals for his advancement at home, but to no avail. Immediately on his return to England in 1766, Lee "deliver'd my letter of recommendation from His Polish Majesty to his brother King" and reminded King George III "of his promise in my favor to Ld. Thanet three years ago." Later, Lee pinned his "principal hopes of success" on the Hereditary Prince soon to arrive in London, but the prince chose not to interfere "as He has not always met with compliance."[7] One wonders whether the Hereditary Prince understood, better than Lee himself, the futility of Lee's petition.

The *philosophes* of the eighteenth century did not necessarily call for the abolition of all monarchies, and many of them, including Voltaire and Diderot, accepted the hospitality of enlightened rulers, as apparently did Charles Lee. Espousing the rights of man in the middle of the century did not require the taking up of arms against one's king; that would come later, first in the American Revolution, where Charles Lee would play his part, and then more frighteningly in the French Revolution. In the 1750s and 1760s, the clarion voices of the Enlightenment sought the ear of kings and princes and attempted to gain acceptance for the policies espoused through royal decree. The results were mixed.

Lee, however, was not a philosopher on a crusade to convert all of the crowned heads of Europe or even the king of Poland to the rising political doctrines of the rights of man. He sought instead a prince to serve in the place of King George III, who had failed to see and reward Lee's merit—one who could tolerate his political philosophy. King Stanislaus served that purpose. Stanislaus, for his part, was a confirmed Anglophile and could suffer Lee in return for English conversation and English political information.

Despite Lee's overwhelming admiration for the Polish monarch, history has offered him mixed reviews. Stanislaus Poniatowski became king of Poland in 1763 through the goodness of his former lover, Catherine the Great of Russia. Poland provided a buffer as well as an entry for Russia to Europe. As a friend on the Polish throne, beholden to the tsar and dependent on the Russian Army to keep his royal prerogative, Stanislaus served a significant purpose for the Russians. He may have appeared a genuine monarch, but even Charles Lee could see that he did not act independently. Stanislaus brought to Poland a touch of the Enlightenment, however. He was a true patron of the arts and identified strongly with English political structures. His trip to England in 1754 as a young man instilled in him a love of Shakespeare and the English rule of law. Lee's perception of Stanislaus—"It is a pity that he has not a better theatre to act on; but really this country is a wretched one"—was based on the inability of the king to act in any way other than the "kind neighbors" of Poland allowed. Years later, when the time to act came to him in 1792, Stanislaus sided with the nobility to overthrow the Polish Constitution and turn the fledgling democracy over to the Russians. For this, he earned the neglect and disregard of generations of countrymen, who saw him as something less than the great man that he appeared to Charles Lee.[8] From their correspondence, it can be deduced that Lee and King Stanislaus were indeed friends or, at least, convivial acquaintances. In addition, this correspondence reveals some of Lee's worldviews, particularly as framed by the rising American spirit.

The Polish king sought out Lee's political observations while Lee was in London in 1767 and 1768. Lee happily obliged with a long letter in October 1767, in large part devoted to the fall of William Pitt and the consequences of his illness in 1767. Lee offers little philosophy, just practical opinions and a fixation on the ins and the outs: he saw Rockingham as the best of the outsiders, but the rest of the opposition were "odious" and "contemptible"; perhaps those in power were no worse than the alternatives. Lee captured the mood of the American colonies precisely and made an exact prediction of the outcome of the agitation over the Stamp Act:

> Nothing could make the American colonists cast off their obedience, or even respect to their mother country, but some attempt on the essence of their liberty; such as undoubtedly the stamp act was, which, if it had remained unrepealed, and admitted as a precedent, they would have been slaves to all intents and purposes, as their whole property would lie at the mercy of the Crown's minister and the minister's ministers, the House of commons, who would find no end to the necessity of taxing these people, as every additional tax would furnish the master with means of adding to their respective wages. . . . If the humours which this accursed attempt has raised, are suffered to subside, the inherent affection which the colonies have for their mother country, and clashings of interests one amongst another, will throw every thing back into the old channel; which indeed is the case already: *but if another attack of the same nature should be made upon them, by a wicked blundering minister, I will venture to prophecy, that*

this country will be shaken to its foundation in its wealth, credit, naval force, and interior population, even without the supposition of a civil war.[9] (emphasis added)

The Polish king, in response, offered a practical solution to the American problem: "I ask you again to tell me, why do they not allow your colonies, to have representatives in the British Parliament? Representation and Taxation would then go together, and the connexion between the mother and her daughters would become indissoluble; otherwise I see no alternative but oppression or entire independence."[10] The king did not think that a separate American parliament would work, however, because it would create "an opposition of interests between the colonies and England, as incompatible as it would be injurious to all parties."

As interesting as this exchange may be, and as accurate on both parts, it fails to reveal the underpinnings of Charles Lee's political thought. Other letters reveal some insights, but not many. Despite all his praise for the Polish court, Lee had no use for Poland, the Polish nobility, or the Polish people. The "gentry," he wrote to one correspondent in England, are "more ignorant, obstinate, and bigotted, than the Hidalgos of Portugal" and those better than the rest "pass their hours in such consummate idleness and dissipation, that our Macaroni club, or Betty's loungers, are, comparatively speaking, men of business and application." Poland boasted an "honest, patriot" king, but it was "a vicious nation." The commoners receive Lee's harshest comments: "Were I to call the common people brutes, I should injure the quadruped creation, they are such mere moving clods of stinking earth."[11] In Lee's defense, if defense of such a statement is possible, he attributes these poor qualities to the sufferings of slavery and concludes that otherwise there cannot be such differences "betwixt man and man."

Lee's references to the "common man" in his correspondence from Europe always come in the context of political vituperation. He failed to see the commoners as people with personal attributes and feelings. This blindness paralleled his inability to see the common American during his time in North America as a soldier in the French and Indian War. He interests lay elsewhere. Lee confessed to another correspondent during his second tour in Warsaw that, in fact, he remained ignorant of the goings on in the country, "as totally a stranger to" the "transactions of this country" as "any man in England." He goes on to describe the fighting between the Russian Cossacks and the "Confederates" as coldly as possible, passing on the tidbit that the Russians had forty or fifty Confederates strip before their execution so as to avoid making "any holes in their coats," inasmuch as the Confederates were so well dressed.[12]

Whatever his situation, Lee always found the time and space in his letters to lambaste politicians back home of every stripe. One common theme is to lament the fallen state of England in the eyes of the world ("from the summit of glory, opulence and strength, to the lowest degree of poverty, imbecility, and contempt");[13] another is to ridicule the current ministers and compare them unfavorably with those he admires; and a third is to hint at a government with as righteous a man as himself at the head ("I am vain enough to think if I had a little weight and credit in Cheshire, I cou'd myself bring about a Glorious Revolution in national affairs").[14]

So, other than lip service to the failings of kings, the nasty effects of tyranny, and the spirit of freedom, where is Charles Lee's political philosophy? One needs to look someplace other than his private writings for a clue. Lee offered no apologies for his tirades, no intellectual or moral arguments for his political conclusions. He was a true believer whose observations confirmed his views. He did not seek out opposing opinions, but carefully associated with those in agreement. His bitterness and disappointment justified his easy dismissal of those in power. Lee was smart enough or lucky enough to have chosen the side of history in ascendancy at the time. As events unfolded in the 1770s, his strident views made him an instant comrade of those moving with events or thinking deeply about the reasons for their positions. He offered a strong voice that dismissed opposing thinkers with a vicious pen. All the better for the Americans that he would soon enrapture, his was a voice from the British aristocracy and the British military ready and willing to take on those institutions.

In fact, however, by the opening scenes of the American political revolution, Charles Lee was a bored and bitter dilettante, traveling around Europe and associating as best he could with people of status who were tolerant of his views. A reading of the early letters from Europe reveals that Lee tired quickly of his position as a "Courtier" (he looked forward to "an *anti-yawning* party"). Poland held little attraction for him, and he sought ways to fill his time while the king and his friends passed theirs in the company of women, "taking snuff, yawning, groaning with ennui, without a syllable to utter." In early 1766, he jumped at the chance to accompany the king's ambassador to Constantinople. But the ambassador moved too slowly for Lee, who soon took up with the faster-moving guard that was "an Escort upon the Grand Signor's treasure, which is annually sent from Moldavia." His impatience nearly killed him. The guard passed through the mountains of Bulgaria without proper provisions, and men and horses were lost to the cold. Lee attributed his survival to the hardening he achieved in his "American Expedition," escaping with only "Rheumatism."[15]

A MILITARY SOCIETY

The concept of a military colony, or a series of such colonies, to be established in the Ohio Valley kept Charles Lee's mind and pen active for at least some of the period upon his return to England after the French and Indian War. Some suggest that Lee pressed this idea on the British ministry and that the rejection of the plan added to his frustration with and disregard for the men running the government.[16] Only a little evidence exists to support this theory, and nowhere does Lee express the wish to return to America for the purpose of founding such an outpost. On the other hand, Lee held on to the idea and used his time after 1778 to write "A Sketch of a Plan for the Formation of a Military Colony," a detailed description for such a settlement.[17] On paper, the colony can be easily visualized; as a practical exercise, however, Lee's dictates for its residents would surely have proved unworkable within just a few years of actual habitation in the American wilderness.

Lee's military colony of 10,000 "men, with their full proportion of officers of different ranks, and children" would subsist on a large circular plot of land equally divided into three concentric circles. Each soldier and officer would be allotted acreage in the center circle and the outer ring (the "pomærium"). The "intermediate" section would be common land for grazing cattle and for "the use of the whole community." Eventually, the pomærium would pass to the children of the community. Women hardly received a mention in Lee's thinking. Their inclusion must be inferred by tangential allusions, such as the bearing of children. All able-bodied men were to work at masculine tasks; only the weak, the deformed, and slaves would perform those "effeminate and vile occupations" such as "tailors, barbers, and shoemakers, and weavers." And all able-bodied men would be required to serve in the militia, on a rotating basis, for "every colony ought to be [military] if they intend to be free."

Military men need to be "softened," Lee understood, "lest they become ferocious in their manners." This duty Lee assigned to a religion of "music and poetry," a pure form of Christianity, as he sees it:

> . . . all good qualities must follow of course: for, without religion, no war-like community can exist; and with religion, if it is pure and unsophisticated, all immoralities are incompatible. Music and poetry, therefore, which ought to be inseparably blended, are the grand pivots of a real, brave, active, warlike and virtuous society. This doctrine I am conscious may shock quakers, puritans and rigid sectarists of every kind; but I do not speak to quakers, puritans, and rigid sectarists. At the first, and from the bottom of my heart, I detest and despise them. I speak to men and soldiers,

who wish and are able to assert and defend the rights of man; and, let me add, to vindicate the character of God Almighty, and real Christianity, which have been so long dishonoured by sectarists of every kind and complexion; catholics, church of England men, Presbyterians, and Methodists.

Lee had an ability to see, and he disdained, the hypocrisy of other men. What he could not see, however, was his tendency to be a true believer in his own logic, no matter how impractical. He would outlaw the "professional priest" but would elect a "grand hierophant, pontifex maximus, or supreme servitor of the ceremonies of divine worship" who would be at least fifty years old and have, as the primary prerequisite, "a distinct and melodious voice." A "chorus of under priests" would assist in the regular ceremonies.

Lee was not a practicing Christian nor an atheist, although his statements that a belief in the divinity of Christ and other "sophistical subtilies" was unnecessary for inclusion in his fold, might lead some to suspect the latter.[18] He simply saw religion—correctly fashioned and administered—as a practical way to soothe the souls of men. In other words, for all of his pretensions, Lee simply refashioned Christianity to serve his worldly purpose, that is, to keep his subjects in line and to prevent self-destruction.

Similarly, Lee attacked the problem of criminality. What had been done to this point in most societies was, of course, incorrect. The death penalty should be eliminated and replaced with servitude and slavery:[19] "The galleys, slavery for a certain term of years, or for life, in proportion to the crime, have accomplished what an army of hangmen, with their hooks, wheels and gibbets, could not." He cites the success of the Grand Duke of Tuscany in such an exercise. Of course, Lee outlaws all "*professional* lawyers" from his colony ("indeed, I should as soon think of inoculating my community for the plague, as admitting one of these gentlemen to reside among us"). Every man would be expected to know and understand the bases on which the community was founded and the laws applicable to him.

Surprisingly, Lee saw tradesmen and merchants in the same light as lawyers and priests. His "community of soldiers and agricultors" would have no need of them. Associating with commercial men leaves "conversation dull, languid and stupid." Too much commerce would simply emasculate men and corrupt republican principles. To compensate, he would allow a fair to run on the outskirts of the community for three weeks or a month each year.

"Coup d'Oeil" and Other Musings

Charles Lee left another treatise, "An Essay on the Coup d'Oeil," that reflects his view of military leadership and, ironically, can be used to discredit his own actions in the field, particularly at the Battle of Monmouth in 1778. He writes of the "coup d'oeil," a military concept that some say is "a present of Nature," and others, like Lee, claim can be learned by diligent study.[20] Lee gives a good definition of this military vision: "The military *coup d'oeil,* then, is nothing else than the art of knowing the nature and different situations of the Country where we make and intend to carry the war; the advantages and disadvantages of the camp and posts that we mean to occupy; as likewise those which may be favourable or disadvantageous to the enemy. . . . It is alone by this knowledge of the country into which we carry the war, that a great Captain can forsee the events of the whole campaign, and, if it may be so expressed, render himself master of them." The "coup d'oeil" is translated as the "stroke of the eye" and suggests the ability to assess the field of battle at a glance, knowing at once the best placement of troops and the commanding positions.

In his essay, Lee cites Greek and Roman military geniuses—Philopoemen, Pyrrhus, king of the Epirots, and Cyrus—and argues that any man can develop this skill through the study of military texts and practice during the periods of peace or military idleness. He urges those who would attain this skill to spend their time "hunting: for, besides giving us a thorough knowledge of the country, and of the different situations, which are infinite, and never the same, it teaches us a thousand stratagems and other things relative to war."

Lee's essay on the coup d'oeil would be of little consequence but for two issues. First, Lee considered himself a great student of war and military strategy. He read extensively on the topic, and his devotion to this subject was clearly made known to his correspondents and acquaintances. Lee's arrogance was such that the essay can be taken as his expression that he had mastered this skill through study and practice. Second, Lee had the opportunity to demonstrate his ability to harness the power of the coup d'oeil at the Battle of Monmouth in 1778. His critics (although not referring to the coup d'oeil concept) claimed that Lee failed miserably in learning the nature of the terrain, placing and advancing his troops, and seizing the moment. Lee, on the other hand, offered a defense of his actions that suggests that only he could see the battlefield for what it was and that his actions saved the day and the Continental Army from disastrous defeat. In counterpoint, George Washington appeared on the Monmouth battlefield to find Lee's troops in disarray, relieved Lee of command, and quickly positioned his men to withstand the advancing British force of considerable strength and experience. It may be the ultimate irony that George Washington demonstrated the possession of coup d'oeil at Monmouth and that Lee clearly did not. Washington was an avid hunter; no evidence exists to suggest that Lee spent any time hunting.[21]

Charles Lee also left other essays that express political views, but with just a few interesting insights into his opinions. One of them, "An Account of a Conversation, Chiefly Relative to the Army," presents Lee taking up the debate with a "grey-headed field-officer" who silences a "subaltern" of "great fire and sentiment." Apparently the subaltern had expressed strong opinions against David Hume (1711–1776), who wrote a history of Great Britain in six volumes between 1754 and 1761 and is thought by many to have been one of the enlightened thinkers of his day. *The History of England* generated considerable controversy at the time, however, owing to Hume's favorable treatment of Charles I, executed for treason in 1649 at the end of the English Civil Wars, and because of his deference to the authority of kings, except in the case of unquestioned tyranny. This caused some, including Lee, to brand Hume as a Tory, despite his agreement with the Whig philosophers on a variety of other issues. Charles I and David Hume were constant foils for Lee's "spleen," and Lee railed against Hume continually throughout his life, making him an object of ridicule and derision repeatedly, especially prior to Lee's taking up the American cause. So this essay, although deftly narrated through the debate of British soldiers, simply served one of Lee's favorite intellectual pastimes.

Again, Lee writes in point and counterpoint rather than presenting a coherent criticism of Hume. The officer had silenced the subaltern, according to Lee, by praising Charles I, suggesting that disparaging the present king was disloyalty, and by stating that such comments were "indecent and ungrateful in those who *eat his Majesty's bread.*" Of course, it is the last (and easiest) argument that Lee takes up. His discourse leads him to several key points: that the king is the "servant of the community"; that the king owes his position to the soldiers' willingness to serve; and that the army serves for "the immediate defence of our mother country against foreign invaders, and the preservation of our colonies and external possessions." He reminds the officer that the present king is simply the successor to a family chosen for the purpose from a "German electorate," and that he owes his position to the people. Indeed, "it might in fact be said with more propriety, that the king eats the officer of the army's bread, than that the officers of the army eat the king's."[22]

In another composition, "A Political Essay," Lee presents an even more powerful statement about kings that could not have gone unnoticed by George III and his ministers: "We will suppose a case: . . . that a community ought not to punish with death any criminal whose existence is not absolutely pernicious, or highly dangerous to the community; and further admitting that a criminal king is the only criminal whose existence can be pernicious or highly dangerous. We will suppose, then, that there should hereafter be formed a community, one of whose fundamental laws should be, that capital

punishment should be confined to delinquent kings alone; . . . I will venture
to affirm that an hundred kings, less guilty than Charles the First, put to death
on the scaffold, would not shock the tenderest nature."[23] This essay, even if
read as speculative musing or historical justification for the execution of
Charles I, could not be ignored. Lee suggests that some societies adhering to
this principle extend the death penalty to the tyrant's entire royal family
to secure tranquillity. Following this analysis, Lee states that applying this
philosophy to the Stuarts would have saved the continent of Europe much
turmoil in the years after the banishment of James II and his sons in 1688.

Clearly, in this last essay we see Charles Lee the firebrand and scourge of
kings, but he offers no specific delineation of the crimes that should be so
punished or the courts that would determine their commission and impose
the sentence.

"Junius"

One of the controversies surrounding Charles Lee, which arose after his death
in 1782, deals with the authorship of the *Letters of Junius*. These letters—
vitriolic attacks on the king's ministers and their policies—were published
regularly in the London *Public Advertiser* between January 1769 and January
1772, and developed an ardent following. The anonymous author decried the
failures of the government, domestically and in foreign affairs, and despaired
the falling stature of Great Britain throughout the world. Junius blistered
any writer who opposed his views, fueling political intrigues with inside
information and gossip.

During the eighteenth century the use of pseudonyms by writers attacking
the ruling powers or seeking to move public opinion was not uncommon.
Junius captured the imagination of the British reading public and held court
for three years without revealing his name. He had an uncanny ability to state
his case in a clear and simple manner, to muster his arguments in support, and
to hold his ground. He pursued his targets—most notably, the Duke of
Grafton, who formed a government after William Pitt stepped down in 1766,
among others—without fear or restraint. When voices would appear in the
newspapers in opposition, Junius would respond and often got the best of the
exchange, at least in the mind of the reading public. Junius focused his radical Whig philosophy on everyday politics in London and expressed his views
with such fervor and disdain that few doubted that exposure of the author
would lead to dire consequences for him and his allies. No candidate among
those who have been suggested as the true "Junius" has yet been universally
accepted, notwithstanding numerous attempts since 1769 to divine his identity.

The dominant issue of the Junius letters concerned the scandalous treatment of John Wilkes. Wilkes was a member of Parliament who openly attacked the king and his ministers and, as a result, was arrested under general warrant in 1763. After the warrant was thrown out in the courts, the government expelled Wilkes from Parliament repeatedly despite his continued reelection. Ultimately, in 1774, he was allowed to take his seat and was elected chamberlain of London. Wilkes became a champion of the people, fighting for parliamentary reform and taking the side of the colonists in America. Junius took up Wilkes's cause and used the platform to state broader demands.

The Junius philosophy can be discerned from a few paragraphs in his first letter, dated January 21, 1769:

> A wise and generous people are roused by every appearance of oppressive, unconstitutional measures, whether those measures are supported only by the power of the government, or masked under the forms of a court of justice. Prudence and self-preservation will oblige the most moderate dispositions to make common cause, even with a man whose conduct they censure, if they see him persecuted in a way, which the real spirit of the laws will not justify. The facts, on which these remarks are founded, are too notorious to require an application.
>
> This, Sir, is the detail. In one view, behold a nation overwhelmed with debt; her revenues wasted; her trade declining; the affections of her colonies alienated; the duty of the magistrate transferred to the soldiery; a gallant army, which never fought unwillingly but against her fellow-subjects, mouldering away for want of the direction of a man of common abilities and spirit; and, in the last instance, the administration of justice become odious and suspected to the whole body of the people. This deplorable scene admits but one addition—that we are governed by counsels, from which a reasonable man can expect no remedy but poison, no relief but death.

The following epistles held to the same line, but with specific attacks on the policies of the ministries and revealing details about the people he sought to dethrone. Junius would be counted among the friends of the American radicals in his opposition to the Stamp Act and his agreement that taxation of the Americans without representation in Parliament violated their basic rights as British citizens.

Could Charles Lee have been the infamous Junius, fuming against the king and his ministers for three years, yet unwilling to reveal himself even to his death in order to avoid the wrath of the king on himself, his family, and his friends? Possibly, but probably not. Compare the above passage from Junius with this excerpt from a May 1769 letter (just months later) to a friend in England and postmarked from Warsaw:

> How miserably fallen she [Britain] is in the eyes of every state! How sunk are we (in a few months I may say) from the summit of glory, opulence and strength, to the lowest degree of poverty, imbecillity, and contempt. Europe is astonished at the rapidity of the change; high and low, men of every order, from the ministers of state to the political barbers, make it the subject of their admiration. How can it happen, say they, that Great Britain, so lately the mistress of the globe, with America in one hand, Asia and Africa in another, instead of the glorious task of giving laws and peace to nations, protecting the weak and injured, checking the powerful and oppressive, should employ her time in trampling on the rights of her dependencies, and violating her own sacred laws, on which her superiority over her neighbors is founded?[24]

Surely, Junius and Charles Lee shared despair for what they saw as the decline of Great Britain and disdain for the same English politicians they deemed responsible. They both possessed a passionate and radical Whig aversion to hereditary monarchs and regal trappings, and both writers lacked restraint, raging at perceived wrongs. Junius and Lee both exhibited excellence at counterpoint attack and reveled in the denigration of their opponents. Once engaged, both were relentless in continuing the argument. Lee had a possible camouflage as well. As we have seen, he was apparently out of the country during much of this time, whereabouts unknown. Few contemporary commentators suspected Charles Lee.

The issue first came up in 1803, twenty-one years after Lee's death, when a letter published by Thomas Rodney of Delaware revealed a conversation he had with Lee in 1773. Lee was then making his first trip through the colonies, and Rodney was one of the men he visited:

> General Lee said there was not a man in the world, no, not even Woodfall the publisher, that knew who the author was; that the secret rested wholly with himself, and forever would remain with him. Feeling in some degree surprised at this unexpected declaration, after pausing a little, I replied, "No, General Lee, if you certainly know what you have affirmed, it can no longer remain solely with him; for certainly no one could know what you have affirmed but the author himself." Recollecting himself, he replied, "I have unguardedly committed myself, and it would be but folly to deny to you that I am the author; but I must request you will not reveal it during my life; for it never was nor ever will be revealed by me to any other." He then proceeded to mention several circumstances to verify his being

the author, and, among them, that of his going over to the continent, and absenting himself from England the most of the time in which these letters were published in London. This he thought necessary, lest by some accident the author should become known, or at least suspected, which might have been his ruin.[25]

Did Charles Lee actually claim authorship of the Junius letters? Thomas Rodney apparently thought that he had. And if he had, why did the world not accept the claim and bring the issue to an end?

No physical proof exists to support Lee's claim, if he made it, and the circumstantial evidence all suggests otherwise. The basic argument against Lee's authorship is simple geography. Junius began his letters in January 1769, and they appeared frequently for the three years thereafter. Oftentimes, Junius responded directly to letters appearing in the prior week by a writer taking him to task. Most observers, steeped in the details of the letters and the politics of the times, believe that Junius must have been someone not only in London at the time but active on the political scene. Many allusions and much of the discourse in the letters deal with contemporary and local London events. It is this urgency that gave the letters their drama and punch for the public. Junius was in the arena speaking to the masses about the spectacle before them.

Charles Lee, by all accounts, was in Warsaw or wandering through continental Europe during most of the period of the Junius ascendancy. Given the distances and the vagaries inherent in eighteenth-century travel, he could not logically be the author. Nevertheless, one ardent supporter of Lee as Junius went to great lengths to track his whereabouts during this period in an effort to prove, though unconvincingly, that Charles Lee was, indeed, Junius. The only other way to explain Lee's putative authorship would be to assume that Lee established an elaborate ruse to make his enemies believe he was on the Continent when all the while he was ensconced in a London hideaway writing his diatribes without the smallest hint of personal fame or approval. In addition, his friends, complicit in this scheme, would have to have assisted the game by maintaining a correspondence with a cipher in distant capitals. Nevertheless, one biographer accepts Lee as Junius ("While it is not easy to pin his name to any particular 'Junius' letter there would seem to be evidence that he wrote not one but probably more"), relying on the "tone rather than anything else"; another dismisses the thought out of hand.[26]

Lee's absence from London may give him cover, but it makes it highly improbable that he was, indeed, Junius. More compelling arguments can be made for Sir Philip Francis, Lord Shelburne, or even Lauglin Macleane,

Lord Shelburne's secretary. Recent reviews, supported by word recognition software, weaken the link to Charles Lee, as does a comparison of the above excerpts. Although the arguments arise from a similar political view, Junius presents a paced, reasoned, and even form of argument in contrast to Lee's charged attacks. It is also possible to conclude that Lee received a copy of the newspaper carrying the Junius letter several months after its publication, while in Europe, and picked up the tone and the substance of the argument in his almost contemporaneous correspondence.

What would be the purpose, then, for Charles Lee to claim in 1773 that he was Junius? Perhaps Lee was flattered by Rodney's suggestion that he was the famous firebrand. Rather than deny the presumption without question, he could have attempted to leave the question open to add to his mystique. Who would know for sure? Rodney, on the other hand, may have heard this non-denial as something more. Perhaps Lee's ambivalence fueled Rodney's vanity in solving the riddle. Or perhaps, Lee knew the identity of Junius, and he was trying to convey that piece of vanity to Rodney. Whatever the cause, Rodney's port-mortem revelation did not raise Lee's public standing but only added to his reputation as someone who shaded the truth to match his own perception of self.

An Eccentric Personality

By all accounts, Charles Lee presented as colorful a figure as any man in the Americas in 1773. His odd appearance, his language—both profane and erudite—his dogs, his European servants, his stories of princes and kings, Russian military campaigns and duels of honor in distant places, all would make for a unique and entertaining dinner guest or traveling companion. In addition, the Americans would surely have heard other stories, such as those about his life among the Mohawks and his Indian bride, or the crossing the Carpathian Mountains with the king's gold. So, aside from striking exactly the right chord with the Americans by his writings in 1774 and 1775, Lee must have also struck the fancy of the Americans by his persona and his person.

Lee was exceptionally well-read and spoke with authority on military issues and British and European politics; he surely dropped names of the great men he had met and dined with such as the king of Poland, the Hereditary Prince of Prussia, or Edmund Burke. If his letters are any indication, his language must have been colorful, filled with literary and philosophical allusions and peppered with Latin, Italian, and French phrases, as well as profanity. He may have presented the hint of nobility, but his peculiar manners, his coarseness in speech, and his lack of personal grooming presented an entirely different persona. The Americans, seeing all of this firsthand, were not horrified, but took to Lee with apparent affection.

If contemporary accounts are to be believed, Charles Lee was less than handsome and poorly groomed. No satisfactory resemblance of him remains, so we must rely on written descriptions. The one picture that appears most often comes from an English broadside or mezzotint produced during the war for the London crowd. It accompanied a number of other prints of the rebels opposing Great Britain. It shows a uniformed man, stout and with a broad face. Unfortunately, this was a stock portrait used by the printers and bears no likeness to Lee.[27] By all accounts, Lee was angular in body and thin-faced, almost to a fault, with a large protruding nose to emphasize his uncomely appearance. A profile caricature drawn by B. Rushbrooke in the early 1770s suggests this exact description. He was of average height and weight for the time and apparently missing several fingers on one hand, allegedly the result of a duel (with swords and pistols) with an Italian several years earlier that left the Italian dead. He must have presented a stark contrast to George Washington, tall and erect, and ever the gentleman, and to many other of the patriots he met, especially those from the South. If Lee dominated a room, it would be by his words, his tone, and his manner, not his physical prowess. The first impressions of Abigail Adams, who met both men in Boston shortly after their 1775 appointment, are telling:

> I had the pleasure of seeing both the Generals and their Aid de camps soon after their arrival and of being personally made known to them. . . .
>
> I was struck with General Washington. You had prepaired me to entertain a favorable opinion of him, but I thought the one half was not told me. Dignity with ease, and complacency, the Gentleman and Soldier look agreeably blended in him. Modesty marks every line of his face. . . . General Lee looks like a careless hardy Veteran and from his appearance brought to my mind his namesake Charls the 12, king of Sweden. The Elegance of his pen far exceeds that of his person.[28]

Abigail's observations, always keen, capture the two men. Notwithstanding his appearance, however, Charles Lee made a lasting impression on her, and she asked after him and his well-being several times in letters to her husband. John Adams also admired Lee but in a frank moment described him as an "Oddity" and a "queer Creature." Lee's constant correspondent, Benjamin Rush, used similar terms in reference to his friend.[29]

Lee seldom traveled alone. He had at least one servant or attendant with him at all times. The most loyal of his entourage was Giuseppe Minghini, who looked after Lee's worldly goods and performed personal tasks as needed.

Lee's letters are filled with references to his servants and his material needs, even in the worst of times. In addition, Lee was accompanied everywhere by several dogs, and he treated them as equals. In letters, he referred to the dogs by name, often not distinguishing them from people or acknowledging their canine nature. Indeed, his fondness for his dogs is documented not just in his own letters but also in the letters of those Americans he visited in this period who had the "pleasure" of dining with the dogs in the room or under the table. Again, Abigail Adams, describes the experience of meeting with Lee and, of necessity, his dogs: "I was very politely entertaind and noticed by the Generals, more especially General Lee, who was very urgent with me to tarry in Town and dine with him and the Ladies present, at Hob Goblin Hall, but I excused my self. The General was determined that I should not only be acquainted with him, but with his companions too, and therefore placed a chair before me into which he orderd Mr. Sparder to mount and present his paw to me for a better acquaintance. I could not do otherways than accept it.—That Madam says he is the Dog which Mr. [Adams] has rendered famous."[30] "Mr. Spada" was a Pomeranian who could not be ignored. Lee would also give voice to his dogs. In a letter to John Adams, Lee passes on that "Spada sends his love and declares in very intelligible language that He has far'd much better since your allusion to him [revealed in an intercepted letter to James Warren], for he is caressed now by all ranks, sexes and Ages."[31] Unfortunately, Mr. Spada was lost in 1776, shortly after Lee's capture in Basking Ridge. In concern for the canine and his master, Abigail Adams expressed her grief to her husband in asking after Lee's treatment in captivity.[32]

By all accounts, Lee's conversation was laced with coarseness, both in language and subject. One biographer of Horatio Gates suggests that the Lee-Gates friendship was in part based on their mutual reliance on colorful language.[33] He also suggests that their falling out just before Lee's death was partly the result Lee's disdain for Gates's wife that exposed itself with a remark at a dinner party at Traveller's Rest, Gates's estate next door to Lee's Prato Rio in Berkeley County, in western Virginia. Lee expressed his contempt for Mrs. Gates in a letter dated June 16, 1781, to Robert Morris ("that Medusa his wife governs with a rod of Scorpions"), so this supposition may, indeed, be accurate.

Lee's regard for his plantation in Virginia, Prato Rio, also reveals some of the strangeness of his character. Clearly, Lee purchased the estate (at the urging of Gates) just before hostilities began in 1775 to secure his stature as an officer committed to the American cause. Lee expressed no interest in the property throughout his service, except for the cost of purchasing the property and maintaining it. When he left the army in 1778, Lee had nowhere else to go but Prato Rio, but he never enjoyed the life of a country farmer, and he surely did not make the manor house a home. The house remained unfinished when he arrived in 1778, with limited interior walls, providing essentially a single room for cooking, eating, sleeping, and recreation. Lee made no attempt to complete the building. Instead, he drew lines on the floor, "creating" rooms to suit his needs. He claimed in letters to Congress asking for assistance that the estate was more of a financial drain than benefit. By 1781, he was making attempts to sell the property, and in his abandonment of the home shortly before his death in 1782 he evinces no concern or affection for the estate. Charles Lee never succeeded in establishing roots during his life, preferring instead to be a vagabond, traveling about Europe and North America in search of his identity. Prato Rio did not change him when he sought exile there in 1778.

Throughout his life, except perhaps in the period after the death of his mother and before his departure for America in 1773, Charles Lee exhibited an excessive anxiety about money. The first letter attributed to him, in October 1754, concerns a dispute with a relative over the entitlement to a legacy of five hundred pounds and his efforts to secure an equal portion of it or foregoing any further contact with the relative claiming the whole. He gave as one of his reasons for quitting England in 1765 his inability to live the lifestyle he aspired to for lack of funds; he was simply awaiting the death of his mother to put him into a comfortable estate. Years later, he wrote to Congress asking for assistance in securing "hard money from New York" (still in British control) and went out of his way to detail the "easy fortune for a private Gentleman" that he had risked to join the patriots in 1775:

> 1stly, I had £480 per annum on a mortgage in Jamaica which was punctually paid—2dly, an estate in Middlesex or £200 per annum for another person's life but which was insured against my own—3dly one thousand pounds on a country turnpike security at four per cent—4thly—£1500 at five per cent on bond—5thly my half pay £136 per annum—besides this about twelve hundred pounds in my Agents and in different debts—in all my clear income besides this money at command was about nine hundred and forty pounds per annum—I had likewise ten thousand acres of land in the Island of St. Johns which had been settled and located at the expense of seven or eight hundred pounds, a mandamus for twenty thousand more in East Florida and a claim as half pay field officer who had served the last War in America in any of the new lands either on the Ohio, Miss'sipi or West Florida—lastly eight hundred ducats pr annum my table lodging and provisions for my horses as Aid de Camp General to his Majesty of Poland whenever I chose to reside in that Country—such was the fortune and

income I staked on the die of American Liberty, and I played a losing game for I might lose all and had no prospect or wish to better it.[34]

As we will see, Charles Lee did not give up this fortune at his commission in 1775 without financial assurances, despite this claim in 1779 that he had everything to lose.

Lee's concern for his goods and his pleasures could also be galling. In 1776, when Washington was racing across New Jersey just ahead of the British and desperately calling for Lee to join his forces, Lee nonchalantly asked Washington to take the time to look for his horse that was somehow left behind near Princeton. In one of his earliest letters after capture by the British in 1776, Lee asked financier Robert Morris to send his servant Giuseppe Minghini immediately, along with his dogs, and Washington dutifully arranged for spending money (as he would have for any similarly situated high-ranking officer) to be forwarded to Lee through drafts on Robert Morris.[35] Lee entreated Morris again in April for Minghini and wrote directly to Minghini at the same time with specific demands: "bring with you as many summer cloaths as you can—silk stockings, linen waistcoats and breeches tights, boots and a new hat—some books likewise particularly Ainsworth's Dictionary & the six French books, l'politique—if any of the Dogs are with you bring them." Expenses were to be paid through Morris.[36] In the last year of his life, Lee placed the following advertisement, which reflects his personal accoutrements during the war and his regard for these belongings:

> A little before General Lee had the misfortune to be taken Prisoner in the year 1776, he left several Trunks, Boxes and Portmanteaux, none of which to his Knowledge fell into the Hands of the British Army, of course they must be in some American Hands; the Articles which he particularly recollects they contained, were as follows: One new Polish Uniform, white faced with blue, one new Uniform of the third Battalion of Phila. Associators, brown faced with white, and Silver Epaulets, five Waistcoats of fine Cloth, a complete Hussars dress of Black Cloth garnished with Fox Skin, several Pair of Silk Stockings, a Spy Glass, but above all, a remarkable Pair of PISTOLS mounted with Steel and inlaid with Gold, with the name KONSKI, ingraved on the Lock. . . . [T]he pistols are of a more Particular Value than any of the other articles, and whosoever delivers them . . . shall receive TWO GUINEAS REWARD.[37]

No evidence survives that suggests Lee retrieved any of these personal articles.

It also appears that Lee was quarrelsome in person as well as in writing. His sobriquet among the Mohawks—meaning "Boiling Water" or a roiling spirit—suggests an apparent temper even as a young man. His biographers list arguments, fights, and litigation from his days in North America in the 1750s through later life. In writing, he could be a persistent and incessant foe, and his tongue and his pen led him to at least two duels.

It may well be that physical ailments contributed to Lee's temper throughout his life, as his letters are replete with complaints of "rheumatism" and gout. His near-death experience in the Carpathian Mountains in 1769 left him in dire condition ("I was delirious for eight days, and given over for three weeks"), keeping him incapacitated for a month before he could move on.[38] The next six months were spent in recuperation, often at resorts. After his arrival in North America in 1773, Lee would refer often to attacks of gout. Perhaps the most embarrassing attack came in January 1776, as Lee was preparing to enter New York City to shore up its defenses. Lee had to be carried into the city in a litter, the pain or discomfort being so great that "I am actually incapacitated from moving my legs by the gout or rheumatism, or mixture of both."[39] And later that year, Lee expressed a desire for the southern command rather than the Canadian command to avoid another bout of the disease.

In spite of all of these quirks, or perhaps because of them, Charles Lee was able to maintain strong and long-lasting friendships with a considerable number of people in England and in the Americas. Several of his English friends were characters themselves, like John Hall-Stevenson, an aristocrat poet of sorts, who founded a society of near reprobates called the "Twelve Monks of Medmenham." One of his associates was Laurence Sterne, the author of *Tristram Shandy.* They partied at Hall-Stevenson's estate, "Crazy Castle," in Yorkshire. Others in England who worked hard to secure Lee the military position he so vainly sought were Lord Thanet and Lord Pembroke, and Sir Charles Davers. At some point, he met the young Edmund Burke and developed a friendship that resulted in the exchange of correspondence over the next years. Once established in America in 1773, Lee developed loyal friendships with Benjamin Rush, Horatio Gates, Richard Henry Lee, and Robert Morris, among others. His correspondence with these men was intimate, and he called on them repeatedly in times of need. And most often, they obliged him if they could. As mentioned above, John Adams retained a fondness for Lee until Lee's death, and his letters and Abigail's letters are filled with references concerning his well-being, especially during his captivity in 1777. As eccentric a personality as Charles Lee was, he could secure and maintain a friendship with persons of like views and open dispositions.

Lee never married, except for his Seneca princess, leaving biographers to speculate about the reason. His letters show an appreciation of the opposite sex, and several suggest or approach the possibility of wedlock. It does not appear that Lee harbored any concerns about subsequent marriage owing to his relationship with his unnamed Native American wife, nor did anyone else. Lee mentions her only once, in one of his first letters to Sidney in 1756, despite later references by friends years later that he had fathered twin boys from the union.[40] With or without knowledge of this marriage, Lee's uncle, Sir William Bunbury, urged Lee's return from North America in 1759 with the prospect of marriage to a local belle ("A great many matches are talked of here in Town, so that if you do not come soon, all our fine ladies will be disposed of").[41] Sister Sidney brought up the possibility throughout Lee's life that he marry and return home. Lee recognized the advantages of finding a life partner and settling down ("What you say is I think on the whole just. When we are arriv'd at a certain time of life, a home is absolutely necessary").[42] But it does not appear that his estate in Chester, or the women available thereabouts, held much appeal for him. Nevertheless, his letters to Sidney are replete with requests for her to pass on "my respects" to numerous maidens. Perhaps the countryside, and the people in it, were just too dull. As seen above, Lee complained to Sidney that "there is not one [man] whose conversation is tolerable" although "Mrs Manwarring" would do to remove his objection if she "wou'd fancy herself a man, and go to the Tavern."

Lee appears to have been rejected by several prospective brides. He found a possibility in Warsaw, a young woman tutored by him in English, only to be rejected: "Why did you not, on some humane pretext, remove me from your side before the flame had acquired such inextinguishable fierceness?" The letter is an offer of marriage ("I cannot see the mighty crime in wishing to unite your fortune with mine") and a plea to identify the flaw in him that prevents it ("I had flattered myself, that time and an unwearied attention to please, would have supplied in me what you find amiss in my person or the arts of conversation.")[43] Lee often remembers to send his regards to the wives of friends and correspondents and occasionally comments on their good and, in his opinion, not so admirable qualities: "Upon my word [Lord Thanet] is singularly fortunate in a Wife, and particularly as she is a woman of great fashion and family, which you know is not the class of women nowadays remarkable for furnishing good domestick wives."[44] His strong opinions, poor hygiene and lack of manners, and his desultory travel would surely have been detriments, but not absolute bars. Lee's earliest biographer goes out of his way to demonstrate Lee's attraction to women[45] but another suggests the possibility that Lee was homosexual.[46] Yet another suggests that Lee may have contracted venereal disease at a young age and this affliction kept him from marriage.[47] Whatever the reason, Lee spent his life (after leaving his Native American princess) as a bachelor, constantly on the move and in the comfort only of his ever-present dogs.

One exchange late in Lee's life demonstrates his willingness to engage in repartee with women as well as men. In a letter dated December 20, 1778, Lee challenges Miss Rebecca Franks to a duel! Her affront was to accuse him of wearing "green breeches patched with leather" to a Philadelphia social affair, a fashion faux pas. The letter, clearly tongue-in-cheek, pokes fun at the lady and Lee himself: "If you had accused me of a design to procrastinate the war, or of holding a treasonable correspondence with the enemy, I could have borne it; this I am used to; and this happened to the great Fabius Maximus. If you had accused me of getting drunk as often as I could get liquor, as *two Alexanders the Great* have been charged with this vice, I should, perhaps, have sat patient under the imputation." He goes on to say in a postscript that, for his part, he is keeping this matter confidential except for "seven members of Congress and nineteen women, six of whom are old maids." Unfortunately, Lee misread his adversary, who took such offense that shortly thereafter he was obliged to send a letter of apology assuring her that the letter was in jest, based on his opinion that "the liberality of your mind and cheerfulness of your disposition were such that you would be pleased with any effort to make you laugh for a moment in these melancholy times."[48] The first letter, just six months after Lee's personal disaster at the Battle of Monmouth, represents the only evidence that Lee sought to laugh in the last years of his life.

CHAPTER 5

A "LOVE AFFAIR" WITH AMERICA

At some point in the summer of 1773, Charles Lee decided to leave England for New York. His correspondence leading up to this decision is missing, or nonexistent, leaving his motives unclear. Perhaps he was bored with the amusements of the European continent. Perhaps his outspoken political opinions made remaining in England uncomfortable. Perhaps he at last realized that his fortune was better tied to the zealots in the thirteen rebellious colonies than laid at the door of the British ministry. Most likely, however, he had time on his hands, and it seemed a suitable occasion to review his holdings in the western hemisphere.

ARRIVAL IN NEW YORK

In 1773, Lee held two substantial land interests in the New World, albeit not within the thirteen colonies. Both were rewards from the Crown that he now so often maligned, but neither was of such significance as to make him a rich man in just the owning: ten thousand acres on the island of Saint John's in Canada (now known as Prince Edward Island) and twenty thousand acres in Florida. The first was awarded in 1764 and the second in 1766.[1] Based on Lee's correspondence and the general economics of the time, it can be understood that these landholdings required more than absentee management. Land speculation at the time required additional outlays of capital for surveys and improvements and attention to adjacent properties and offerings. Working the land required personal attention or at the least the hiring of trustworthy managers and the maintenance of farmers. Little reward came from ownership by itself. All of this can be seen clearly in the last of the preserved letters that we now have to Charles Lee before his departure for New York in 1773. And this letter may explain the trip.

Apparently Lee had written to an old friend and business associate, Walter Patterson, whose good fortune placed him as the governor of St John's. Lee wanted advice on his holdings there, and what better source than the governor of the island? We can discern the questions only from the answers provided. Patterson wrote a long letter from St John's in November 1772, in three parts: first, thanking Lee for writing after such a long time and for the "flattering letter, from you"; second, answering in detail Lee's questions about his property; and, third, questioning Lee's claim that Patterson owed him money.[2] The meat is in the description of Lee's estate:

> You desire to know if it is worth your while to lay out any money on your lands in this Island. I answer yes. You have half of the very best lot on this Island, or at least as good as any; and were I in your circumstances I would be proprietor of the whole of it; in that manner I would lay out the first money. There are many good French who live upon it already; but for want of titles to the land, they do not improve it as they might, these would commence a small rent immediately, for which you ought to appoint an Agent, . . .
>
> . . .
>
> But after all Lee, what is there to hinder you from taking a view of the place yourself, nay of bringing your own agent, don't you think, the cultivating of your lands and improving your constitution and fortune, is a much more rational, and perhaps I might say sensible employment, than scampering all over the Continent of Europe in search of dam'd Hungarian fevers. Come Lee, and leave Hume to cramb his history down the throat of his countrymen, for few others read it.[3]

It is not likely that this letter from Patterson alone prompted Lee to leave England. But coupled with reports from those he met after arriving in New York that he was intent on a trip to inspect his Florida holdings (by way of the Ohio and Mississippi Valleys), it is clear that Lee had more than American politics on his mind at this time. As we have seen, finances were always an issue with Lee, but for the most part his concerns centered on the immediacy of wealth rather than its cultivation. His wanderings on the Continent demonstrate that he was not in need of money to travel or to care for himself. His 1779 listing for the Congress of the moneyed properties he held in 1773 (see chapter 4) provides a clear picture of the ease of his finances at this time. We can be sure by the "Hume" reference that Lee had not forgotten to send his friend his recent diatribe against David Hume that he was so very fond of and was passing on to others as well. Lee refers to this paper on Hume in a long letter several months earlier to his sister Sidney. In the same letter he discussed his health ("I intend to consult the famous Physician Tissot of Lausanne on the subject of my disorder"), his travel to Dijon, and his temper and its impact on his life ("I have just enough merit to condemn and detest myself"). He took the time to ask for numerous relatives ("How does my Aunt Williams? . . . The Gwynynog family and Charlotte amongst the rest?"). But notably, this letter does not mention the struggle of the American colonies. All of the political references are decidedly British, the only non-British reference being to the "cantons of Switzerland . . . where the Clergy are not taught to anathematize the Champions of their Country, and consecrate the Tyrants."

Lee spent his first month in America living with Thomas Gamble, a friend from the Forty-fourth Regiment and now a successful businessman in New York. After Lee left New York, Gamble assumed that he was making his way to his investment properties. He tried to track Lee down in June 1774 and thought he might be "gone to the West-Indies" or Carolina, discovering at last that he was in Virginia. Gamble also referred to Lee's land in Florida and mentioned that he was still awaiting an answer to correspondence with the governor of that territory.[4] Lee may have shared with Gamble an entertaining letter he received in September from Thomas Baldwin, a friend who had just returned from "Bermudas." The letter must surely have ended any plan that Lee had to visit the Caribbean. Baldwin complained that "Candles burned dim, cockroaches and innumerable Ants filled every room, not only of our own house, but every house we entered." He continued, "The Air is never free from clouds . . . very shrill Mosquitoes attack you from every quarter. . . . The water is putrid in a few days [and t]here are no Markets thro' the Island."[5]

Lee's interest in investment properties that would require substantial attention waned quickly after his arrival in New York. He put aside the arduous Florida adventure, claiming, whether in fact or as expedience, an attack of the gout. Just as likely, Lee was dissuaded from this trip by events in America and his welcome in New York, given that he did, indeed, travel over the next weeks. He must have realized that the hotbed of agitation that was America in 1773 better suited his disposition, because he simply changed his itinerary for a more appealing survey of the land and politics of the colonies west and south.

As with most of what we know about Charles Lee, observers can debate whether he sailed to New York in 1773 as a resolute believer, determined to bind his life and his fortune to the American cause, or as an opportunist who found his destiny upon arrival. Lee's earliest biographer may be the original source for the theory that Lee came to America in 1773 specifically to support the growing sentiment for independence. Edward Langworthy stated without question in 1792 that Lee was an outspoken supporter of the colonies while in Europe ("These circumstances are mentioned, as they serve to demonstrate that a zeal for the welfare of the Colonies, from the General's earliest acquaintance with them, had been a ruling principle of his life") and traveled to America to be ready to serve ("and the General concerted a design of taking a part in the favour of America in case it came to an open rupture"), but the evidence, at least for the latter claim, remains thin.[6]

Surely Lee felt that he had a peculiar knowledge or understanding of America, owing to his adventures in the French and Indian War; his letters show that he had followed American affairs and the political discourse that it generated throughout Europe in the past several years; he offered his opinions on American affairs whenever he had the opportunity; and, of course, he was well acquainted with the political thinkers and writers who challenged the right of kings and railed against the dictates of tyrants. But from 1764 to 1773, Charles Lee was a desultory and dissolute Englishman about Europe, not a firebrand of American political activism. All of his fuming and ranting was aimed at British policies in general and the personal qualities of King George III and his advisers, in particular. His tirade against David Hume's history of England might have stirred a few intellectuals in Philadelphia had it been available, but it certainly would not have elicited the least interest for Bostonians railing against the tax on tea.

Another indication that Charles Lee was not focused on the political agitation in America upon his arrival in late 1773 was his first foray into public political discourse. A sketch of several European rulers that has been attributed to Lee appeared in *Rivington's Gazetteer* in November, and certainly Lee would have been one of only a few in New York at the time with sufficient first- and secondhand knowledge of King Stanislaus, Joseph II, and Catherine of Russia to write or comment on political matters in eastern Europe. The timing all but confirms his authorship. Lee loved political discourse in word and paper and surely continued thinking and writing on his long voyage from England in the fall of 1773. And so it is telling that his first published piece in America dealt with European politics instead of current American events.

There does not appear to be a triggering event that caused Charles Lee, amid his leisure on the Continent or while writing tirades about English politicians, to make a mad rush to America to join in the coming storm. His correspondence does not show such a transformation. His actions immediately upon landing in New York suggest otherwise. He did not take the time or make the effort on the long sea voyage from England to New York to pencil a manifesto of American rights and demands. The turning force may have occurred *after* his arrival in New York: the Boston Tea Party.

Lee's host in New York, Thomas Gamble, was a committed Tory. Their early conversations apparently dealt with European affairs.[7] It does not appear to be coincidence that Lee's rhetoric and focus shifted sometime between November and the end of the year. On December 16, 1773, just weeks after Lee's arrival in the colonies, hooligans dressed as Indians dumped His Majesty's tea into Boston Harbor, igniting passions that would not be checked. Within months of his arrival in New York, Lee transformed his rhetoric and his person from a European to an American orientation. It happened so quickly that his friends could not see it. When Lee left for the southern colonies after the Tea Party, his host, Thomas Gamble, left for Boston at the solicitation of their former commander, General Thomas Gage. By June, Gamble was back in New York searching for Lee and wondering why he stopped short of Florida, in Virginia. Gamble reported on the good fortune of Gage to have command in Boston and then on the number of troops being readied in England to quell the disturbance.[8] Lee had, by then, moved in the opposite political direction.

To a man as vain and ambitious as Lee, the Boston Tea Party could easily have seemed propitious timing or even destiny. That he followed its lead is no discredit. Whether the Tea Party was the trigger or not, sometime shortly after his arrival in New York in 1773, Charles Lee realized, as did the Americans who greeted him, that their causes conjoined in a beautiful way.[9]

TRAVELS THROUGH THE COLONIES

The eighteen months after his arrival in New York were surely the pinnacle of Charles Lee's life. Not in New York a month, Lee was heralded by *Rivington's Gazetteer* as a "sincere friend to liberty in general, and an able advocate for the freedom and rights of the colonies in particular." He then traveled to Philadelphia, Maryland, and Virginia, meeting and conversing with men active in the political agitation against England and in the early stages of expressing themselves and making their personages known to a wider audience. He was back in Philadelphia by the early summer of 1774 and then moved quickly through the middle states to Boston. He returned to Philadelphia by September in time for the meeting of the First Continental Congress. At each stop he made the acquaintance of more of the men who would soon be taking up pens and arms against the king.

It may not be too much an exaggeration to suggest that during this period Charles Lee began a "love affair" with America. When he had left North America in 1760, "America" was a conglomeration of colonies and territories owned by the English king that needed civilizing and control. Its borders were unclear, its leaders nonexistent, its manners a coarse reflection of the empire. Charles Lee, as we have seen, did not even notice the Americans (other than the colorful Native Americans). On his return, thirteen years later, Charles Lee discovered so much more. The colonies were beginning to unite, the borders had become secure, leaders and a distinct political philosophy were developing as one. In a word, the colonies had matured. The country now had allure, not only handsome, but fresh and sassy. Charles Lee could not help but notice and, fortunately for him, America returned the infatuation.

Lee's arrival in America in 1773 was propitious. He soon became a darling of the press and impressive to the colonials. Here was a man in his prime (he was only forty-two at the time), a major general in the Polish Army, a war hero in Portugal, a sophisticate of continental Europe, a confidante of kings, and an adventurer not afraid of upholding his honor in duels to the death. But most important, here was a member of the British aristocracy and the British military—willing, able, and known to be a scathing critic of the king! It is any wonder that doors opened for Lee? He may have had letters of recommendation from Benjamin Franklin or other notables, as some suggest, but Lee's own self-promotion and vivid personality would surely have been enough to move him along in the right circles. He had friends in America, rebels and Tories alike, and we have seen that his friends could not refuse him even if given cause. He could tell stories that few others in America could, and his biting tongue must have enlivened many an evening of political discussion.

To further the cause, America desperately needed military minds to legitimize its threats to England. Officers of rank—and officers of regulars—were in limited supply, and Lee carried the rank of major general from the king of Poland, lieutenant colonel in the British regulars (albeit on half pay), and adviser to the Russian Army. America needed military men, and despite Lee's limited field engagements, he had credentials—with European flair. American political leaders accepted those credentials on face value, not needing or wanting to look deeper. America eagerly embraced Lee as a military genius in return for his apparent love for the cause.

Of course, there were flaws in the two parties that each ignored in the other. The rough-hewn Americans were not the elite of Europe, and the fledgling political structure of the colonies left a lot to be desired. And as a young creature, America would prove fickle. On his side, Lee was not high in the aristocracy, and his manners and bearing left him woefully short of European sophistication. He could not bite his tongue even when he could see the destruction that it would bring. Nevertheless, America and Charles Lee shared a common mantra—"the rights of man"—and a common enemy—King George III. These shared views forged a strong relationship that blossomed in 1774 and played out in Lee's appointment as major general in the Continental Army in June 1775. The remnants of this bond held firm for Lee to the end of life.[10] Only his flagrant disregard for moderation after the Battle of Monmouth in 1778 caused him to fall short when he called on his friends. At his death, long before the worse would be discovered, he received honors from the people he served, and even his enemies held back from outright condemnation.

PHILADELPHIA AND BOSTON

Lee threw himself into the forefront of attention in 1774, beginning a campaign that simultaneously showcased Charles Lee and advanced the American cause. He appeared at all the right places, met with the right people, and said the right things, all orchestrated to keep the momentum going. His timing, whether the result of luck or effort, could not have been better. In Philadelphia in January–February 1774, Lee met with Charles Thompson (later secretary of the Continental Congress) and Richard Bache (Benjamin Franklin's son-in-law). He attended a meeting of the Friendly Sons of St. Patrick as well. He then traveled south through Delaware and Maryland, following the careful directions and a description of the country given to him by Thompson, and eventually arrived in Williamsburg, Virginia, by March. Here he met Richard Henry Lee, George Mason, Colonel William Byrd, and Thomas Jefferson, among others. While in Virginia, news of Parliament's Coercive Acts reached the Assembly as these newly rising stars of that province were gathering. Lee may have had a hand, along with Jefferson, in the Assembly's adopting of a fast for June 1 in support of its Massachusetts brethren.[11] He left Virginia in late May, making his way back to Philadelphia.

While in Philadelphia, Lee thrust himself into the agitation surrounding the election of delegates to the First Continental Congress with the publication of an essay in the *Pennsylvania Journal* signed "Angus Americanus." He called for a boycott of British goods and an embargo of American goods to England as one way to pressure the British government to grant the rights that Americans demanded. As he moved to New York, this essay was reprinted there.[12] He then made his way up to Boston. Here, in the crucible of American agitation, he would meet Samuel Adams and John Adams.

When he was in Boston, Lee thought about visiting with British General Thomas Gage, the newly appointed military governor and commander of the English forces in Boston, and his former commanding officer in the Forty-fourth.[13] He decided against the visit. Perhaps it would look odd or send the wrong message to his new American friends. Instead, he met with some of the British troops garrisoned in the city. This could be interpreted as gathering intelligence on the strength of the British forces. Nevertheless, Lee confronted Gage by public letter, chiding the king's diplomatic and military representative in the colonies for his role in enforcing the policy of the royal court against the rights of the Americans. Poor Gage found himself in a situation exceedingly more demanding than his talents could handle: he lacked both the authority to broker a peace and the will to quell the growing agitation with force. His failure to act decisively simply encouraged the zealots in the city to apply more pressure. He surely did not need a subordinate officer bringing him to task for fulfilling his duties.

As an officer on half pay and a recent seeker of promotion and a military post, Lee played fast and loose with the allegiance an officer owed to the Crown and his paymaster. He begins his open letter with his characteristic obsequious flattery: "whether it is to my credit or discredit I know not—but it is most certain that I have had a real affection for very few men—but that those few, I have lov'd with warmth and ardor. You, Sir, amongst these few, I swear by all that's sacred, have ever held one of the foremost places. I respected your understanding, lik'd your manners and perfectly ador'd the qualities of your heart."[14] It is for this reason, Lee continues, that he is perplexed and appalled by the general's continued support for the "present diabolical measures with respect to this Country" that have been imposed by the "present Court of G. Britain." Others, nobler than Gage (in Lee's examples "My Lord Chatham ... for a time" and "poor York"), were similarly entrapped, seduced or duped. Lee prays that "God Almighty" may extricate General Gage from the "clutches" of the fiends who have put him in such an untenable position. It is hard to see how such poorly veiled insults could bring about any change in Gage. What would Lee have him do? Could Gage walk away from this command in disgust at his country's foreign policy without bringing his career to an end and, perhaps, bringing even more serious consequences on himself?

One must wonder what Charles Lee would have done had their positions been reversed—had Lee received the rank desired before 1773 and been sent to the colonies on behalf of the king (on full pay) to put down the nascent rebellion. Here, in 1774, with no chance of advancement or call to action, he could play the role of a scold to those in positions he just recently coveted. At the writing of this letter, Lee had yet to forgo his half pay and would not do so until he received a commission in the American service and assurances that his assets would be protected by taking the commission. For sure, this letter was intended to impact readers other than General Thomas Gage.

It enhanced Lee's credentials as a spirited supporter of the rights of man and colorful opponent of the court: "As to North, my opinion of him is this, and (I have known him a long time) that did he hear of a single freeman in the remotest corner of the World, he wou'd willingly put his country to the expense of furnishing forth an Army and fleet for the sole pleasure of destroying that single freeman."[15] Without a doubt, Lee recited the letter with glee over the next several months as he continued his travels through the colonies.

Even with taking the time to make General Gage his unwitting foil in Boston, Lee was able to make it back to Philadelphia to be on hand for the convening of the First Continental Congress in September 1774. Here he would cultivate his new friendships with the leaders he had met in the previous eight months and receive introduction to others. Without doubt, he was a presence in Philadelphia. John Adams lists "General Lee" among his dinner companions.[16] He may even have taken some part in the work of the Congress, although without any official standing, owing to his close relationship with the leaders gathered there.[17]

At the conclusion of the Congress, Lee continued his travels. In Annapolis, Maryland, he met the pamphleteer Daniel Dulaney and then Charles Carroll. In late December 1774, he spent five days at Mount Vernon with George Washington. It may be that Lee had made Washington's acquaintance years earlier at the disastrous British defeat at the Monongahela, but no evidence of such a meeting can be found. In any event, they had met just months earlier at the First Continental Congress and would be continuing their discussion of the politics of the day and, most likely, the need for and the organization of a military force to resist further British aggression. Sometime in early 1775, Lee met with another military man, Horatio Gates, at his estate called Traveller's Rest, in Berkeley County, Virginia. Gates had written to Lee on Lee's first pass through Virginia and succeeded in capturing his attention on this trip. In addition to a discussion of military issues, Gates was trying to interest Lee in property near to his estate that he wanted Lee to purchase. Lee made a second trip to Mount Vernon in April to talk further with George Washington. Both men would leave Mount Vernon for the convening of the Second Continental Congress in Philadelphia. Washington, a delegate to the Congress, was ready in his uniform of buff and blue to accept the leadership of an American army if offered. Lee may have had similar expectations.

THE GENIUS OF CHARLES LEE

It is during this period, the eighteen months from December 1773 to May 1775, that Charles Lee claimed his genius. He tied his strong will and quick-witted mind to a noble fight. The combination lifted him in the company of men and helped to embolden the cause of the Americans. His presence, his pen, and his courage brought him the recognition and esteem he so surely felt he deserved his entire life. His rank, his stature, and his colorful past gave him entrée, but his voice for the revolutionary cause during this period endeared him to thousands of patriots for the rest of his life.

For sure, Lee played to the crowd, but the crowd loved the show. He was also "over the top" at times, as in his chiding letter to General Gage. The tone is simultaneously obsequious and condescending (suggesting that they were as close as brothers "twin'd at Birth"), making it difficult to read without whining. His unceasing attacks on the court and the king were biting and sarcastic. But his call for the downfall of the royal court outweighed his rhetorical faults. His appearance in all of the right places and his meetings with all of the right people were calculated for an end. Charles Lee had found *his* cause within the American cause and realized that he could become a revered leader of that crusade. His inability to sustain this ardor for the American cause in the face of difficulties and setbacks—or the inability to restrain his ego and ambition—would eventually overwhelm him, but in 1774–1775, he endeared himself to the Americans moving inexorably toward a confrontation with Great Britain.

Charles Lee reinvented himself in 1774. One of the first changes that manifested itself is a newly acquired appreciation of Americans. He finally noticed the people who populated the thirteen colonies in North America, and he could not resist extolling their virtues (even if, occasionally, reminding his reader that these virtues were not always present). He openly acknowledges this change of opinion in a letter to his friend, Sir Charles Davers, written in Philadelphia in September 1774:

> I have now lately run through the colonies from Virginia to Boston, and can assure you, by all that is solemn and sacred, that there is not a man on the whole continent (placemen and some high churchmen excepted) who is not determined to sacrifice his property, his life, his wife, his family, and children, in the cause of Boston, which he justly considers as his own. . . .
>
> . . .
>
> The character of New England men, seems to me to be totally changed since we knew 'em. Instead of gasconade, laziness, self-sufficiency, and poltroonery, I am confident in the present cause will prove most formidably brave. Their rage for war is increased; in every town are formed companies of cadets, who are as perfect as possible in the manual exercise, evolutions, and all the minute manœuvres practiced by the troops of Europe.[18]

Lee goes on to tell Davers, presciently, that Canada will not join with the colonies but that France and Spain will be enjoined if a fight begins, in the hope of securing the rich commerce to result. He also comments on military leadership: "You will ask, where they will find generals? But I ask, what generals have their tyrants? In fact the match in this respect will be pretty equal."

Lee's change of heart about the character of "New England men" would be amusing if we take it as a passing guise. But he repeats it in a focused and clearly worded letter months later to the eminent Edmund Burke and also includes praise for their fighting in the French and Indian War:

> There is one more circumstance which we gentlemen in red never chose to remember, viz.—that in all our defeats and disgraces, particularly in those upon the Ohio, the provincials never led the fight, but were the last to leave the field. But be these things as they will, if I have any judgment, the people of New England are, at this day, more calculated to form irresistible conquering armies, than any people on the face of the globe. Even the appearance of their individuals is totally changed since I first knew them. Formerly, they had a slouching, slovenly air. Now, every peasant has his hair smartly dressed, is erect and soldier-like in his air and gait. This change struck me very much in passing through the provinces of Massachusetts and Connecticut. It must be attributed to the military spirit which they breathe, and their companies of cadets formed in all the towns of any considerable size.[19]

Was Lee right about the change in the Americans? Or was his 1750s vision impaired by his arrogance and his present vision equally impaired by his sudden infatuation? Perhaps he needed to explain his change of heart, for surely he had earlier expressed views in word and on paper that now did not fit in his new scheme of the world. Clearly, Americans had come of age in the years during which Lee had been gone, but the change could not have been as dramatic as he described. Whatever his reasoning, Lee took every chance to describe the virtues of his newly acquired family and to warn his old friends of the dangers of ignoring his opinion.

In addition to his change of heart about the character of the Americans, Charles Lee picked up several specific themes at this time and developed them in print. Most likely, he discussed these same ideas repeatedly with the men of the Revolution he met in his travels throughout the country. In person, his flamboyant rhetoric and colorful personality must have added to the sting of these themes:

• That King George III was a tyrant who had trampled the rights of his subjects to such an extent that he no longer commanded respect.

- That Parliament and/or the king's ministers had accepted the king's transgressions without question, to their dishonor.
- That free men fighting for their families and their rights establish the strongest force.
- That the king's army was not an unbeatable force.
- That Americans could match British regulars in the field.[20]
- That the British Army had no greater generals than could be found in America.

All of this was music to the ears of the American zealots. The first several premises simply echoed the political theories underlying the American cause. The remainder were unique and necessary if the vast majority of Americans were to be called on to fight. The idea that rustic colonials could match British regulars in the field was considered ludicrous by the British and their supporters in the colonies, which made Lee's assertions on this subject all the more compelling. The message was clear: *the British government was corrupt politically and could be beaten militarily.* The fact that these themes were openly espoused by a British military officer was extraordinary and gave all of his arguments, even the familiar political rationale, added punch.

Charles Lee was a British-born aristocrat with the courage to challenge the king in the colonies. He stood out and quite alone. He was also a British military officer of rank (still on half pay) willing to question the readiness and strength of the British military. Who else in the colonies at that time had the military stature and courage to make these claims? Again, Charles Lee stood out. His opinions made a difference. His views were adopted and woven into the arguments for the cause. Americans needed to believe not only that their cause was just but that their fight could be won. Lee's voice provided the support necessary.

These ideas can be seen in Lee's private and public letters. Clearly, as discussed above, Lee had changed his view on the characteristics and stature of American fighting men. Their numbers, their skill with weapons, and their willingness to fight for their liberties were formidable. He hammers this theme in all of his letters to Britons. In the Davers letter in September 1774, Lee states that "[t]he Boston company of artillery is allowed to be equal of any" and that that colony alone could raise "an army of 60,000 men." He provides a chart tallying 746,000 people in the four colonies of Rhode Island, New Hampshire, Connecticut, and Massachusetts. In a letter the next month addressed to a "Duke," he refers to "two hundred thousand strong body'd active yeoman ready to encounter all hazards and dangers, ready to sacrifice all considerations rather than surrender a tittle of the rights which They have deriv'd from God and their Ancestors." He warns as well that these men are armed and know how to use their weapons.

His conclusion, if it escapes his reader, is stated clearly in his December 1774 letter to Edmund Burke: "In short, sir, it is my persuasion, that should the people of England be infatuated enough to suffer their mis-rulers to proceed in their measures, this country may scorch her fingers, but they themselves will perish in the flames." Earlier in the year, his warning to General Gage in Boston could be read as treasonous, written by an officer on half pay to the British king:

> I know not whether the People of America will be successful in their struggles for Liberty, I think it most probable They will, from what I have seen from my progress through the Colonies—so noble a spirit pervades all orders of men from the first estated gentlemen to the lowest Planters, that *I think They must be victorious—I most devoutly wish They may*—for if the machinations of her enemies prevail, the bright Goddess Liberty must like her Sister Astrea utterly abandon the Earth, and leave not a wreck behind— She has by a dam'd conspiracy of Kings and Ministers been totally driven from the other Hemisphere—here is her last asylum—here I hope she may fix her abode.[21] (emphasis added)

Surely, General Gage passed on this sentiment to the British high command, just as Charles Lee himself was passing it on to any American within earshot.

But Lee went even further when addressing Americans by denigrating the fighting ability of the men who could be expected to fight on the field for the British. At some point in 1774, he answered directly and publicly the claim of the Reverend Myles Cooper, president of King's College, that the British were so good that they could not be beaten.[22] The reverend was a Loyalist who issued a paper urging the American firebrands to pull back or risk disaster. His paper was titled "A Friendly Address to All Reasonable Americans on Our Political Confusions; in Which the Necessary Consequences of Violently Opposing the King's Troops, and of a General Non-importation, Are Fairly Stated" and received considerable attention in the press. Lee's blistering response—political theory wrapped up with a personal attack and scathing ridicule of the writer and his arguments—received the greater acclaim. All of his themes were brought to bear in this tour de force, "Strictures on a Pamphlet, Entitled, 'A Friendly Address to All Reasonable Americans, on the Subject of Our Political Confusions,'" and the Americans embraced his arguments. Lee turns the reverend's perceived goal on its head right at the beginning of his response by challenging Cooper's attempt to discourage the Americans: "The design of his Pamphlet, is manifestly to dissolve the spirit of the union, and check the noble ardour, prevailing throughout the continent; but his zeal so far outruns his abilities, that there is the greatest reason to think that his Reverence has laboured to little effect."[23]

Cooper claims that "all the maritime powers of the world would not dispossess Great Britain of the empire of the sea, even when America is separated from her." Lee answers that Britain would be hard-pressed to produce a "single frigate" or to man it without the "timber, iron, planks, masts, pitch, tar or hemp" and without the "nursery for seamen" that America provides. Cooper claims that Britain can call upon its own regulars, Hessians, Hanoverians, Canadians, tribes of savages, and able generals to crush any rebellion and reduce Canada with 7,000 men. Lee responds that these 7,000 will face "200,000, of the most disorderly peasantry upon earth . . . animated in defence of every thing they hold dear and sacred." And besides, the British no longer have the "genius" of General Wolfe in the service or anyone like him. As to the Hessians and Hanoverians, Lee recites all of the political and financial difficulties that the British Crown will face in bringing them to America and predicts that "in less than four months not two [of 10,000] would remain with their Colours," preferring instead to become "useful and excellent citizens" on this continent. In the next eight years, many of the German mercenaries proved Lee right. Lee dismisses, somewhat incorrectly, Cooper's assertion that 40,000 Loyalists would rise and fight with the British. In fact, more than that number may have answered that call during the war.

But Lee's strongest arguments are saved for the regulars, universally feared for their fighting abilities. In characteristically colorful language he tells the Americans that they are a paper tiger:

> Great Britain has, I believe, of infantry at home, (comprehending Ireland, and exclusive of the guards), fifteen thousand men. They find the greatest difficulty in keeping the regiments up to any thing near their establishment; that they are able to procure are of the worst sort. They are composed of the most debauched Weavers, 'prentices, the scum of the Irish Roman Catholics, who desert upon every occasion, and a few Scotch, who are not strong enough to carry packs. This is no exaggeration; those who have been lately at Boston, represent the soldiers there (one or two regiments excepted) as very defective in size, and apparently in strength. But we are told that they shall be regulars, and regulars have an irresistible advantage. There is, perhaps, more imposition in the term regular troops, than in any of the jargon which issues from the mouth of a Quack Doctor. I do not mean to insinuate that a disorderly mob are equal to a trained disciplined body of men; but I mean, that all the essentials, necessary to form infantry for real service, may be acquired in a few months. I mean, that it is very

possible for men to be clothed in red, to be expert in all the tricks of the parade, to call themselves regular troops, and yet, by attaching themselves principally or solely to the tinsel or show of war, be totally unfit for real service. This, I am told, is a good deal the case of the present British Infantry. If they can acquit themselves tolerably in the puerile reviews, exhibited for the amusement of Royal Masters and Misses in Hyde Park, or Wimbledon Common, it is sufficient.[24]

Here, in one paragraph is the genius and notoriety of Charles Lee in 1774. He tells the American yeomen, in terms they can understand and enjoy, that the British can be beaten. Coming from John Adams, Benjamin Franklin, or even George Washington, such a statement would not have the sting and could not be believed. But Lee was a British officer who had served with and commanded such troops. The farmers, merchants, and young firebrands could accept that Lee knew what he was talking about and could not be dismissed.

In fact, Lee's ridicule of British regulars was heresy. To some extent, the strength of British troops depended on their reputation. The bayonet charge, common at the time, depended on terror as much as on ruthless slaughter. For Lee to strip away this layer of invincibility was, in fact, to put these troops in grave danger. But he continues further in the same vein. He talks specifically of the troops sent in the French and Indian War. Although they were "well dressed" and "well powdered" and the "perfect masters of their manual exercises," they "*knew not how to fight*" (emphasis added). (Presumably this includes Lee as well, but he does not go there.) After three years of "repeated losses and disgraces" and only after forgetting all they were taught as regulars did they, indeed, become a formidable fighting force. The American militia, on the other hand, were "frequently crowned with successes" in that war, knew how to handle weapons and the mundane instruments of war ("spades, pick-axes, hatchets, &c."), and with three or four months of training could be *100,000* men strong.[25]

Here we have the standard Charles Lee formula for short-term political success: flatter your friends, dismiss and ridicule your enemies, and offer a blueprint for success. Here's his plan:

Let one simple general plan be adopted for the formation and subdivision of your battalions; let them be instructed only in so much of the manual exercises as to prevent confusion and accidents in loading and firing; let them be taught to form, to retreat, to advance, to change their front, to rally to their colours; let them be taught to reduce themselves from a line of fire to a line of impression, that is, from two deep to four, six, or eight. This is all so easy and simple, that it may be acquired in three months. Let some sort of this plan be adopted, I say, and there is no doubt but that, in the time I have prescribed, you may have an army on foot of seventy, eighty, or an hundred thousand men, equal to all the services of war.[26]

Military language. Military knowledge. Military expertise. And what about officers? Lee repeats his comment to Sir Charles Davers that the sides are equal on this score. Even if the Americans have "no able officers," neither do the British. Peacetime has provided no "practical lessons," and British officers do not use their idle time reading about tactics and strategy. On the other hand, Lee considered himself well-read on military strategy, but he avoids any reference to his own availability to the American patriots in his response to Cooper's "Friendly Address."

Lee's "Strictures" have been examined as a political document and as the exposition of his acceptance of the political agenda of the American cause. This misses the mark. The several paragraphs on the evils of tyrants and tax ation without representation offer nothing new or significant. Rather, it is the calculated comparison of the strengths of the opposing forces by a renowned military man and the flattering assertion that the Americans can defeat the British that makes it compelling. Lee gives short shrift to political theory in favor of military victory. He is talking to the American fighting man and giving him reason to be hopeful that the cause is winnable, not merely just. Nevertheless, Lee claims that he wishes to avoid "the calamities of a civil war." But "remonstrances, petitions, prayers, and supplications" will not work. He urges the Americans to prepare for civil war as the surest means of preventing it: "to keep the swords of your enemies in their scabbards, you must whet your own."

"Strictures" gives us another window into the talents and psyche of Charles Lee—his biting tongue and acerbic wit. At this point in his life it served him well, even though earlier and later it did him more harm than good. The Americans were upstarts, cocky, itching for a fight. Fine theories on the rights of man gave cover but no lift for the spirit. For the men who would do the fighting, Lee's typical style played to their desire to mock and taunt the opponent, to strut and stride before superior force, and to dare the fight. Lee talks directly to these yet unassembled troops. Was the author of the "Friendly Address" a clergyman? Lee, like everyone else, knew this to be true, but it was more fun to conjecture: "I know not whether the author is a Layman or an Ecclesiastick, but he bears strongly the characters of the latter. He has the want of candor and truth, the apparent spirit of persecution, the unforgivingness, the hatred to Dissenters, and the zeal for arbitrary power which has distinguished Churchmen in all ages, and more particularly the *high* part of the Church of England."[27] Did "his Reverence" mean to scare and intimidate the Americans with visions of "Hessians, Hanoverians, royal standards erected, skilful Generals, legions of Canadians, and unnumbered tribes of savages, swords flaming in the front and rear, pestilence, desolation and famine"? If so, he is misguided—the Germans won't come, and those that do will desert at the first opportunity. Did this "divine Exorcist" claim that Loyalists in the thousands would rise up in support of the king? Lee becomes ecstatic:

> Dreadfully formidable they must be indeed! There would resort to it; let me see, (for the respectable town of Rye, have declared themselves a kind of neutrals, *rather than friends to the government;*) there would resort to it, Mr. Justice Sewell, the honourable Mr. Paxton, Brigadier Ruggles, and about eight or ten more *mandamus* Council-men, with perhaps twice their number of Expectants, and not less than twenty of the Hutchinsonian Addressers; these the four Provinces of New England alone would send forth. New York would furnish six, seven, or probably eight volunteers, from a certain knot, who are in possession or expectation of contracts, and the fourth part of a dozen high-flying Church of England Romanised Priests.[28]

As Lee sees it (and surely his readers joined in the vision), the "Reverend Pontifex himself" would be at the head of this frightening army.

CHAPTER 6

FOREIGN OFFICERS IN
SERVICE TO AMERICA

Charles Lee's love affair with America was consummated on June 17, 1775, when he was named a major general in the Continental Army. Lee did not stand alone as a former British officer named to a high post in the newly formed colonial armed forces. His good friend Horatio Gates was named adjutant general, and Richard Montgomery received a commission as a brigadier general. Both, like Lee, had served as officers in the British military. The remaining officers commissioned in June 1775—Philip Schuyler, Israel Putnam, David Wooster, Seth Pomeroy, William Heath, Joseph Spencer, John Thomas, and Nathanael Greene—were all American. No other nations were represented in this initial round of commissions, but Congress was soon inundated by seasoned officers and soldiers of fortune from all over Europe. Most of them served the new country with courage and distinction.

COMMISSION AND INDEMNITY

Lee's appointment was striking. On June 17, 1775, he still remained a lieutenant colonel in His Majesty's service, albeit on half pay. His American commission required him to take up arms against officers he served under and men he commanded; he would be one of the leaders of armed rebels against his king and country. Despite all that came later, Lee's acceptance of this commission in 1775 showed enormous courage and resolve. He would risk his fortune and his life in the American cause. Although Gates and Montgomery had been born in Britain and had served in the British military, they did not face the same choices that confronted Lee. They had decided somewhat earlier to live in America and had limited ties to Britain by this time. Putnam and Schuyler were both born in North America, and their families and fortunes were centered there. Both men had militia experience in the French and

Indian War; Schuyler served as a delegate to the Second Continental Congress. So too, the brigadiers beneath them. None of these men needed to resign a commission. They had lived their lives in North America and had no immediate family of stature residing in England or property easily confiscated there. Only Charles Lee, among the first group of officers appointed by the Continental Congress or leading militias, had so openly defied the king and the British government in the press. Lee was an officer of rank going to the other side.

For all his posturing prior to the June 1775 selection, however, Lee did not jump at the commission offered him. As mentioned earlier, Lee at his most egotistical moments saw himself as the commander in chief and was miffed that he landed not only behind Washington, but behind Artemas Ward as well. He held his tongue (at least at first). Perhaps he knew that commander in chief was a long shot, owing to his English birth, and that Ward would not be long in the field. Whatever his reasoning, he accepted this ranking. Nevertheless, another more practical issue surfaced at this point that needed to be resolved. Lee would risk life and limb, but he wanted to protect his financial assets from confiscation. He asked the Continental Congress for indemnification for losses he might suffer as a result of his acceptance of this commission. This was an extraordinary request. Giving Lee this protection could create a precedent for Congress that might restrict its maneuverability in the future. But Lee was a tremendous catch, a stick in the eye to the king and an example for other British officers to follow. Lee was persuasive on the financial issue. He had just recently extended himself to purchase an estate in Virginia, "Prato Rio" near General Gates's "Traveller's Rest," and he would be unable to complete the purchase or maintain the property if Britain took punitive action against his assets in England. His friends in Congress took up his case and, in fact, the matter was resolved relatively quickly.

The congressional resolution adopted June 19, 1775, reads as follows:

Upon motion Ordered, That Mr. [Patrick] Henry, Mr. [Thomas] Lynch, and Mr. J[ohn] Adams, be a committee to wait upon Genl Lee, and to inform him of his appointment, and request his answer, whether he will accept the command.

Committee returned and reported, that they had waited on Genl Lee, and informed him of his appointment, and that he gave for answer: That he had the highest sense of the honor conferred upon him by the Congress; that no effort in his power shall be wanting to serve the American cause.— But before he entered upon the service he desired a conference with a committee to consist of one delegate from each of the associated colonies, to whom he desired to explain some particulars respecting his private fortune.

Where upon Mr. [John] Sullivan, Mr. S[amuel] Adams, Mr. [Stephen] Hopkins, Mr. [Eliphalet] Dyer, Mr. P[hilip] Livingston, Mr. W[illiam] Livingston, Mr. [George] Ross, Mr. [CÆsar] Rodney, Mr. [Thomas] Johnson, Mr. [Patrick] Henry, Mr. [Richard] Caswell and Mr. [Thomas] Lynch were appointed a committee to confer with Genl. Lee. The committee returned and reported that they had conferred with Genl. Lee, who had communicated to them an estimate of the Estate he risqued by this service;

Whereupon, Resolved, That these colonies will indemnify General Lee for any loss of property which he may sustain by entering into their service, and that the same be done by this or any future Congress as soon as such loss is ascertained.[1]

Critics can claim in hindsight that Lee refused to make the commitment to America that he needed to make, that he placed his financial well-being above the cause. But if critics arose at the time, they did not prevail—and for good reason. Lee was in a class by himself. Granting him what he asked for made sense to those who saw his actions as open treason to the Crown. American-born colonists who had no property in England might eventually lose their fortunes, but England would need to bring the fight to them. Former military men who were not under commission to the king might expect some leniency if the cause went awry; Lee needed victory to survive. This financial self-interest at the crucial moment, however, does lend fuel to the fire of historians and critics of later generations. They look back on Lee's life and his choices and weave a pattern of self-interest and opportunism. This view may indeed be correct. Lee did no favor for his legacy, which would be tarnished in much greater degree by his later actions, by demanding favorable financial treatment at the moment of truth. And, once again, his demand contrasts with George Washington's declaration to forgo a salary for his service.

Once this bit of financial maneuvering was out of the way, however, Lee commenced his service to the American cause in style. He resigned his commission and forfeited his half pay in a public letter to "The Right Honourable Lord Viscount Barrington, His Majesty's Secretary of War," dated June 22, 1775, and published in the colonial newspapers:

My Lord,

Although I can by no means subscribe to the opinion of divers people in the world, that an officer on half pay is to be considered in the service, yet I think it a point of delicacy to pay a deference to this opinion, erroneous and absurd as it is. I therefore apprise your Lordship in the most public and solemn manner, *that I do renounce my half-pay, from the date hereof.* At the same time I beg leave to assure your Lordship, that whenever it shall please his Majesty to call me forth to any honourable service against the natural hereditary enemies of our country, or in defence of his just rights and dignity, no man will obey the righteous summons with more zeal and alacrity than myself; but the present measures seem to me so absolutely subversive to the rights and liberties of every individual subject, so destructive to the whole empire at large, and ultimately so ruinous to his Majesty's own person, dignity and family, that I think myself obliged in conscience as a Citizen, Englishman, and Soldier of a free state, to exert my utmost to defeat them. I most devoutly pray to Almighty God to direct his Majesty into measures more consonant to his interest and honour, and more conducive to the happiness and glory of his people.

> I am my Lord,
> Your most obedient and humble Servant,
> CHARLES LEE[2]

Lee makes the fantastic claim, for his time, that an officer in the service of his sovereign (as Lee accepts his position to be for the purpose of this argument) can pick and choose the wars that he will fight, based on his individual interpretation of the interests of the sovereign. Lee's hair-splitting discourse over whether an officer on half pay owes any duty only distracts from the arrogance of his position. Surely, this manifesto, as intended, made for great reading and built upon the reputation that Lee had cultivated for himself in the colonies as a freethinker and an advocate for the "rights and liberties of every individual subject."

Just eighteen months hence, this timely resignation would prove to be invaluable in saving Charles Lee from the hangman's noose.

The congressional indemnification also turned out to be of practical value. In July 1776, after he had presided over the successful defense of a land and sea invasion against Charleston, Lee was soliciting supporters to write to the Continental Congress urging them *to fund* the indemnification. He apparently raised the issue with John Rutledge, the governor of South Carolina, at this propitious moment because his attempts to draw against his accounts in England to complete the purchase of Prato Rio were returned unfulfilled. Lee faced the loss of the farm and public embarrassment. If the Congress had expected their magnanimity in 1775 to be no more than a conciliatory gesture, they were sorely mistaken. Now, just one year later, Lee was asking that the indemnity be fulfilled. To their credit, the members did not flinch from their commitment and quickly authorized the appropriation of $30,000. A committee was appointed to take up the question raised in a letter from Governor Rutledge. Notably, Richard Henry Lee, Charles Lee's strong advocate in the Congress, was one of the two committee members. The Congress waited for Lee's return from the south and on October 7, the day Lee appeared before the body to report on the victory at Charleston and the state of military affairs in the southern colonies, voted to advance the money:

> That this Congress, having a just opinion of the abilities of General Lee, applied to him to accept a command in their service, which he readily agreed to, provided the Congress would indemnify him against any loss, which he might sustain in consequence thereof, he having, at that time, a considerable sum of money due to him by persons in the kingdom of Great Britain, which he was resolved to draw from thence as soon as possible. That the Congress unanimously concurred in his proposal: That General Lee accordingly entered into their service; that he has since drawn bills upon his agent in England, which bills have been returned protested. That General Lee, having purchased an estate in Virginia, the purchase money for which has been long due, is likely to sustain, by means of the protested bills, many injuries, unless this house prevent the same by an advance of thirty thousand dollars: Whereupon,
>
> Resolved, That the sum of 30,000 dollars be advanced to General Lee, upon his giving bond to the treasurer to account for the same, and taking such steps, in conjunction with Robert Morris, Esqr. on behalf of the Congress, as will secure the most effectual transfer of his estate in England, to reimburse the Congress for the advance now made to him.[3]

As can be seen, the monies were to be refunded if Charles Lee was able at some point later to reclaim his English assets. His sister, Sidney, ultimately repaid the advance after Lee's death in 1782.

Other Foreign-Born Officers

Charles Lee was not the only foreign-born officer to serve in the Continental Army. Indeed, at one point the flood of foreign officers stretched the patience of George Washington who had to deal with their pretensions of rank and stature as well as the jealousies of American officers who found foreigners in the way of advancement. The reasons that these men sailed to America were varied. For some it seemed that it was simply a matter of putting their skills to work or securing a rank that would otherwise be unavailable; for others it may have been personal glory; and for still others it was the efforts of the French to support a war against its rival Great Britain. The list of foreign-born officers is long, and most of these men served the nascent country well, some giving their lives in the cause. Again, Charles Lee stood apart. In spite of his pretensions and financial demands, Lee presented himself to Congress as a willing participant *before* the fighting began and publicly took up the political cause as well. Although many of the others shared some similarities with him, no one else offered as much to America. No other foreign officer created the political stir that attended Lee.

Let's look at the non-British group. Many of the adventurers pouring into the colonies at the outbreak of the war had military credentials; others just claimed so. After a period, Congress and Washington were overwhelmed and had to close the door. France was encouraging "volunteers," and many soldiers of fortune presented themselves to the American diplomats in Paris— Silas Deane and Benjamin Franklin—seeking high rank for joining in the fight. Clearly, every foreigner presenting himself could not be what he claimed, but these men could not be vetted, were oftentimes demanding and arrogant, and soon angered the American officers by their rank and trappings. Congress could not just ignore them, however, for fear of annoying the French government. Richard Henry Lee, in a letter to George Washington dated May 22, 1777, advised him that Congress had tried to staunch the flow, which originated from a "desire to obtain Engineers, and Artillerists," but which led to applications from men with "sagacity enough quickly to discern our wants, and professing competency in these branches." Nevertheless, "they were too quickly believed."[4] At least one of these adventurers, Thomas Conway of Ireland, would provide considerable difficulty for Washington. Others, notably Frederick von Steuben, the Baron Johann de Kalb, and the Marquis de Lafayette would serve the country with honor and distinction. The American cause was not the primary reason for their appearance on the scene, nor did these men take up the political debate in letters or the press as did Charles Lee. Several of them, notably Lafayette and Thaddeus Kosciusko, eventually embraced the ideals of the American Revolution with passion, but not at first.

The most interesting foreigner was the Marquis de Lafayette. He had no military experience or expertise at all and came to American with Baron de Kalb, ostensibly seeking glory. Twenty years old and without credentials, Lafayette wanted a command and the rank of major general. He received the rank from an obliging Continental Congress, but had to wait some time for a command. He began his service as a "volunteer" and through the force of his personality was able to inveigle himself into Washington's officer corps. When he eventually gained a command, Lafayette became a crucial member of Washington's inner circle. Why Washington chose to bestow his favor on the young and unproven Frenchman with no obvious military skills remains somewhat a mystery and is usually explained by reference to the relationship that arose between them. The two men developed a mutual affection shortly after introduction, and Washington must have soon seen something in the Marquis to keep him on at first and then add him to his staff. Obliging the

French, always a political concern for the rebels, may also have played into acceptance of Lafayette.

Two words describe Lafayette's participation in the American Revolution: glory and loyalty. Lafayette first approached the Americans in France in late 1776 with his dream of sailing to America to join the Revolution. He received a letter of introduction to the Continental Congress from America's agent in France, Silas Deane. It does not appear, however, that Lafayette was driven by political ideals, the "rights of man," or the need to fight against tyrannical oppression. As a French aristocrat, he was naturally inclined to oppose all things British; as a French aristocrat, he also would have landed in a difficult position by publicly espousing the political theories that underpinned the American Revolution, and he did not. This came later and to select audiences. His contemporaneous letters to French correspondents emphasize his passion to fight the enemies of France.[5]

It appears that the Marquis's ambition for personal glory also drove his passion to join the fight. He arrived in America in June 1777, too late to add to the rhetoric of the cause but still early enough to share the glory of the victory that he envisioned. Indeed, the ship he clandestinely purchased to make his way to America was the *Victoire*. And if glory was the reason for Lafayette's commitment to the American cause, he achieved his goal. His single-mindedness, his dynamism, and his valor propelled him to an important role in the fight. In his first action at Brandywine in September 1777, Lafayette suffered a dangerous leg wound that required two months for recovery. He saw more action in New Jersey in late 1777; at Barren Hill, the Battle of Monmouth, and at Newport, Rhode Island, in 1778; and at several southern venues in 1781, including Yorktown. Militarily, Lafayette had to learn on the job, but he eventually proved an effective officer in the field.

Charles Lee would have met Lafayette for the first time at Valley Forge in 1778, after the suffering of the winter and as the spring thaw brought word that Clinton would be moving his headquarters from Philadelphia to New York. Lafayette and Lee did not share a mutual respect. The Marquis mistrusted Lee. Lee, for his part, saw Lafayette as an impetuous boy who should not be involved with the Continental Army. Their relationship would last only until the Battle of Monmouth in June 1778. Sir Henry Clinton chose to march his troops across New Jersey from Philadelphia to New York, and Washington, looking for a fight after the winter at Valley Forge, was determined to make the passage difficult. He shadowed Clinton's force until they were close enough for an engagement at Monmouth Courthouse, New Jersey. Lafayette eagerly took command of the vanguard troops when Lee refused. At the last moment, Lee reconsidered and demanded the command based on rank. Washington reluctantly obliged. Lafayette could not and did not object. Their opinions on what happened at Monmouth could not be in greater conflict. More on this later.

If personal glory drove Lafayette to America, his personal loyalty to George Washington sealed his commitment. Once welcomed into Washington's circle, the Marquis never wavered in loyalty to the commander in chief. He had to wait for a command, had a command taken from him at the last moment before battle, and was tempted to abandon Washington for another command. He remained loyal to Washington to the end, without question. This trait distinguishes Lafayette from Lee, as well as many other American officers, foreign and native born. Of course, some of those whose loyalty wavered saw themselves in Washington's place. Lafayette, despite his vainglory, was hardly at a point in life where he could aspire to that ambition. Charles Lee was, and his ego certainly prevented unflinching loyalty to Washington. Lee's loyalty to any living man was always in question and always depended on a material quid pro quo.

Joining Lafayette aboard the *Victoire* in 1777 was a German-born soldier of fortune working for the French authorities, the Baron de Kalb. Although he appeared to be of nobility and carried the title of baron, Johann de Kalb was, in fact, born to a peasant family in Hüttendorf. Like others of his time, he was able to remake himself, assuming the bearing as well as the title of aristocracy. By age fifty-five, Kalb had served with several German units in the French army. He served with such a unit in Europe during the Seven Years' War. Missing out on promotions after that war that could secure him, he was offered the opportunity to travel to America to size up the situation in 1768. The French wanted to know if American disillusionment with the British Crown was real. Kalb provided an accurate report of the situation and perceived that the colonies would at some point break with Britain. He returned to France for further instructions, but internal politics sidelined him until late 1776. At this point, the French once again aimed to stir the pot in America. He was to go to America as a "volunteer" (retaining his position in the French military, nonetheless) and assist in the delivery of arms and aid. Like Lafayette, Kalb had entered into a contract with one of America's envoys in Paris, Silas Deane, for commission as a major general upon arrival in America.

In December 1776, the Baron de Kalb and the Marquis de Lafayette boarded the *Victoire*, both seeking the rank of major general. Based on his extensive travels in America in 1768–1769 and his ability to speak English, Kalb proved invaluable to Lafayette. Lafayette's perseverance in gaining entry to the Continental Army and his friendship with Washington likewise aided Kalb, who received his commission as a major general several months after

Lafayette had received his own, in September, and Kalb then began an active role in the field. He had come to respect the commercial and independent spirit of the Americans and eagerly joined in the cause. He spent the winter of 1777–1778 with Washington's troops at Valley Forge and gave his life for those ideals at the Battle of Camden in 1780, shot several times and bayoneted as he lay on the ground.[6] Although Kalb came to America as an agent of the French, he died an American hero on the battlefield.

Another German was Friedrich Wilhelm von Steuben. This master of discipline proved invaluable to George Washington at Valley Forge, transforming his ragtag army into a true fighting force by means of training and drills. Steuben also began his service to the Continental Army as a volunteer, until named a major general in May 1778 as a reward for his efforts. Before the end of the war, he came off of the drill field to serve in the southern campaign and was at Yorktown for Cornwallis's surrender in 1781. Steuben began life in Prussia and he became attached to a military unit, like Charles Lee, at an early age, about sixteen. Well-trained, he served during the Seven Years' War and thereafter, but by 1777, he was without a commission. He came upon Benjamin Franklin in France. Franklin was impressed and obliged Steuben with a letter of introduction to the Continental Congress. His appearance in America was hailed because of his background, and he was sent to Washington at Valley Forge even though he could not speak English and had to give his orders through an interpreter in French. Steuben became a citizen of the United States after the war and was granted a farm of 1,600 acres by the State of New York, in Oneida County. He was awarded a pension by Congress in 1790 and died in November 1794.

Another French officer, Thomas Conway, caused George Washington considerable consternation. This Irish-born soldier had spent most of his career in the service of the French Army. After twenty years of service, he held the rank of colonel and received a recommendation from Silas Deane in 1777 to the Continental Congress. By his own words, he came to America "to increase my fortune and that of my family." His military record and apparent skills were obvious, however, and he had an advantage over others sent by Deane in that he spoke English. He received the rank of brigadier general from the Congress in May 1777 and major general before the year was out. His service for America was short-lived, however, and full of controversy. He acquitted himself well at both Brandywine and Germantown, but it was his penchant for intrigue, not any lack of military ability, that roiled Washington and his friends. Conway arrived in America at about the same time as Lafayette and Kalb, but the latter two had received commissions as major general based on their agreement with Silas Deane. Conway immediately objected, claiming that he outranked Kalb in the French Army. He eventually received his commission and appointment as inspector general of the army, but he soon began to undermine George Washington's authority.[7]

It is Thomas Conway for whom the infamous Conway Cabal is named—the so-called conspiracy among officers in the Continental Army and members of the Continental Congress who saw Washington as a failure in the first years of the war and were looking for a replacement. Conway did not approve of Washington's running of the army and was not discreet in letting his views be known. At one point it appeared that Conway might be named to the Board of War created by the Continental Congress in October 1777, but Congress avoided this direct confrontation with Washington. Ultimately, they appointed Horatio Gates, the military darling in 1777 after his decisive victory at Saratoga. Some saw Gates as a replacement for Washington, and Conway encouraged this. The matter came to a head when Washington learned of a letter from Conway to Gates that questioned Washington's ability. Washington demanded an explanation from Gates, who forwarded the letter to Congress. This public airing of dirty laundry hurt Conway and Gates more than Washington, who was busy tending to the desperate army at Valley Forge.[8]

Conway offered his resignation in March 1778 and was surprised to find it accepted. He looked to return to France, but his exit was almost too late to save his life. One of Washington's ardent supporters, a commander of Pennsylvania militia, John Cadwalader, challenged Conway to a duel for his intrigues and shot him through the mouth on July 4, 1778. Near death, Conway wrote an apology to Washington, but then recovered to make his return to France. He lived until 1800, serving as a governor of French territories in India and as a Loyalist officer in the French Revolution.

Like Thomas Conway, Charles Lee was also a confidante of Horatio Gates. And, like Conway, Lee would see Washington as a liability by late 1776. Indeed, Lee's capture by the British in December 1776 probably kept him from playing a role in Conway's intrigues against Washington. Had Lee avoided capture and remained on the scene, he might have been considered as a replacement by those looking for an alternative. In two interesting parallels, Charles Lee would also fight a duel with a Washington surrogate, only much later in the war, and escape wounded but with his life; and, a letter from Lee referencing a letter critical of Washington was inadvertently read by Washington. Unlike Conway, however, Lee never apologized to Washington for his actions.

Three other foreign-born officers should also be mentioned: Thaddeus Kosciusko, Casimir Pulaski, and Louis Lebègue Duportail. All three of these men came through the French channel maintained by Silas Deane and

Benjamin Franklin in 1777. Duportail was a French Army engineer; Pulaski and Kosciusko both served in the Polish Army and had made their way to France looking for positions to continue their careers.

Duportail began his Continental Army service as a colonel in July 1777 and rose to major general (brevet) in November 1781. He served admirably and then returned to France, only to be driven out by the French Revolution. He emigrated to America after 1791 and lived out his life near Valley Forge in Pennsylvania. Pulaski joined the Continental Army in the fall of 1777 and saw action at Brandywine, Germantown, and Haddonfield, New Jersey. Named brigadier general by Washington in September 1777, Pulaski created and commanded the first troop of cavalry in the Continental Army. He was killed at the Battle of Savannah in October 1779. Kosciusko began as a volunteer in August 1776 with the rank of colonel and eventually rose to brigadier general (brevet) in 1783. He had the distinction of a recommendation from Charles Lee, who knew him or knew of him during his stints with King Stanislaus in the period before coming to America in 1773. Kosciusko's skills as an engineer, greatly needed by the Americans, served Horatio Gates to advantage at Saratoga and helped Nathanael Greene down south later in the war. Kosciusko embraced the ideals of the Revolution and is warmly regarded by Americans for his service. He spent the remainder of his life after the war trying to bring those ideals to his native Poland.

It does not appear that any one of these foreign-born officers came to America exclusively to advance political theories on the "rights of man" or the independence of America from the British Crown, and none had achieved much renown prior to the fight. For the most part, the path into the Continental Army for these officers wended through the national interests of France. Personal glory and military position, in addition to the interests of France, were the main forces driving these men. Nevertheless, all of them served with distinction and, with the exception of Thomas Conway, without intrigue. They arrived after the fighting started. Although some adopted the political underpinnings of the Revolution, not one was primarily motivated by these ideals. American historians, again with the exception of Conway, remember these men fondly and honor their service. Not one wavered in the commitment once made. Lafayette, of course, has become a symbol of American-French cooperation.

GATES AND MONTGOMERY, STEPHEN, MERCER, AND ST. CLAIR

Although the most colorful and the highest ranking, Charles Lee was not the only former British officer of regulars in the Continental Army. He shared that distinction with Horatio Gates and Richard Montgomery. All three men saw action as British officers in the French and Indian War. Twenty years later, all three turned against the Crown and fought for the rights of the American colonists in the Revolutionary War. In some ways, the journeys of Montgomery and Gates parallel Charles Lee's path to war against his sovereign, but their lives also contain differences that foreshadow their destinies in American history. Richard Montgomery, killed in the fight to take Quebec in December 1775, is remembered as a revered figure in the history of the war. Horatio Gates's military fortunes brought him both the glory of the 1777 victory at Saratoga and the despair of the 1780 defeat at Camden. But Gates remains an honored figure in American history as well.

Horatio Gates and Charles Lee shared a similar personal history. Both men were born in England, were ushered into the military at an early age, were advanced in action through the French and Indian War, and then found themselves stymied as the British Army retrenched in the period of peace that followed. Their lives crossed a number of times, and at some point, probably when Lee arrived in the American colonies in 1773, their acquaintance turned into a true friendship that would last almost until Lee's death in 1782. In June 1775, in the same resolution that named Charles Lee major general, third in command, Congress named Horatio Gates adjutant general of the Continental Army.

Gates was born in Essex, England, several years earlier than Charles Lee, but his family had no pretensions of British nobility. His father was a butler in a household of means, and Horatio was fortunate enough to be taken under the wings of people of influence, including Horace Walpole and Edward Cornwallis.[9] As a result, he found a home and advancement in the military. He joined the British Army as a lieutenant in 1745, and his first service came in Germany during the War of Austrian Succession. He purchased a captaincy and received an assignment in North America as an aide to Edward Cornwallis, who was posted at Nova Scotia. Gates fought at Monongahela in 1755 under General Edward Braddock and alongside of many of the men who would serve on both sides in the Revolutionary War, including George Washington, Charles Lee, Daniel Morgan, and Thomas Gage. Gates fought well and was wounded in this disastrous defeat for the British. Later in the war, Gates saw action at the capture of the island of Martinique in the West Indies in 1761. He rose to the rank of major.

After the war, Gates returned to England. Like Lee, he became enamored of Whig philosophies and maintained social ties with freethinkers in England.[10] And, also like Lee, Gates could not parlay his service in the French and Indian War into an active commission of substance in the British military. Gates's response to this personal misfortune, however, was significantly different from Lee's. Perhaps the level of their respective upbringings in England led to this deviation in the paths taken. Lee had relatives with some power and influence at court and relied on them, and his personal lobbying, to get the position he sought. When Lee's efforts proved unsuccessful, he turned bitter. Gates had few political connections to rely on and chose to give up the suit and rely on himself. He had married Elizabeth Phillips in 1754, and he sold his commission when promotion failed to come after years of trying in the 1760s. By 1772, he determined to make his life in the American wilderness and sailed for the colonies. He purchased 650 acres in Virginia (now in Jefferson County, West Virginia) and established "Traveller's Rest," a working farm that would anchor him until his death in 1806. From 1773 to his commission in 1775, Gates faithfully worked at making the farm a lifetime home and source of income. When it became clear that hostilities could break out between the colonies and Great Britain, Gates made his loyalty to America clear and, like Lee and others, made a pilgrimage to Mount Vernon to discuss the situation with George Washington."

Gates and Traveller's Rest played prominent roles in the life of Charles Lee. Gates immediately renewed his acquaintance when Lee arrived in New York in 1773. In addition to their mutual service at Monongahela, Gates and Lee had met at least once in London in 1768 at the home of Benjamin Franklin. These two men had much in common. Both apparently enjoyed a rough manner, an unkempt appearance, and off-color speech and allusions. On a more theoretical plane, one Gates biographer suggests that Lee and Gates shared an understanding that an army of citizen-soldiers could be a tool to effect social change.[12] Significantly, each would stand in a duel to defend his honor, Gates against fellow officer James Wilkinson in 1778 and Lee several times throughout his life. In 1775, Gates provided Lee with his American legitimacy. Gates encouraged Lee to obtain a land stake in the colonies and then found Lee a farm to purchase near to his own. Unfortunately for Lee, Prato Rio, as he called it, would never provide the anchor or the solace that Traveller's Rest provided for Gates.

From 1775 to 1782, the lives of Gates and Lee appeared to run again on parallel lines. Both received prominent positions in the Continental Army in 1775, both doubted the competency of George Washington in the earlier going of the war, both ran afoul of Washington's authority, and both would eventually face a military inquiry and forced retirement in Virginia. His early victory at Saratoga gave Gates considerable political strength. In 1777, the Continental Congress, thrilled with his victory and unsure of Washington, appointed Gates head of the Board of War. Washington suspected that Gates was conspiring against him along with General Conway. In late 1777, Washington learned of a letter from Conway to Gates with less than flattering comments about his leadership as commander in chief. It was Washington's cold shoulder after that intrigue that forced Gates into an early retirement to Virginia. A year earlier, in another eerie similarity, a letter from Lee to Adjutant General Joseph Reed was inadvertently opened by Washington, revealing their mutual concerns about Washington's leadership. Lee's capture days later may have blunted Washington's wrath toward Lee, but the letter's contents clearly shook his confidence in Reed, whom he considered a trusted aide.[13]

Despite the obvious parallels, several factors separate Lee and Gates during this period. First of all, Lee had lived much of his life prior to his 1773 arrival in New York on the European continent, such that his experiences after the French and Indian War were distinctly different from those of Gates. Lee did not have any substantive landholdings to anchor him in the Americas and no wife and family. He remained an officer, on half pay, in the British military at the time he received his commission from the Continental Congress. Lee embraced the American cause in 1773 as a political philosophy and then took it up as a political struggle; Gates, on the other hand, understood the cause from the perspective of an American working the wilderness of Virginia to make a living and raise a family. Gates's political contributions to the cause pale in comparison with Lee's, but his convictions and dedication to it were rooted firmly in an American experience and the desire to maintain the life that he had created for himself and his family.

So too, although both Horatio Gates and Charles Lee were out of the war by 1778, having run afoul of George Washington, they pursued different avenues thereafter. Gates found some comfort at his estate in Virginia, but his neighbor did not. Gates understood that an open debate with Washington would not serve him well, and he bided his time. His tact and his patience worked in his favor. Congress called on Gates in June 1780 to lead the army in North Carolina. Gates welcomed the opportunity to contribute once again, but unfortunately his military career effectively came to an end after the rout of his army at Camden, South Carolina, in August 1780, and his less than glorious run from the field (for a distance of several miles) to avoid capture. Camden demonstrated Gates's shortcomings as a field general, and the resulting court of inquiry put his command in suspense until its conclusion in 1782. The verdict exonerated Gates, but his retirement was the actual result.

Richard Montgomery's short but glorious career as a brigadier general in the Continental Army prevents any significant comparison with the life of Charles Lee after 1775, but his early life presents some striking similarities.

Montgomery was born in Ireland in 1738, seven years after Charles Lee. His father served as a member of Parliament, and young Richard was well-educated at Trinity College, Dublin. Montgomery's military career also began at a young age, in 1757, and he soon found himself in North America during the French and Indian War. He served under James Wolfe at Louisbourg, Jeffrey Amherst at Lake Champlain, and with William Haviland at Montreal. Like Lee, Montgomery saw action at Fort Carillon (later Ticonderoga) in 1758, and, like Gates, he served in the Caribbean, including Martinique, in 1762.

Back in England after the war, Captain Montgomery also sought military advancement without avail, despite his strong political connections. Perhaps his struggle came because his friends were among the leading lights of liberalism, such as Edmund Burke and Charles James Fox. At some point, Montgomery must have given up his quest for military advancement in the British Army and made choices more parallel to those made by Gates than by Lee. When Montgomery returned to North America in early 1773, he immediately bought property near New York City and married a local woman of means, Janet Livingston. Montgomery did not carry the military cachet of Charles Lee, even though he may have seen more action in Canada, the Caribbean, and against the Indians during the Pontiac rebellion. His highest rank was captain, and he sold his British commission in 1771 before he left for New York. Although Montgomery did not shy away from politics, he was not a political firebrand. When he arrived in New York, just months prior to Charles Lee, he concentrated his energies on finding a wife and an estate. Once secure in his newly adopted homeland, Montgomery became involved in politics and took an active role in the cause. In May 1775, he was sent as a delegate to the Provincial Congress in New York. Just weeks later, the Congress appointed Montgomery one of the eight brigadier generals commissioned in June 1775. Six months later he was dead, killed under the walls of Quebec in the failed attempt early in the war to take that city and bring Canada into the fight on the side of the colonies. He had taken actual command in the field upon the illness of General Philip Schuyler, but even working with Benedict Arnold, Montgomery could not coax a victory out of the ill-timed attack.

Another British-born officer serves as both a parallel and a contrast with Charles Lee. Adam Stephen was born in Aberdeenshire, Scotland, about 1721. Stephen studied medicine and entered the British military as a naval surgeon, seeing action in Europe in 1740. He then emigrated to America in 1748 and practiced as a physician in Fredericksburg, Virginia. Stephen commanded Virginia militia in the French and Indian War, serving alongside George Washington, and eventually received a captain's commission in the British

Army, which Washington never did. He also served with Washington and Lee at the disastrous Battle of Monongahela in 1755. He challenged Washington for a seat in the Virginia House of Burgesses in 1761 (and almost won) and served with the militia again in 1774 during "Lord Dunmore's War." Congress commissioned Stephen as a brigadier general in May 1776, and he fought valiantly at Trenton. He eventually became a major general, but his career came to an abrupt end after the American loss at the Battle of Germantown in 1777. In the fog and confusion, his troops fired on Anthony Wayne's men, and the incident was blamed on Stephen, who was not with his troops for a period during the battle. A court-martial led to a conviction for "unofficerlike behaviour" and for often being intoxicated; he was permanently dismissed from the army. Like Gates and Lee, Stephen retired to his farm in Berkeley County, Virginia, and for a short time after 1778, the three discharged generals were neighbors and companions. Like Gates, but unlike Lee, Stephen kept to himself his disdain for George Washington and the treatment he received. As a result, Stephen's neighbors recognized his contributions to the war and his strengths, electing him a member of the Virginia House of Delegates (1780–1784) and a member of the Virginia convention that ratified the Constitution in June 1788.

Two other men also served as officers in the British military prior to the Revolutionary War, but their careers offer little comparison for a variety of reasons. Hugh Mercer was a Scottish-born solider who fled to America in 1746 after fighting with Bonnie Prince Charles, the Jacobite pretender to the British throne, who was defeated that year at Culloden. When the French and Indian War began, he joined the British forces as a colonel and saw action. Like Montgomery, Mercer was commissioned a brigadier general in June 1776. He fought at the Battle of Trenton but was killed just days later in the early fighting at Princeton. Arthur St. Clair, also born in Scotland, served as a lieutenant in the French and Indian War. He resigned his commission in 1762 and settled in Pennsylvania. After receiving an American commission as a brigadier general in 1776, St. Clair fought with Mercer at Trenton and Princeton. He was given command of Fort Ticonderoga in 1777 but chose to abandon the fort in the face of an advancing British force of greater size. His refusal to fight, despite the odds, caused a public furor and led to a court-martial, which exonerated him. Nevertheless, his military career in the war came to end. He subsequently served as a member of the Continental Congress, from 1785 to 1787, and then as the first governor of the Northwest Territory in 1787. At the head of a federal army in 1791, St. Clair suffered a stunning defeat against a smaller Indian force, causing great embarrassment to President George Washington and effectively ending his service to America.

One of the factors that distinguishes Charles Lee from all of these contemporaries is the *appearance* that he had significantly greater military experience. In fact, Charles Lee's actual military experience may not have differed from that of Gates, Montgomery, Stephen, Mercer, or St. Clair, except for the fact that he maintained the pretense of continuous military service after the French and Indian War. His actual field actions did not outshine any of these men. His service in Portugal was short-lived and not large-scale for either the British military or himself personally. He went on half pay in 1763 and served in no British military capacity thereafter. Lee made much of his attachment as a military adviser to the king of Poland and his stint with the Russian forces fighting in eastern Europe, but most of his time in Europe was spent in boredom or desultory travel. Whether any of his military exploits after Portugal were of any consequence is a matter of conjecture.

Nor did Charles Lee have any significant military experience in commanding large bodies of men. His highest rank in active service was as a lieutenant colonel, notwithstanding the honorary title of major general he received from the king of Portugal after his exploits at Vila Velha. Lee presented himself as an ardent student of all things military and, clearly, he was a voracious reader of military histories and strategies. The leading men of the Revolution wanted to believe that Charles Lee was a military genius and accepted his military expertise without question. Lee must have been impressive in face-to-face discussions of military matters with the patriot leaders, conveying a confident knowledge based on his reading and service. The British public, press, and officers, on the other hand, were at best ambivalent about his credentials. Based on contemporary correspondence, it appears that no leading American challenged Lee's inflated view of his genius. Charles Lee offered the whole package. He was a British officer of social standing (if not a noble by birth), still in the pay of the Crown (albeit half pay), and he took up the cause in print.

Gates and Montgomery, Stephen, Mercer, and St. Clair chose America as a homeland before they chose to stand and fight for the independence of the colonies. Charles Lee's commitment was reversed and, therefore, half-hearted. Lee may have shared the political beliefs of the revolutionaries, but he never shared their experience in America. He remained an Englishman right up to his disembarkment from the *London* in 1773. As we have seen, during the French and Indian War he ignored the settlers on the frontiers of the colonies, the militia who fought beside him, and the merchants along the seaboard in North America. His purchase of a farm in Virginia in 1775 appears to have been an afterthought, the sudden awareness that his claim for high command could not be forthcoming without a commitment to the American way of life. He shared many experiences and personality traits with Horatio Gates, but Charles Lee was no farmer, and his futile retirement to Prato Rio in 1780 proved that beyond a doubt.

Unlike Gates and Montgomery, Stephen, Mercer, and St. Clair, Lee was not fighting for America; he was fighting for Charles Lee. He shared an enemy with the American revolutionaries in the person of King George III and the ministers advising him. In America, Charles Lee found an entire continent filled with men who agreed with him that the king and his ministers were bumbling idiots at best and tyrannical authoritarians at worst. Lee's actions, even after throwing in with the Americans, demonstrate this viewpoint. Early in the war, Lee approached and tried to convince others in the service of the king to abandon their sovereign's misguided policies and allow Lee to mediate the dispute. Lee's admirers in America politely ignored these attempts or chalked them up to his overinflated ego. Later on, these attempts may have had more pressing personal motivations.

When comparing Lee with the other British officers who fought against the Crown, and even with the French, German, and Polish officers who came into America's service, one must wonder whether Charles Lee ever adopted *America* as a cause. Surely, in 1776, as the political and military contest was being engaged, he urged the Continental Congress to declare the independence of the colonies and to be quick about it. Perhaps from his commission in June 1775 to his capture in December 1776, Lee could see the bigger picture, but in a long letter to Patrick Henry, dated May 7, 1776, he treats the issue of independence as a debating point: "Having weigh'd the arguments on both sides, I am clearly of opinion, that we must (as we value the liberties of America, or even her existence) without a moments delay declare for Independence." For the most part, he argues a European question and comes to the conclusion that the Continental Congress cannot wait for France or Spain to adopt its cause. They will eventually, he argues, because it serves their interests. Congress should act immediately from a practical point of view—the men in arms need to be supported with equipment and need to know that Congress shares their desire for independence. "[B]y procrastination our ruin is inevitable," Lee declares.[14]

Just days later, Lee wrote to Richard Henry Lee, his main connection in the Congress, and this short letter, dated May 10, is telling:

> My Dear Friend,
> Your brother and I think, from the language of your letters, that the pulse of the Congress is low, and that you yourself, with all your vigour, are by collision, somewhat more contracted in your hopes than we wished to have found. If you do not declare immediately for positive independence,

we are all ruined. There is a poorness of spirit and languor in the late proceedings of Congress that I confess frightens me so much that at times I
regret having embarked my all, my fortune, my life, and reputation, in their
bottom. I sometimes wish I had settled in some country of slaves, where the
most lenient master governs. However, let the fate of my property be what
it will, I hope I shall preserve my reputation, and resign my breath with a
tolerable degree of grace. God bless you. I cannot write more at present.
'Ah, Cassius, I am sick of my many griefs.'

Yours, most entirely,
Charles Lee

Reading Lee's letters in the heat of the moment, one might not suspect a
want of passion for the cause. He argues compellingly for a Declaration of
Independence to advance both political and the military objectives. Reading
these letters after the fact, however, one can easily make the case that his
commitment was personal and pecuniary. Like many other men, Lee was
searching for a campaign that matched his political philosophy and simultaneously could advance his career. The American cause provided that vehicle,
and he would do all he could in 1775 and 1776 to make it successful. His
commitment, however, would be tested shortly thereafter.

BENEDICT ARNOLD

One more officer in the war, this one American-born, needs to be listed in
comparisons with Charles Lee. This man, of course, is Benedict Arnold. The
American Revolution provided a score of heroes, with George Washington
the indisputable shining star. It produced a single villain: Benedict Arnold.

The villainy of Arnold stands out for a multiplicity of reasons: he demonstrated considerable military skill and suffered serious wounds in the struggle
for the American cause; he abandoned it in the heat of the fight and in a way
that threatened men under his command; he abandoned it for greed, or
advancement, or the wishes of his wife, not personal or political conviction;
after he turned, he fought against the men he served and led; and, he eluded
capture during the war and lived out his life in England and Canada. Arnold
remains America's most notorious traitor. His courage and valor in the battle
for independence could not be denied. As a result, his turn away from the
cause was received with great anguish. He led his men through hundreds of
miles of wilderness to reach Quebec in the fall of 1775, facing disease and star-
vation along the way, and led them again in the rush to the walls to take the
city. He suffered a severe leg wound in that fight and reinjured the leg the next
year at Saratoga when he placed himself in the heat of that battle despite

orders to stay in the rear. His actions at Ticonderoga, Crown Point, Quebec, Lake Champlain, and Saratoga were heroic as well as skillful.

Charles Lee has not received the general public opprobrium attached to Arnold, despite some telling comparisons in their actions. Lee also held a high rank, higher indeed than Arnold, and his treachery during the period of his captivity in Manhattan may have been equally as significant as Arnold's at West Point. Lee's actions at Monmouth, if ascribed to treacherous motives, may have also proved devastating if not curtailed. The events of history, however, have unfolded in a way that has prevented Lee's designation as a clear villain. First of all, despite his high rank and esteem in the colonies, Charles Lee was not considered of military importance to the British. British military officers held an uneven opinion of Lee, with some newspaper pundits suggesting after his capture in 1776, sarcastically, that Britain would be better off returning Lee to the Americans for the remainder of the war. No one on either side of the fight doubted the military skill or personal courage of Benedict Arnold. Second, Lee's apparent treachery was not uncovered during the war and has never been completely accepted. A treason uncovered after the passage of seventy-five years and the passing of all the men who fought in the political and military battles surrounding it leaves its assessment solely to historians. The men who served alongside Arnold at Quebec and Saratoga must have felt his betrayal the deepest. Perhaps the impact would have been more telling for Charles Lee had he remained in the fight to the end of the war and reveled in the ultimate victory, or alternately, gloriously died in battle. Instead, by 1858, when Lee's actions were uncovered, he was already viewed as only a secondary player in the drama. What a difference in the legacy of this man had his actions, even giving him the benefit of all doubts, been discovered in 1777 or 1778!

CHAPTER 7

AMERICA'S SOLDIER

George Washington and Charles Lee were both in Philadelphia in June 1775 to accept their commissions from the Continental Congress. Independence was more than twelve months away and not a foregone conclusion, but the American soldiers across from the British regulars in Boston needed more than Artemas Ward to bolster their confidence. Boston was under siege. Men had already died for the cause. If the Americans were to continue their opposition to king and Parliament, they needed officers to lead the men attempting to chase the British from the city that started the fight.

Congress could delay a vote for independence, but the body could no longer deny the needs of the men they had placed in danger. In Philadelphia on June 15, Congress appointed George Washington commander in chief of the American forces and, over the next two days, appointed four major generals (Ward, Lee, Putnam, and Schuyler) and an adjutant (Gates). In Boston on June 17, the British stormed Breed's Hill in an attempt to breach the defenses of the farmers and merchants at its crest. In the bloody confrontation many Americans were killed, but they gave worse than they got, and now the British soldiers and their officers knew that the Americans meant to make a stand. Washington and Lee would shortly be on their way.

As we have already seen, Charles Lee was not completely happy with his position behind Ward. He demanded financial assurances from Congress, which agreed to accommodate him.[1] Nevertheless, Lee must have reveled in the euphoria of this bold step toward independence by his newly found country. The naming of officers energized the rebels, and the movement of Washington and his entourage became an event. The new heroes began their journey from the City of Brotherly Love to Boston with a parade at the company's departure. They picked up an escort through New Jersey, met with the appropriate people in New York City, so as not to antagonize the large Tory population still hoping for reconciliation, and finally reached their destination on July 2. Once at Cambridge, just outside Boston, Washington set about to make the defenses guarding his troops as formidable as possible. In this effort, he looked to Charles Lee for support.

Boston

In the twelve months after his appointment in June 1775, Charles Lee provided invaluable service to the American cause as both a military leader and a political provocateur. Lee wrote extensively during this period, and in reading his letters it is obvious that his sense of self was high and his spirits buoyant. He had attained a high military command in an important war; he was respected by both the military and the political leaders of the cause; he would become a substantial landowner and had the guaranty of the government to support the credit he extended to make the purchase.

As he moved through the mid-Atlantic colonies with Washington, Lee was received by men and women as a military genius and a man who could do great things. He was energized, and his letters reflect his commitment to the effort at hand. Politically, he goaded and prodded those hesitant to declare independence and make the break with Great Britain. Militarily, he was unquestioned in his judgments and his actions. Significantly, in this period and perhaps for the only time, he felt so self-assured that he could shrug off slights that at other times would have sent his temper flaring. As the weeks passed, Lee's letters also reflect the growing dangers of his high spirits. He became increasingly certain that the mantle of genius thrust upon him was deserved, and his advice to those who would listen became increasingly uncensored by his better judgment.

Lee needed a high level of energy. Washington designated him to command the left wing of the Cambridge defenses, and Lee took the task seriously. In one letter to Dr. Benjamin Rush, he claimed that he spent twelve hours that day on horseback reviewing the fifteen miles of line around Boston.[2] By all accounts, Lee acquitted this duty well. If he complained, it was about the shortage of engineers. This would be a constant complaint by Lee over the next twelve months, the lack of engineers.[3] He did not consider himself well-versed in defenses, and that may have been the source of the irritation. Where he thought that engineers would come from is a mystery. The colonies did not have a cadre of men trained in battlements and defenses waiting in the wings for the war to begin. It took months to find men for this duty, and the major part ultimately fell to foreigners who had the necessary experience, including Duportail and Kosciusko, who had not yet arrived. Lee would be on his own for a while in this arena.

Despite the hours he spent in the field and at the battlements, Lee made time during this period to maintain correspondence with a number of friends and supporters, notably Dr. Benjamin Rush and Robert Morris. His correspondence with Rush was political; his correspondence with Morris was financial. But it in these letters that we hear some of Lee's opinions on the men he was to command. For the most part, Lee liked what he saw of the men in the ranks, but doubted the abilities and commitment of the line officers. His letters are peppered with compliments and high expectations for the common soldier, especially if he could be outfitted with adequate equipment and officers. These private thoughts match his public proclamations before his commission that the British would be surprised by the strength and skill of the men who would fight for independence. Lee also raised the concern that the recruits in Boston might suffer a lack of confidence if they were continually kept behind the barricades.[4] Let them fight and show their worth.

As to the officers, however, Lee had little good to say. He placed some of the blame on Congress for the poor pay for officers, but his opinion was clear: "—the men (as I observ'd before) are excellent materials, but the lower order of officers are execrable. They are intriguing, factious, and dastardly—this I speak with exceptions—but the bulk deserve the epithets—Our new Army will I hope and believe be good. We purge it daily."[5] Lee suggested that some of the officers who were dismissed for inability tried to "dissuade the soldiers from re-enlisting."[6] These observations, however, appear sound and could well be expected from a lifelong military man put in charge of farmers and merchants under military command for the first time.

Lee's correspondence with Robert Morris concerned financial matters. Morris served as an agent for Lee in the purchase of land in Virginia that became known as Prato Rio. The seller was a man named Jacob Hite, and Lee was alternately exasperated and excited about his dealings with Hite. The deal would finally be consummated in December 1775 but not without considerable back-and-forth over the terms and conditions.

Lee's most important correspondent, and the one who caused the most stir in camp and among the rebels leaders in Massachusetts, was his former superior officer, General John Burgoyne, second in command of the British troops that Lee now faced every day. Probably even before he arrived in Boston, Lee was working on a letter to Burgoyne, ostensibly to wean the soldier to the side of the Americans. It may be that Lee was just having fun, making Burgoyne the foil for his public goading of the British ministry. On the other hand, Lee believed himself a persuasive man and may well have thought that if he could convince Burgoyne to talk with him, he could broker a settlement of the conflict. Either notion—winning over Burgoyne or negotiating a resolution—was close to preposterous given the military and political situation in April 1775. Indeed, several times in the next three years, Lee would forcibly try to place himself in such a position. The American rebels, on whom Lee depended for support, were not eager to reach a negotiated agreement, and Burgoyne (like Gage before him) had little authority to make concessions and surely saw Lee's efforts as inept. Nevertheless the British generals maintained an open channel to see if they could learn something valuable. Lee's polemic reads more like a justification of his own position than a realistic attempt to win over Burgoyne. Surely it read well to the American crowd, and it does not take much imagination to picture Charles Lee at dinner reciting it word for word for an attentive audience, along with personal anecdotes about his days under Burgoyne's command in Portugal and his personal triumph at Vila Velha.

Lee's letter begins with flattery ("There is no man from whom I have received so many testimonies of esteem and affection; there is no man whose esteem and affection could, in my opinion, have done me greater honour"); moves to politics and the corruption of the British government ("a wicked and insidious court and cabinet"); pays homage to the American revulsion against taxation without representation ("I am convinced that no argument . . . can be produced in support of this right"); and offers his opinion of the ultimate outcome of the conflict: "You cannot possibly succeed. No man is better acquainted with the state of this continent than myself. I have ran through almost the whole colonies from the North to the South, and from the South to the North. I have conversed with all orders of men, from the first estated gentlemen, to the lowest planters and farmers, and can assure you that the same spirit animates the whole. Not less than one hundred and fifty thousand gentlemen, yeoman, and farmers, are now in arms, determined to preserve their liberties or perish."[7] This letter continues Lee's appeal, not to Burgoyne (whom Lee could not have had any delusions of dissuading from his military obligations), but to the American soldier and to the common man supporting the Continental Congress, hoping that they have a chance to win against Great Britain. Lee made sure that the letter was printed in the newspapers so that the true audience could read it. At the end, Lee adds one more thought about America: "In short, this is the last asylum of persecuted liberty."[8]

Thrown the gauntlet, Burgoyne proved himself up to Lee's challenge. He answers Lee point for point without conceding any ground ("a King never appears in so glorious a light as when he employs the executive powers of the

state to maintain the laws") and then nicely turns the tables on Lee by accepting his offer to meet across the lines.[9] Lee now faced a dilemma. Could he
casually accept Burgoyne's offer while his commanding officer, George
Washington, camped just miles away? Could he go without permission from
Washington or the authorities in Massachusetts who had enthusiastically
greeted him just weeks earlier? What could he discuss with Burgoyne? Lee
had no negotiating authority for Washington, the Massachusetts Provincial
Congress, or the Continental Congress. He faced a more personal dilemma as
well. His public appeal to Burgoyne elicited a public response, and the officers
and men under his command and the Massachusetts authorities began to
question the purpose and value of such a meeting and Lee's motives in asking
for it. Would Lee reveal the army's defenses, intentionally or unwittingly?
Would he try to negotiate away the gains they had made for some lukewarm
freedoms? Lee had succeeded, in just a few weeks, in undermining his
professed loyalty to the cause.

Lee extricated himself without harm to his reputation. He asked the
Massachusetts Provincial Congress for permission to meet with Burgoyne.
Concerned, but unwilling to slight their new hero, the Congress grudgingly
gave their permission. Lee then politely turned down Burgoyne's offer to
meet by suggesting that it would appear unseemly. Everyone involved saved
face. Looking at the written exchanges it is impossible to determine if
Lee's actions were coolly calculated and smoothly executed or whether he
stumbled into an awkward situation and righted himself unconsciously.
Regardless of which way it is viewed, the episode of the Burgoyne letters
demonstrates the hubris of Charles Lee at this moment in his life. He lectured
his former commanding officer in public and set himself up in a meeting
where he would be at least his equal. He saw himself the equal, if not the
superior, of every man on the scene.

Reading Burgoyne's other letters and dispatches, however, one comes
away with a different perspective, and one that would have rankled Charles
Lee from head to toe if he were privy to them. Burgoyne did not see Lee as his
equal. He saw Lee as a meddler, perhaps a traitor, and useful only to the
extent that he could offer insight into what was happening in America and
among its councils. He would meet with Lee to further his duty to the Crown
and perhaps to turn him back to a useful loyalty to the king. Lee, of course,
did not let this exchange end without more lecturing. He sent a private letter
to Burgoyne warning that France and Spain would support the American
cause and followed this with another letter on the occasion of Burgoyne's
leaving Boston to return to England. In this letter, Lee denied that the
Americans wanted independence and stated that their ties to Great Britain are

"dear to them," albeit being rendered "asunder" by the British ministry. He flattered Burgoyne that he had the opportunity to immortalize himself as the "saviour of your country," urged him to entreat the ministry to retreat from its American policy, and told him "to address yourself to the people at large" if the ministry refused to listen.[10]

In this period, Lee also felt so secure in his position that he could laugh off personal slights and slights directed at his beloved dogs. Given his pride and his tendency to quarrelsome affairs of honor throughout his life, his reactions in 1775 appear an aberration. John Adams had the misfortune of having a letter to James Warren intercepted in July and published in the Tory press. This episode caused Adams considerable consternation and political anxiety because of his deprecating comments about John Dickinson of Pennsylvania, the author of "Letters from a Farmer," and some off-the-cuff remarks about Charles Lee, whom he describes as "the Oddity of a great Man" and "a queer Creature." Adams also refers to Lee's love of dogs and states that "if you love him" you must "forgive a thousand whims for the Sake of the Soldier and the Scholar."[11] Lee's response was politically magnificent. He used the opportunity to praise Adams, excuse away his comments as compliments, and solidify his relationship with this key player in the unfolding American drama: "As you may possibly harbor some suspicions that a certain passage in your intercepted letters [may] have made some disagreeable impressions on my mind, I think it necessary to assure you that it is quite the reverse. Until the bulk of mankind is much altered, I consider the reputation of being whimsical rather as a panegyric than sarcasm, and my love of dogs passes with me as a still higher compliment." And he performed the task with humor and humility: "Spada sends his love to you, and declares, in very intelligible language, that he has fared much better since your allusion to him, for he is caressed now by all ranks, sexes, and ages."[12]

How can it be that this master of arrogance and sarcasm could withhold his pen's wrath? Clearly, Lee felt more secure in his person and his position in 1775 than at any other time in his life.

NEW YORK

By late 1775, Washington apparently felt secure enough in his defenses around Boston to allow Charles Lee to move to another theater of the war where work also needed to be done. In December, Lee departed for Rhode Island to assist the locals in shoring up their defenses on the belief that a detachment of British troops would be heading there soon. The governor feared for Newport, where Tories held considerable sway.

Washington could spare Lee, but no troops. Lee headed south with a small retinue, essentially his guard and some riflemen. He also carried with him a loyalty oath. In addition to making recommendations for defenses of Newport, Lee insisted that the most notorious Tories sign the oath, declaring that they would not aid the king's troops or assist them in their "tyranny and villainy." Without troops to enforce the oath, Lee's actions only had the effect of solidifying opposition to the newly formed colonial government. Lee's foray to Rhode Island was short-lived and notable only for the oath.[13] He soon returned to Cambridge.

Now Washington anticipated that the British would head for New York City, another haven for Tories and Loyalists, and he accepted a plan Lee presented to shore up the defenses of that city. Lee looked forward to continuing his harassment of those Americans opposing the armed conflict with Great Britain and reveled in the assignment. He had been railing in his letters about the New York Tories, especially Royal Governor William Tryon, and he anticipated taking matters into his own hands if Congress and the local colonial authorities were loath to do so. Lee called for a direct and forceful approach in dealing with New York Tories and their governor: "What in the Devil's name possesses the Congress in not giving orders to seize that Scoundrel?"[14] Lee detailed his plan in a long letter to several members the Continental Congress and George Washington. He boasted to Robert Morris that his letter was "long and presumptuous" but necessary. The plan contained three parts: disarm "all the manifestly disaffected," not just the Tories, and give the arms to the Continental troops; require all of the same to post a bond equal to one-half the value of their estates "as security for their good behaviour"; and, administer "the strongest oath that can be devised." Lee favored loyalty oaths to confront those who were cold or lukewarm to the cause as a way to "distinguish the desparate fanaticks from those who are reclaimable" and to neutralize the former by removing them to the interior, where they could no longer be a danger.[15] A cadre of vicious revolutionaries in New York, led by Isaac Sears, was more than willing to oblige him in this effort.

As to the "scoundrel" Tyron, Lee had already made his opinions known to New Yorker Alexander McDougall, in response to the suggestion that the citizens of New York feared shelling by the British ships in the harbor: "You are, it seems, afraid of your Town in the first place I do not believe that They dare fire upon it—but if it was earnestly their intention you have I think, the means of preventing it—seize by one bold stroke this Tyron and all of his associates—then, assure the Capt of the Man of War that the first House he sets on fire shall be the funeral pile of his Excellency—and You ought really to execute your threats—if you do not adopt this method I am confident that you will repent it—if the seizure of his Person cannot be effected by public authority, you may work on some glowing young Particulars to the undertaking[.]"[16] Weeks later Lee suggested that the city be destroyed if it could not be held.[17]

In January 1776, Lee asked for the New York command. After several months in Massachusetts, the defenses Lee helped to erect satisfied George Washington, and Lee had little active military work to perform. On January 5, Lee addressed a letter to his commander that began with the admission that the prospect of leaving New York City defenseless was "so terrible, that I have scarcely been able to sleep from apprehension." Lee advised Washington that he should not quibble about whether he had authority to move on New York, but to take action. Congress expects action and would be "inspired by decision." Of course, Lee saw himself as the man to carry out the task:

> I would propose that you should detach me into Connecticut, and lend your name for collecting a body of volunteers. I am assured that I shall find no difficulty in assembling a sufficient number for the purposes wanted. This body, in conjunction (if there should appear occasion to summon them) with the Jersey Regiment under the Command of Lord Stirling, now at Elizabethtown, will effect the security of New York, and the expulsion or suppression of that dangerous banditti of Tories, who have appeared in Long Island, with the professed intention of acting against the authority of the congress. Not to crush these serpents, before their rattles are grown, would be ruinous.[18]

Washington anticipated that the British would soon leave Boston for New York and enthusiastically accepted Lee's plan, but only after checking with John Adams, who happened to be in Watertown, as to his authority to undertake the action. Washington thereupon commissioned Lee "to put the city in the best position of defence" and to disarm those persons on Long Island "justly suspected of designs unfriendly to the views of Congress." Washington clearly trusted Lee and specifically tells him to use his best judgment, because "it is impossible with propriety to give particular directions" in the matter.[19]

It might be expected, given his bravado, that Major General Lee would march into New York astride a stallion with a battalion of men ready to clean the town of the Tory vipers. Alas, it would not be so. First, the weather made preparations and transportation difficult. Next, Congress wavered at the prospect of confronting the Long Island Tories, causing Lee to complain to Washington that Congress ordered the Connecticut volunteers disbanded and the Tories "unmolested."[20] And, needless to say, not everyone in New York looked forward to the appearance of Charles Lee or Connecticut troops in their city. The New York Committee of Safety feared for themselves and the inhabitants of the city. British ships in the harbor may have posed a threat, but they allowed New York merchant vessels to pass the line in and out of the city. Severe action by the rebels would surely change that situation. Besides, the defenders of the city were almost without gunpowder, and hostilities would force families to flee out of town and into the cold. These patriots begged Charles Lee to spare them until at least the beginning of March. They asked that he stop short of the colony's borders and proceed alone into the city to discuss his plans.

Sitting in Stamford, Connecticut, with 1,200 men of "zeal and ardour," Lee fumed. He wrote to Congress on January 22 to let them know that coddling the Long Island Tories was a bad idea, that the British had specific designs on New York, and that losing the city would "cut the Continent in twain" and prevent coordinated action thereafter between North and South. He wrote to the Committee of Safety to assure them that his entry into their colony would be for defensive purposes only, but he could not resist rattling the sword by repeating his earlier threat: "If the ships of war are quiet, I shall be quiet; but I declare solemnly that if they make a pretext of my presence to fire on the Town, the first house set in flames shall be the funeral pile of some of their best friends."[21] By late January, Congress appointed a three-man committee to go to New York City to negotiate a peace between Lee and the Committee of Safety.

Lee crossed into New York on February 2, but his entry into the city on February 4 was anything but majestic. The bad weather and a debilitating case of gout hampered his movement, and for most of the trip Lee was carried on a litter. He was accompanied by 300 Connecticut men, and Lord Stirling brought over a detachment of New Jersey troops as well. Additional Connecticut and New York militia brought the command to 1,700 men. General Henry Clinton appeared with several ships in New York Harbor on the same day. The Committee of Safety had accepted troops in the city, but the inhabitants were nervous and anxious. Despite his irascibility, Lee quickly made peace with the locals by accepting a plan for defenses that made sense to all of the parties involved. Aggressive actions were put on hold in favor of defensive actions. Lee also immediately made contact with General Clinton, on board one of the British ships. Clinton had no immediate desires on New York, letting everyone know that he was heading to the Carolinas with his troops. His appearance in the harbor just made for greater anxiety and the departure of many women and children from the city.

It did not take Lee long, however, to determine that defending the city would be impossible if the rebels could not control the harbor. At best, they could try to prevent occupation of the city by British troops. To this end, attempts were made to blockade passage between Long Island Sound and the East River at Hell's Gate and across the water at Hallet's Point and to maintain a route between Long Island and Manhattan. Batteries were placed at the entrance to the harbor along the East River at Catherine Street (Waterbury's Battery), on a hill above this battery (Badlam's Redoubt), and below Wall Street (Coenties Battery). Fortifications were also to be built across the water on Long Island. On the Hudson River side of Manhattan, large ships could not be thwarted, so defenses focused on making the taking of ground expensive in men and materiel if British troops landed.[22]

Lee began these works with the 1,700 men at his disposal, but he would soon be leaving the city. It appears that his active approach to the New York command may have been part of the reason that he was considered for and awarded the command of the army to be sent to Canada. The New Yorkers may have suggested Lee to prevent him from doing damage to their situation. He was a likely choice for the post in any event because of his familiarity with Canada from the French and Indian War and his fluency in French. Washington hinted at this transfer in a letter as early as January 30, and the Continental Congress made the appointment on February 17, just days after Lee's arrival in New York City.

Lee received letters from John Hancock, John Adams, Benjamin Franklin, Benjamin Rush, and Robert Morris, praising him on his selection to go to Canada and wishing him well. Their comments were effusive. Franklin opened his letter with "I rejoice that you are going to Canada," but John Adams was over the top: "We want you at N. York—We want you at Cambridge—We want you in Virginia—But Canada seems of more Importance than any of those places, and therefore you are sent there. I wish you as many Laurells as Wolf and Montgomery reaped there, with a happier Fate. Health and long Life, after a glorious return."[23]

COMMON SENSE AND RADICALISM

Over the next several weeks, Lee's correspondence overflowed with congratulations on his good fortune. Several letters, like that of his faithful correspondent Benjamin Rush, alluded to the glorious deaths of previous generals assigned to the northern battlefields: "Should your blood mingle with the blood of Wolfe, Montcalm, and Montgomery, posterity will execrate the plains of Abraham to the end of time."[24] Lee's concerns for his person, however, were more immediate. He let his correspondents know that he was honored by the appointment but that his most recent battle with the gout, which he believed was brought on by the cold and nasty weather in Connecticut, dampened his enthusiasm for the Canadian post. He might prefer a southern assignment.[25] Notwithstanding his physical misgivings, Lee set about preparations for his new command while still concerned with duties unfinished in New York.[26] His pressing need was men to defend the city. He wanted 3,000 men to build and arm the camp planned for Long Island and told George Washington that 5,000 were needed for the overall defense. Enlistments among the Connecticut men would expire in just days, and the threat of Governor Tryon's return to the city bedeviled him.

The most interesting event during this period, however, had to be the dinner that Lee hosted for Thomas Paine, the author of the pamphlet *Common Sense*. Lee first got notice of the work from Horatio Gates in a letter dated January 22, 1776, and within days he was recommending the work to George Washington: "Have you seen the pamphlet—*Common Sense*? I never saw such a masterly, irresistible performance. It will, if I mistake not, in concurrence with the transcendent folly and wickedness of the ministry, give the Coup de grace to Great Britain. In short, I own myself convinced, by the arguments, of the necessity of separation."[27] Paine's attack on the British monarchy, his defense of the rights of man, and his fervent call for an immediate separation echoed sentiments spoken and written by Lee over the previous twelve months. John Adams, among others, proposed to introduce Paine, "a Countryman of yours, and a Citizen of the World," to Lee. Apparently, Paine was going to New York and wanted to meet "a Gent[N] whose character he so highly respects."[28] Indeed, the meeting took place on February 24, according to a letter from Lee to Benjamin Rush: "—your Mr. Payne din'd with me yesterday, I am much oblig'd to you for the introduction—He has genius in his eyes—his conversation has much life—I hope he will continue cramming down the throats of squeamish mortals his wholesome truths."[29] These two men, both radicals, each urging in his own way the separation of the colonies from Great Britain, most probably enjoyed each other's company.

The meeting with Thomas Paine, coupled with his experiences with the Tories in New York City, surely reinforced Lee's political theme of the moment. During the period from his appointment as major general in June 1775 through June 1776, Lee pressed all of his correspondents to move Congress toward a declaration of separation from Great Britain. He used reason, biting sarcasm, and military necessity to make his case, and his frustration with the snail's pace of the political efforts could not be suppressed. The Congress was still debating a vote on independence, and many felt that the only way to achieve it was through unanimous vote of the colonies.

The New York delegation posed a significant obstacle to unanimity. Surely, a Congress split on this overriding issue would have difficulty governing, but the New Yorkers were scared as well as divided. In New York City, the citizens could see the British men-of-war in their harbor and feared that any aggressive revolutionary action would put them in personal danger and could destroy the city. Even the revolutionary Committee on Safety favored a measured approach. Taking a strong, and perhaps violent, stand against New York Tories in the opening months of 1776 was not considered by all as the right approach.

Lee disagreed. He urged immediate preparations for war and did not care if some colonies thought it unnecessary. He chastised New Yorkers for their hesitation, and as always, his language was colorful and to the point. As early as January 1775, in a letter to Robert Morris of New York, Lee scolded the laggards:

> I am sorry your Province cannot be prevailed upon to arm themselves as I think it absolutely necessary in the present crisis ... either the ministry must precede or they must persist if they recede your Province will incur disgrace in having shewn less spirit than the others . . . , but you have always in my opinion been in pursuit of a chimera absolute unanimity which cannot be expected in a society of any considerable extent that dam'd slow heavy quakering Nag your Province is mounted upon ought to be flogg'd and spurr'd though she kick and plunges. If it had not been for the smart whip of my friend Mifflin I believe she never would have advanced a single inch. Virginia and Maryland ride most noble mettled coursers—[30]

Later in the year, Lee offered the same advice and expressed the same impatience to Richard Henry Lee after a weak "Address to the King" by the Virginia Congress: "That callous tyrant must have his fears alone worked upon. If I did address him, I would do it in the following style: 'Sir, if you do not withdraw your troops upon receipt of this, we will absolve ourselves from all allegiance to you, and we will divorce ourselves forever from Britain, whose patience in suffering such tyranny as that she has experienced through your whole reign, renders her totally unworthy to be the presiding power of a great Empire.'"[31]

This direct approach surely gained him support among those ready to break away and eager for the fight such action would bring. One month later, it was John Adams he was hectoring "to shew firmness" and not to go "hobbling on, like the Prince of Lilliput, with one high-heeled shoe, one low one, for you will undoubtedly fall upon your noses every step you take."[32] By January 1776, Lee was convinced that "the inexorable bloody disposition of the King" was forcing the colonies to break away.[33] As noted above, however, Lee's exhortations appear to have a more practical than ideological foundation.

Charles Lee's radicalism expressed itself in other pragmatic ways as well. He could not shake his obsession with the Loyalists in New York. He perceived them a threat that could undermine the entirety of the effort to defeat Great Britain on the ground. He did not understand how men who had fomented the revolution could live side by side with people clearly, in his eyes, abetting the enemy. Lives were at stake. Severe measures needed to be taken, and he would take them, notwithstanding the outcry that he knew would result. He announced his intentions, and with each exchange of letters, Lee ratcheted up the rhetoric and the effort.

Aware that his position in New York was coming to an end, Lee lectured the Provincial Congress on the treatment of Tories posting bonds for their liberty: "The liberation of the notorious enemies of liberty and their country, on giving bonds for their good behaviour, appears to me in our present situation, extremely ill-imagined. It is so far from security, that it is rather adding virus to their malignancy. The first body of troops that arrives will cancel these bonds. Some vigorous, decisive mode must now be adopted, of discovering on whom you may depend, on whom not. The crisis will admit of no procrastination."[34] Lest he be accused of not acting on his own advice, the next day Lee directed Isaac Sears to administer a loyalty oath to these "banditti" and to seize all who refuse to sign and "send 'em up to Connecticut where they can be no longer dangerous." To make sure the job is done, Lee sends a copy of the oath he used in New England.[35] Lee informs Congress of his directions for the oath and decries the effectiveness of the bonds, adding for color that the British troops cancelling the bonds of the Tories will be "the first Regiment of our Gracious Sovereigns Cut Throats."

The Provincial Congress of New York recoiled. A "Mr. Samuel Gale" had been apprehended and sent off to jail in Connecticut. The Congress not only wanted to know the charges but rebuked Lee as to his authority to take such action: "It may not be improper to remind you, Sir, that the right of apprehending, trying, and punishing citizens who violate the resolutions of Congress, or act inimical to the liberties of America, is by the Continental Congress delegated to the Provincial Conventions in the respective Colonies."[36] And further, Lee's soldiers were firing on boats going in and out of the city. Lee apologized for not referring Gale "to you, his proper judges," but did not back away from his campaign to rid the city and Long Island of Tories. Based on intelligence that he received, Lee labeled Gale "a most dangerous man" who posed a threat just by his presence on Long Island. Lee did not seem to care if he was considered "foolish, rash or precipitate."

He reiterated his intent to clear Long Island of Tories with this rationale: "When the enemy is at our door, forms must be dispensed with."[37]

Just days later, Major General Charles Lee presented Congress with a thorough "Report on the Defence of New York, March, 1776." He gave a detailed account of his efforts to fortify the city. He correctly foresaw that the "possession and security of Long-Island is certainly of still greater importance than New-York" and listed the efforts made to defend the island. Nevertheless, Lee ends the report with another diatribe on the delicate treatment of Tories on Long Island and ends with this chilling paragraph of the actions needed to be taken: "I do not imagine that the disarming of the Tories will incapacitate them from acting against us, as they can easily be supplied by the ships. *I should, therefore, think it prudent to secure their children as hostages.* If a measure of this kind (hard as it may appear) is not adopted, the children's children of America may rue the fatal omission [emphasis added]."[38]

For all parties concerned, it appears that Charles Lee left New York City in early March 1776, not a day too soon. The outcry about his tactics had made its way to the Continental Congress and a "public resolve" issued by that body rejected the loyalty oaths as a legitimate method for dealing with Tories.[39] Friend Richard Henry Lee sought to soften this reprimand by assuring Lee that the Congress deliberately did not point its finger at him and acknowledged the difficulties he faced in trying to defend the city.[40] Lee recognized that his measures were harsh and the reprimand expected, but he defended his actions as the result of "an immoderate zeal for the rights and safety of this country."[41] In the spring of 1776, Charles Lee was too valuable a military commodity to risk losing over a dispute about the treatment of Tories in New York.

One aspect of Charles Lee's writing during this period cannot be ignored. He was surely full of self-confidence and self-importance. He went out of his way to say more than once that he would take personal responsibility for the actions pursued under his orders and advised his subordinates that if the actions were questioned, they should be attributed to him. He cloaked this self-importance in the necessity of war and the "liberties" of the American people, but he was so convinced of his own worth that the opinion of Charles Lee was sufficient by itself to justify any actions taken.

Major General Charles Lee would depart New York City in March, but he found himself traveling south, not north to Canada.

A SOUTHERN COMMAND

It appears that a combination of factors diverted Charles Lee from a command in Canada, despite his evident advantages. George Washington stated the arguments for the Canadian post succinctly: "I was just about to congratulate you on your appointment to the command in Canada, when I received the account that your destination was altered. As a Virginian I must rejoice at the change; but as an American, I think you would have done more essential service to the common cause in Canada. For, besides the advantage of speaking French and thinking in French, an officer who is acquainted with their manners and customs and has travelled in their country must certainly take the strongest hold of their affection and confidence."[42] Nonetheless, the egos of several generals (Philip Schuyler, for one) caused them to lobby for the northern post, and Lee's high estimation in the minds of the southern delegates to the Continental Congress caused them to secure Lee once it became clear that the British would focus their forces on the southern colonies rather than New York. Lee's griping about his gout may also have been a factor in the switch. Whatever the reasons, Charles Lee may have received the better opportunity, at least in the short run of the next several months.

Lee left New York City, was in Philadelphia on March 11 to visit his friends in the Congress, and then traveled through Baltimore on his way to Virginia, arriving at the capital in Williamsburg just three weeks after leaving New York. Along the way he had the time to pick up intelligence on the happenings south. He railed against the southern royal governors just as he did against Tryon in New York and picked up where he left off in calling for harsh action against Tories, this time those who lived under the protection of British vessels along the coast. Shortly after his arrival in Virginia, he ordered the arrest of the royal governor of Maryland, Robert Eden, on the pretext that he had documents that came from the British ministry. Apparently, the Committee of Safety in Annapolis questioned Lee's authority in Maryland, and his decision to send the orders to the Baltimore Committee, not the Annapolis Committee, irked them even more. Eden eluded capture and left for England shortly thereafter.[43]

In Williamsburg, Lee commandeered the college building for a military hospital. He was at first rebuked, but the action was ultimately ratified by the Virginia Provincial Congress. At his urging, Tories were removed from their homes and transported north and west, out of harm's way, out of the sphere of any British spies looking for information, and unavailable to troops that might advance looking for succor.[44] Lee ordered the burning of the houses of particularly flagrant Tories in Portsmouth and Suffolk, and he took prisoners. In a letter to Edmund Pendleton, president of the Virginia Committee of Safety, Lee invited rebuke if his actions exceeded his authority, but Pendleton allowed the necessity and acknowledged Lee's restraint in "that you confined the conflagration at present to the houses of a few of the most notorious offenders." Nevertheless, Pendleton suggested that the matter be thoroughly debated before further actions were taken.[45] Running throughout these exchanges in Virginia, as in New York, is a tension surrounding the extent of Lee's authority and whether his professed willingness to abide by civil authority was genuine or just a cover for the continued trespassing of that authority.

Lee did not find himself in an enviable position in the southern command. Tories were everywhere, the British fleet was appearing at various locations along the coast, the deposed royal governors were encouraging the slave population to rise against the patriots in return for freedom, and the colonial troops were disorganized and scattered. Lee described his predicament in colorful terms to Washington in early April 1776: "I am like a dog in a dancing school—I know not where to turn myself, where to fix myself. The circumstances of the country, intersected by navigable rivers; the uncertainty of the enemys designs and motions, who can fly in an instant to any spot where they chose with their canvass wings, throw me or would have thrown Julius Caesar, into this inevitable dilemma. I may be in the North, when (as Richard says)[46] I should serve my sovereign in the West. I can only act from surmise and have a very good chance of surmising wrong."[47] Lee had a good military fix on the situation, and during this period he worked well in concert with the many officers under his command and the several committees of safety. He called for more engineers and for clothes and arms for the men in the field; he encouraged the building of armed rafts that could at least challenge the British ships in the rivers;[48] he tried to instill discipline in the men in the field; he penned an appeal to the "Young Gentlemen of Virginia" to form a troop of cavalry; and, he appointed officers for a company of artillery. Lee received appeals and requests for advice from every corner of the command.

CHARLESTON

The defense of Charleston, South Carolina, represents the high point in Lee's career as an American soldier. The British committed more than fifty ships and 2,000 troops to the conquest of this important southern port town. The capture of Charleston early in the war would have changed the British strategy, and the unfolding of the American Revolution would have been quite different from the story now told. As with all Charles Lee lore, the importance of his role depends on the historian and is often viewed in light of Lee's subsequent actions. At the time, however, Lee came away from Charleston an American hero, his reputation as a general significantly burnished.

Detractors have argued that Lee played an insignificant role in the battle or stole the thunder of the local heroes or got in the way and almost prevented the American victory. These kinds of claims fall flat. Lee was sent to the southern theater to coordinate the Continental Army and local troops, to prepare defenses, and provide military insight. He performed those duties, and he performed them well. The American victory at Charleston came about owing in equal parts to luck, hard work, and bravery by all involved, including Lee. There should have been and there was enough honor and glory to cover all of the participants. The road to Charleston, however, was not without difficulty and controversy for Charles Lee, as always.

It became clear in May 1776 that the British were making for Charleston with the intention of taking the town. When Henry Clinton appeared in New York Harbor in February with troops from the evacuation of Boston, he told Lee and everyone else that he was taking his troops south to the Carolinas. He picked up the royal governors of both North Carolina and South Carolina, apparently for the purpose of reinstalling them in their authorities with support from a fleet arriving from England under the command of Sir Peter Parker. The rendezvous finally took place in May at Cape Fear, North Carolina. The combined force then moved south along the coast to Charleston. In all, the force numbered about fifty ships and transports and appeared outside the bar of the harbor by June 1. By this time, Lee was already making his way to the city and ordering troops from several corners of his command to the spot. He arrived in the first days of June and immediately began assessing the situation. The South Carolinians were furiously working to finish the fort on Sullivan's Island in the harbor. The British had already landed troops on nearby Long Island, and the ships were approaching the bar.

The governor of South Carolina, John Rutledge, was not yet committed to American independence but surely wanted to defend his territory. The first issue to be resolved in the defense of Charleston was the issue of command: who would be the commander of the troops? Charles Lee was the highest ranking Continental Army officer, of course, but the troops were South Carolina and North Carolina militias. The concept of an overriding Continental Army control of forces was just taking shape in the hostilities, and it had not yet been enforced in battle. Lee raised the issue right away, as he should have—the officers and the men under them needed to know whom to obey, and any coordinated effort demanded a chain of command. Rutledge recognized the exigencies of the situation and almost immediately named Lee the top military officer in the city.[49]

The governor's early and decisive action made the defense of the city possible. Lee's military instincts made him argue for the abandonment of the half-finished fort in Charleston's harbor, but the local defenders would not budge on the issue. On this issue, the governor retained authority and disagreed with Lee. Once Lee recognized that his advice would not be taken, he surveyed the work on the fort, provided support and advice for the work yet to be done, and set the tone for command when action started.[50] This is not to say that all that he commanded was put into action by his subordinates. Some of his orders could not be carried out because of the circumstances, and others were simply ignored.

The commander of the troops most immediately in harm's way—that is, the troops building and charged with defending the fort on Sullivan's Island— had his own ideas about how to proceed. This was Colonel William Moultrie, and he moved at his own pace and direction when his ideas clashed with those of Lee. For one thing, Moultrie refused to build the defensive protections Lee ordered for the rear of the fort. Lee was rightly concerned that one or more British ships would be able to make their way around the back of the island for a clear firing line on the fort's artillery positions. As late as June 22, Lee expressed deep concerns to Governor Rutledge about the ability to rely on the fort for the defense of the city, asking bluntly whether "it will be prudent to risk so many men, and encounter so many difficulties in attempting to support it."[51] Lee even considered removing Moultrie from command just days before the fight.[52] Governor Rutledge remained just as adamant, so much so that the day before the battle he sent Colonel Moultrie the following message: "General Lee wishes you to evacuate the fort. You will not do it without an order from me. I would sooner cut off my hand than write one. JOHN RUTLEDGE."

Colonel Moultrie had no doubts. Whether his conviction was based on solid judgment or stubbornness cannot be ascertained. In any event, when the time came to fight, Moultrie demonstrated exceptional coolness and bravery in confronting the overwhelming naval and land forces he faced. He deserved and received enormous credit for the ultimate victory. He also benefited from an extraordinary stroke of luck. No question, however, he was aided by the advice of Charles Lee before the battle and by the fact that Lee held the command and coordinated the combined forces before and throughout the fight. Lee was also lucky—that Moultrie ignored Lee's military intuition that the fort could not be defended.

The British battle plan on June 28 called for the 2,200 troops under Henry Clinton on Long Island, just east of Sullivan's Island, to attack Fort Sullivan by land while the ships bombarded the fort from the sea. Only a fairly narrow stream divided the islands. Lee stationed a troop of South Carolina Rangers to defend the strait along with North Carolina regulars. Nevertheless, in the days prior to the fight, it appeared that capture of the fort and, ultimately, the city could be a relatively simple task for the combined British forces. Peter Parker had eleven ships in the fight with 270 guns, including the *Bristol* and

Experiment, with 50 guns apiece. Even in hindsight, a cold analysis of the land and sea forces available to the British leads to no other conclusion. Fortunately for the Americans, the British did not reconnoiter or execute the land assault well, their ships performed poorly, and a natural phenomenon that no one on either side anticipated played a major part in the battle.

The naval bombardment began at about eleven o'clock, with the British gunships taking up positions in two parallel lines within cannon distance from Fort Sullivan. But the ships received no support from the British troops on Long Island. The British had neglected to survey the stream that needed to be forded. On the day of the fight, this small stream became a torrent, effectively denying access to Sullivan's Island. A relatively small contingent of Americans stood across the stream on Sullivan's Island and were able to hold off the British without the need of reinforcements. The British land troops were not a factor in the battle.

The ships — including the *Thunder*, the *Bristol*, the *Experiment*, and the *Solebay*—began pouring fire into the fort. The fusillade was enormous but, despite its fury, had no effect. The Americans had built the fort, to the extent that it was completed, with palmetto trees and sand. At some points, the walls were sixteen feet wide and ten feet high—parallel rows of piled palmetto logs filled in the center with sand. The 450 men available to Moultrie manned thirty-one guns placed along the walls. Instead of battering and eventually destroying the walls of the fort, the British cannonballs simply sank into the soft barrier walls or flew over the heads of the men into the empty center of the fort. The "walls" of the fort were unaffected. The frustration aboard the ships at the futility of these naval efforts must have been enormous. At the same time, the accuracy of the American cannons, bravely manned by the South Carolinian defenders under the constant shelling, wreaked tremendous damage on the attackers.

The cannonade lasted for twelve hours. On the British side, it was constant. The Americans paced their firing to preserve their ammunition. Charles Lee spent most of the day on the mainland, concerned about an escape route for the men. He had prepared to give the order to spike the guns and save the men if the situation required such drastic action. At one point in the day, he crossed over to Sullivan's Island "in a small boat, in order to animate the garrison in *propriâ personâ*," only to find the men in good spirits and willing to stay the course.[53] He had fretted for days before the fight about the lack of an escape route and feared that the men would be slaughtered if their only recourse was by boat (which it was). This legitimate military concern never came into play, however. When the firing ceased, Moultrie had lost only twelve dead and twenty-five wounded.

The situation was considerably different on board the British ships in the harbor. Fire from the fort had devastating effect. The flagship *Bristol* lost 100 men killed or wounded, including Peter Parker, who was wounded twice; Lord William Campbell, the royal governor of South Carolina, who died from his wounds; and the captain, who lost an arm. The captain of the *Experiment* also lost an arm and an equal number of other men dead or wounded. Had one or more of the British ships been able to maneuver around the back of the fort, as Charles Lee feared, the barrage would have been significantly more effective, and the Americans, lacking an escape route, might have been routed. But the ships sent to complete this task—the *Sphynx*, the *Actæon*, and the *Syren*—could not make it to their destination. They foundered on the shoals. Two finally freed themselves, but the *Actæon* was now of no use to the British and was eventually scuttled.

Despite their overwhelming numbers, their military prowess, and the inherent weakness of the defenders, the British could not take anything positive from this encounter. By the end of the day, they had suffered an enormous defeat, although it was not readily apparent. Lee fretted that they would regroup and make a second attempt. Instead, the ships reassembled over the bar and eventually high-tailed it from Charleston. The British would not attempt a similar assault on a southern city for the next five years. Eventually, in 1780, the British captured Charleston, but by then it was too late to make a significant difference in the outcome of the war.

Charles Lee shared the luck and the glory with Colonel William Moultrie. In letters to the president of the Virginia Convention, Benjamin Rush, General Gates, and George Washington immediately after the battle, Lee lavished praise on all concerned, particularly Colonel Moultrie and the fighting men: "I think it but justice to publish the merits of Col. Moultrie and his brave Garrison. Col. Thompson of the South Carolina Rangers acquitted himself most nobly in repulsing the troops who attempted to land at the other end of the Island. I know not which Corps I have the greatest reason to be pleased with—Muhlenberg's Virginians, or the North Carolina troops—they are both equally alert, zealous and spirited."[54]

The Americans had escaped an impossible situation. Lee had assessed the situation correctly in the days he had available to prepare the city for the onslaught. He raised concerns about the readiness of the fort; he spurred Moultrie on in constructing the fort and fortifying it; he brought to the task all of the resources—state and continental—that were available; he applied discipline to the various efforts running simultaneously; he fretted endlessly about leaving the men on Sullivan's Island without an escape route; he coordinated the forces left to him on the mainland if the British succeeded in taking the fort and confronted the city proper. Without question, Lee expressed doubts about the defense of the city, and he was probably right in most respects. It does not appear that anyone—especially Lee and Moultrie—anticipated the beneficial impact of the palmetto logs on the outcome of the battle or could have foreseen and planned for the British blunders. Had the British land troops been able to cross over to Sullivan's Island and assault the fort directly, had the fort been built with wood that could not absorb the cannonade, had the British ships not foundered and instead had made their way behind the fort, Lee's concerns would have become readily apparent and realized, and the outcome would have been quite different. In that case, despite his clearly expressed concerns, Lee would most assuredly have been tarred with part of the blame. He was right to revel in a true turnaround of events.

CHAPTER 8

REJOINING
WASHINGTON

Charles Lee finished up his southern command shortly after the victorious defense of Charleston, South Carolina. And before he could do much damage to his burnished reputation. George Washington needed all the help he could get to drive the British from New York, or, more specifically, to keep from losing his army and the war in New York. Lee was called back in August 1776.

In the days and weeks after Charleston, Lee pursued several causes. First of all, he made sure that all of his superiors and friends knew of the events in Charleston. He continued, quite correctly, to keep a vigilant watch on the British ships and men in the Charleston area and throughout the district under his command. He urged the completion of the fort on Sullivan's Island and the creation of a navy that could patrol the rivers that interlaced throughout the southern theater. At the same time, he revived his plea with Congress for a corps of cavalry to protect the southern colonies. Major General Charles Lee was thoroughly engaged in his work as commander of the southern theater during this period, and the number of letters he wrote and received testify to his activity.

SUMMER 1776

The most active role Lee played in the early summer of 1776 was the pursuit of a strategy to prevent Indian and English attacks in the remote areas of the Carolinas and in Florida. Fears of the British, their Indian allies, and escaped or captured slaves frightened the rebels at the southern end of the colonies. The Creeks menaced the borders of the Carolinas and were agents of the English in Florida. Lee received emissaries from Georgia seeking help, and the governor of Georgia encouraged forays into Georgia and eastern Florida. Lee moved from Charleston to Savannah to gain better intelligence of the enemies he faced and to arm and lead an army into eastern Florida to put an end to this continual threat. To create a formidable force, he pestered Governor Rutledge of South Carolina to release his militia into Georgia and Florida.

Notwithstanding all of this activity, Lee found the time to renew his appeal to Congress for financial support. Just days after the repulse of Sir Peter Parker and General Clinton, Lee made a desperate plea to his financial mentor Robert Morris and urged him to "exert yourself in concert with my other Friends particularly Rutledge, the Lee's, Dickinson and the Adams's," to free him from debt. Perhaps he understood that timing was important in these matters and that the time was now ripe. His July 2 letter could not be more direct. "In short my situation with regard to circumstances is more whimsical and disagreeable than any man's on the Continent. I have really nothing that I can call my own—the half of the Estate pay'd for is more properly yours than mine. I have this morning been conversing with Mr. Rutledge on the subject—He is of the opinion that the Congress ought of their own Accords at least to have advanced the whole purchase money of this Estate—that it is delicate to keep me in this most rigid state of dependency than other men."[1] The "Estate" that Lee refers to is the land in Virginia that General Gates had brought to his attention and urged him to purchase. Congress had already voted to guarantee his purchase, but Lee wanted more definitive action. He urged the payment of the mortgage to stop the running of interest and "likewise one thousand pounds or five hundred to set the Estate agoing." He insisted that he had maintained his end of the bargain he made with the Congress, but he fretted that the Congress was "composed not only of mortal but changeable men."

The status of his finances was not the only personal issue bothering Charles Lee, and his concern about monetary matters may have been triggered by a letter he received earlier from confidante Richard Henry Lee. This letter, written from Philadelphia on May 27, contained some intelligence that sent Lee into a froth. A letter "from London" contained the following: "A General of the first ability and experience would come over if he could have any assurance from the Congress of keeping his rank, but that being very high, he would not submit to have any one but an American his superior, and that only in consideration of the confidence due to an American in a question so peculiarly American."[2] Richard Henry Lee vouched for the letter's authenticity and wanted Lee's opinion of who the man could be. Washington, Gates, and Mifflin guessed Major General John Beckwith.[3] It is not clear when Charles Lee received Richard Henry Lee's letter, but he restrained his pen in correspondence until after the battle of Charleston. He replied with a vengeance on July 19, 1776.

Lee's response to the news reveals his own assessment of why Richard Henry Lee had asked his opinion: "[T]he palpable meaning of your letter is, to prepare me for a cession of my rank in favour of some impudent adventurer." Charles Lee's opinion of Beckwith cannot be doubted: "I am not, I believe, naturally proud; I do not think myself conceited of my talents; but to be put in competition, much more to be spurned aside, to make room for so despicable a character as Beckwith, a generally reputed coward, (and a b——d syco-phant,) I say, to be kicked out of my station for such a creature as this, would swell a man more humble than myself into a trumpeter of his own merits. Great God? Is it come to this?"[4] If, indeed, Richard Henry Lee was testing Charles Lee to see if he would object, he clearly received his answer! Lee goes on for two pages of outrage and throws in another request, that should he be over-ranked, he be returned to the "easy fortune which I have forfeited" so that he could retire from the service. After all, "Have I, sleeping or waking, employed a single thought, but for [America's] welfare, glory or advantage?"

Whether this issue of another British officer's out-ranking Lee had legiti-macy or not, the event did not come to pass. Lee continued with his duties. On August 7, Charles Lee sent a letter to Congress that he was moving to Georgia to direct the foray into eastern Florida. The next day, Congress sent a letter to Lee advising him that the British had combined all of their forces in New York, creating a serious threat. John Hancock commanded that Lee "repair as soon as possible to the City of Philadelphia there to receive such Orders as [Congress] may think proper to give you."[5] It is unclear when Lee received Hancock's order, but he had appeared in Savannah by the 18th, and he acknowledged a congressional letter of praise, dated July 22, in a letter dated August 23. The order to return goes unmentioned, and his correspon-dence in the following days suggests that the August 8 letter was still on its way. Lee continued to secure Georgia and did not leave until September 9. His letters are filled with military advice and concern for the arming and pro-visioning of the southern troops. He prepared a detailed report to the Board of War and Ordnance on August 27, which included a demand for some measures to prevent the "extortion" engaged in by "Merchants Mechanics Farmers and Planters" on the sale of "public necessities."[6]

Lee also found the time to write to the French governor at Cape François, Haiti, urging him to send supplies—small arms, clothing, powder, cannon, and medicine—to help the American cause, which he declared was also in the "interest of France." This letter, dated August 30, provides a unique view of Charles Lee *by Charles Lee* just before the most profound events of his life:

> It will be necessary in addressing a letter of this nature, so abruptly to your excellency, that I should inform you who the writer is. I have served as

lieutenant-colonel in the English service, colonel in the Portuguese, afterwards as aid du camp to his Polish majesty, with the rank of major general.
Having purchased a small estate in America, I had determined to retire, for
the remainder of my days, to a peaceful asylum: when the tyranny of the
ministry, and the court of Great Britain, forced this continent to arms, for
the preservation of their liberties, I was called, by the voice of the people, to
the rank of second in command.[7]

NEW YORK, 1776

By the time Charles Lee returned to the northern colonies, in October 1776,
George Washington's position on the New York islands was more than precarious. By late July, the British had gathered together more than 40,000 men
and more than two hundred ships at the entrance to New York Harbor to
confront the rebels in New York. Washington needed all the troops and all
the capable officers available. In August, 20,000 British regulars landed on
Long Island, and over the next several days Washington nearly lost the
Continental Army and the war in intense fighting. With only half as many
men, and outmaneuvered, Washington's forces became overwhelmed, and at
the end of fighting on August 29, they were trapped in a defensive position at
Brooklyn Heights. Generals John Sullivan and Lord Stirling were captured.
Only a daring nighttime retreat across the East River saved the remainder
of Washington's army from further battering or complete destruction. The
impending arrival of Charles Lee, fresh from a victory in South Carolina, was
welcomed by Washington and everyone else.

Lord Howe delayed his assault on Manhattan at this point to see if the
Americans were ready to capitulate. He asked for and received a delegation
from the Continental Congress—John Adams, Benjamin Franklin, and
Edmund Rutledge—but the meeting on Staten Island on September 11 proved
futile. Howe then resumed the campaign and occupied lower Manhattan on
September 15, moving Washington's army north. Over the next several days,
the Americans retreated further, routed by a British landing on the eastern
side of the island at Kip's Bay. Backed up to Harlem Heights, the Americans
held their own in a fight on September 16 but eventually had to continue
north and off Manhattan Island to White Plains. At this point, in early
October, Lee joined Washington and was absorbed back into the command
of the Continental Army, now second only to Washington, with the resignation of Artemas Ward in March. Lee took command of one of four divisions,
and Washington and Howe battled again at White Plains on October 28. Lee's
division saw limited action in this engagement, and again the British got the

best of the Americans. Nevertheless, Washington was able to move his troops further west and away from Howe, who then withdrew to Manhattan.

In October 1776, the public perceptions of the two men at the top of the command in the Continental Army could not have been more different. Washington was reeling from the blunders and losses suffered from the day the British landed troops on Long Island two months earlier. Congressmen and fellow officers questioned Washington's military skills and his ability to lead the battered army that was disintegrating from losses and desertions. Lee, on the other hand, returned from Charleston a hero, having vanquished the British Army and the Royal Navy. On his way north, as always, Lee stopped in Philadelphia to meet with his supporters in the Congress. He heralded his return north with a lecture to Congress on the overtures by Lord Howe. This letter would be of little importance, except for subsequent events that evince such a different approach by Lee on this particular subject. The letter starts with this definitive sentence: "The ridiculous idea, that Lord Howe has some reasonable terms to offer, and that the Congress are desirous of their being communicated to the people, gains ground every day."[8] Lee's advice on the issue of sending emissaries to meet with Howe is to send no one. Howe, he says, will not offer terms but rather will require "unconditional submission," and to accommodate his request would "convey an idea that [Congress] did not consider independency absolutely fixed." If Congress must send someone to satisfy the "unreasonable and weak," then it should send "some gentlemen in the simple character of individuals who are supposed to have influence" to demand Howe's terms. He follows up this advice with a warning about the inability of Washington to prevent the British from landing at South Amboy and marching to Philadelphia. "For Heaven's sake, rouse yourselves; for Heaven's sake, let ten thousand men be immediately assembled and stationed somewhere about Trenton."

At this point in his career, Charles Lee was at the height of his self-importance. And although some self-satisfaction with his station and his efforts to date was justified, his sense of self begins to erode his limited sense of self-restraint. In a letter to General Horatio Gates, he reveals his dissatisfaction with the position of the army, which he blames on Congress—"*inter nos* the Congress seem to stumble at every step."[9] He suggests that Washington should threaten resignation to end the interference of Congress in military matters. Two weeks later, he tells confidante Benjamin Rush that the army is ready for the task but that "all the resolves of Congress relating to Military affairs are absurd, ridiculous and ruinous."[10] And he tells Benjamin Franklin that "if America is lost, it is not in my opinion owing to want of courage in your soldiers, but pardon me, to want of prudence in your highmightinesses."[11]

One of the most telling decisions facing Washington at this point was whether to hold or abandon the remaining American stronghold in Manhattan, Fort Washington, across the Hudson River from Fort Lee on the Palisades in New Jersey. The patriots had hoped that these two fortified positions, named for their ranking commanders, could block or at least impede British navigation of the Hudson River. They proved ineffective for this purpose, but some of Washington's officers saw the forts as valuable for their strategic locations, especially General Nathanael Greene. Charles Lee disagreed. The Manhattan fort held substantial armaments and munitions, as well as 2,800 men. Washington called a council of war to determine whether the New York fort could be held against a British assault. He had his doubts, but he deferred, in a divided vote, to Greene and several others who insisted that the fort could stand. Unfortunately, Washington and Lee held the correct opinion, and the fort and its men and materiel were lost on November 16. By this time, Washington had already crossed the Hudson with 2,000 men and could only watch from Fort Lee as the battle unfolded. Anxious, Washington crossed over the river to Manhattan at one point, but had to return, realizing that there was nothing he could do to save the doomed fort. Lee remained with the other half of the army at North Castle, north of White Plains, while Washington surveyed his options and his next move.

Lee complained to his correspondents before and after the loss of Fort Washington that defending the fort was futile. Just before the fort fell, he wrote to Joseph Reed, adjutant to Washington, questioning "what circumstances give to Fort Washington so great a degree of value and importance as to counterbalance the probability or almost certainty of losing 1400 of our best Troops."[12] Just after, Lee let Benjamin Rush know that he had advised against a defense of Fort Washington, and he knew that he was talking out of school in his criticism of the decisions made: "The affair at Fort Washington cannot surprise you at Philadelphia more than it amazed and stunned me. I must entreat that you will keep what I say to yourself; but I foresaw, predicted, all that has happened; and urged the necessity of abandoning it; for could we have kept it, it was of little or no use. Let these few lines be thrown into the fire, and in your conversations only acquit me of any share of the misfortune—for my last words to the General were—draw off the garrison, or they will be lost."[13] Perhaps Lee can be excused this fit of pique— Washington had agreed with him on the uselessness of the fort and the chances of defending it. Nevertheless, we begin to see Charles Lee's growing discontent with the way events are unfolding and the beginning of the growing distance, geographically and militarily, between him and George

Washington. In the coming days Lee's actions reflect his belief that his opinions should carry more merit than any others.

A short letter to Benjamin Rush also reveals two more important strains running through Lee's mind at this time. First, he chides Congress for its despicable treatment of the soldiers under his command: the soldiers did "not want courage," only full bounties and blankets. The letter ends with the stoic reprimand: "Strip even yourselves of blankets." The other potent statement in the letter presents an ominous proposition. He suggests that he could solve the country's problems if given unlimited authority: "I could say many things—let me talk vainly—had I the powers I could do you much good—might I but dictate one week—but I am sure you will never give any man the necessary power—did none of the Congress ever read the Roman History?"[14]

Delay

General Washington had divided his army. He took the troops under his command, 2,000 men, and crossed the "North River" in the early days of November 1776. He left Charles Lee with 7,000 men and General William Heath with 3,000 men in New York, in case Howe decided to move toward New England. Lee's army was safely camped at North Castle, and Heath guarded the Hudson River Highlands. Howe decided to follow Washington into New Jersey, however, and soon captured Fort Lee on November 18. The Americans were barely able to abandon the fort, avoiding another disaster like the loss of men and munitions at Fort Washington. Washington now could see that his depleted force, threatened with expiring enlistment terms, could not face the British head on. He desperately needed to protect the men he had with him by combining his forces once again so that he could at least offer legitimate resistance if a confrontation could not be avoided. To this end, he sent for Horatio Gates's forces returning from Fort Ticonderoga in upstate New York and for Lee's forces as well.

Much has been made of Charles Lee's delays in rejoining Washington's command. Some suggest that he deliberately disobeyed direct orders; others, that he was positioning himself for a master stroke against the British to propel himself into command of the army over George Washington. This moment in time presented the greatest threat to Washington's command. He had lost the Battle of Long Island, abandoned Manhattan, lost Forts Washington and Lee, and, to most observers, was in full retreat before the British. A number in Congress and up the line of the Continental Army command questioned his judgment or his will, especially after the loss of Fort Washington with its 2,800 men. The Congress had just recently appointed a

War Board, perhaps as a check on Washington's authority, and members were jockeying to place their supporters in key positions.

Notwithstanding all of the maneuvering in the army and the Congress, Charles Lee's actions between October and December 13, 1776, were not very suspect. He had command of the greater half of the army, and he assiduously guarded his prerogatives in that role, as any in command might. He had military options to consider that could enhance his standing, if successful, but that also could help Washington's position and the interests of America. And, as some have pointed out, Washington's orders left some room for interpretation. It is Lee's careless correspondence and ego that raise issues of insubordination and the irritated tone in Washington's later letters that suggests he was dissatisfied with Lee's actions.

Washington advised Lee on November 10 that he would cross the river to meet with "the probability of [the enemy] having designs upon the Jerseys."[15] He provided a detailed letter of instructions, but no *orders* for Lee to follow. He could not be sure what the British intended and specifically left Lee's movements to Lee: "I shall give no directions, therefore, on this head, having the most entire confidence in your judgment and military exertions." In fact, Washington was concerned that the Jersey movement might be a feint on the part of the British with the intention of weakening the New York position and the army under Lee's command. He warned Lee to be aware of this possibility. At the end of the letter, Washington considered what should happen if the British "remove the whole, or the greater part of their force, to the west side of Hudson's River." In that case, Lee should follow "with all possible dispatch," leaving only the militias and invalids to cover New York and north.[16] Washington wrote again two days later and cautioned Lee about defense, given that Howe had not moved his troops.

When Washington wrote yet again on November 16 to advise Lee of the loss of Fort Washington, his military concern was the protection of the forts north of Manhattan that covered the passes through the Highlands—the last avenue of retreat for the troops in New York should disaster strike. General Heath was given this duty, and Lee was admonished to give this issue his most urgent attention. No mention is made of removal to New Jersey.[17] On that same day, Colonel Reed, on behalf of General Washington, asked for Lee's opinion: "The General has requested me to suggest to your Consideration the Use or Propriety of retaining your present Post under all Circumstances & would be glad to hear from you on the subject."[18] As an obedient subordinate, Lee responded in detail three days later:

> My objections to moving from our present position are, as I observed before, that it would give us the air of being frightened; it would expose a

fine fertile country to their ravages; and, I must add, that we are secure as we could be in any position whatever. We are pretty well disencumbered of our impediments, which I propose depositing on or about Crumb Pond, which (though I confess I have not reconnoitered the place,) from its situation, must be full as safe, and is more centrical than Peekskill. If on further examination it has any material disadvantages, we can easily move from thence. As to ourselves, (light as we are) several retreats present themselves. In short, if we keep a good look out, we are in no danger; but I must entreat your Excellency to enjoin the officers posted at Fort Lee to give us the quickest intelligence if they observe and embarkations of troops in the North River.[19]

No question, both Continental Army troops and the British troops were on the march during these several days in November 1776, and the situation was in flux. The British landed troops in New Jersey in the days that these letters were exchanged, but Washington had given Lee flexibility, and flexibility in trusted officers during times of uncertainty has its merits. On the 20th, Lee finally received a direct request from Washington, through William Grayson, to move his troops to New Jersey: "His Excellency thinks it would be advisable in you to remove the troops under your command on this side of the North River, and there wait for further orders."[20] It could be that Washington's direction to Grayson was more forceful than Grayson's presentation to Lee or, perhaps, Washington deliberately couched his direct orders in these more gentle terms. Whatever the situation, Lee did not ignore this request. He immediately wrote to General Heath, stationed at the Hudson River Highlands, to move 2,000 troops across the river to support Washington. Lee stated his reasoning: "I have just received a Recommendation not a positive order, from the General, to move the Corps under my Command to the other side of the River. This recommendation was I imagine on the presumption that I had already moved nearer the Peekskills, there is no possibility of crossing over Dobb's Ferry, or at any place lower than Kings Ferry, which to us would be such an immense round, that we cou'd never answer any purpose."[21] Lee tells Heath at the end of this letter that he will replace the 2,000 men as soon as he is able.

Lee's correspondence with General Heath during this period provides a parallel situation and delightful reading as well. Heath apparently saw his command as separate from Lee's and his line of command directly to George Washington, much to Lee's chagrin. Lee tried in several letters to bring Heath in line but reached his boiling point on November 26 with this tirade: "I perceive that you have formed an opinion to yourself that shou'd General Washington remove to the straights of Magellan, the instructions he left with you upon a particular occasion, have to all intents and purposes invested you with a command separate from, and independent of any other superior." Lee went on in the same vein to suggest that "if any misfortune shou'd happen" from a refusal to follow Lee's orders, "you must answer for it" for, in the absence of the commander in chief, "I must & will be obey'd."[22] Ironically, Washington sides with Heath in his letter dated December 3 to Lee: "As to bringing any of the troops under General Heath, I cannot consent to it. The posts they are at, and the passes through the Highlands, being of the utmost importance, they must be guarded by good men."[23]

Those who would vilify Charles Lee for his actions during this period read his letter to General Heath as Lee's dissembling to his own advantage, by creating doubt through his own hand that he had received a direct order and instead directing the reduction of troops from an area that Washington had declared inviolate. Giving Lee the benefit of the doubt, however, his correspondence demonstrates that he abhorred the idea of moving detachments back and forth across the river with each movement of the enemy.[24]

But at this point in time—November 21, 1776—the atmosphere changed. Washington perceived that he was in a desperate situation in New Jersey; several of his subordinates were losing their respect for his command; and some of these officers were making overtures to Charles Lee and others, perhaps in anticipation of Washington's removal or defeat. Lee came to see himself in a position of strength, in command of the stronger half of the Continental Army and in a safer and more strategic position than his commander. On this day, two very different letters were written to Charles Lee. Washington wrote to relate the loss of Fort Lee and his position: "[W]e have no accounts of [the enemy's] movements this morning; but as the country is almost a dead flat, and we have not an intrenching tool, & not above 3000 men, & they much broken and dispirited not only with our own ill success, but the loss of their tents and baggage, I have resolved to avoid any attack, tho' by so doing, I must leave a very fine country open to their ravages, or a plentiful store house, from which they will draw voluntary supplies." Lee could not have been encouraged by this despondent account of his superior's position. Washington continued with indecision about Lee's position. He starts by stating that he is not sure whether he still wants Lee to cross the river. He then answers the concerns that Lee had raised a few days earlier, arguing that he believes the British are committed to the Jerseys and that a show of protection for this territory and Congress in Philadelphia was surely needed. In the end, he states his desire clearly: "[U]nless therefore some new event should occur, or some more cogent reason present itself, I would have you move over [the river], by the easiest and best passage."[25]

Contrast Washington's letter with the letter penned by Colonel Reed, also urging Lee to cross over to New Jersey, "where the principal Scene of Action is laid":

> I do not mean to flatter, nor praise you at the Expence of any other, but I confess I do think that it is entirely owing to you that this Army & the Liberties of America so far as they are dependent on it are not totally cut off. You have Decision, a Quality often wanting in Minds otherwise valuable & I ascribe to this our Escape from York Island—from Kingsbridge and the Plains—and I have no Doubt had you been here the Garrison at Mount Washington would now have composed a part of this Army. Under all these Circumstances I confess I ardently wish to see you removed from a Place where I think there will be little Call for your Judgment & Experience to the Place where they are like to be necessary. Nor am I singular in my Opinion—every Gentleman of the Family the Officers & soldiers generally have a Confidence in you—the Enemy constantly inquire where you are, & seem to me to be less confident when you are present.
>
> . . .
>
> Oh! General—an indecisive Mind is one of the greatest Misfortunes that can befall an Army—how often have I lamented it in this Campaign.

Reed then proposes that once the situation settles down ("as soon as the Season will admit"), Lee should go to Congress with several others, point out the defects of the army and "form the Plan of the new Army."[26]

Consider the impact that these two letters, authored on the same day, must have had on Charles Lee, whose ego and ambition ruled his intellect and emotions.

Lee answered Reed's letter the same day, acknowledging that he has received Washington's letter as well. Lee repeated his main reason for refusing to move—the need to travel too far for a passable crossing—and advised Reed that he ordered Heath to move 2,000 men across the river. Lee did not respond to Reed's flattery in this letter, but rather in a separate letter three days later, agreeing, albeit by generality, that *Washington* had proved indecisive: "I receiv'd your most flattering letter—lament with you that fatal indecision of mind which in war is a much greater disqualification than stupidity or even want of personal courage—accident may put a decisive Blunderer in the right—but eternal defeat and miscarriage must attend the man of the best parts if curs'd with indecision."[27] But now Lee added another reason to delay crossing the Hudson River. He told Reed that he intended to carry off the British Light Horse encamped in a nearby exposed position. Only weather had prevented doing so already. To Lee's credit, he conveyed the same information about his intended foray to George Washington on the same day.[28]

The descent on the Light Horse never occurred, and Charles Lee did not cross the Hudson River until at least December 6, 1776. The correspondence between Lee and Washington over this two-week period is brittle. From Washington in Newark on November 24: "I perceive by your letter to Colonel Reed, that you have entirely mistaken my views in ordering Troops from Gen. Heath's Division to this Quarter. . . . Col. Reed's second letter will have sufficiently explained my intention upon this subject, and pointed out to you that it was your division which I wanted & wish to march."[29] Lee responded that his orders to Heath were "only for expedition's sake" and he did not intend to "leave the Highlands unguarded." He offered another excuse for not leaving, however. This time, he blamed the recent activities of local Tories and the belief that considerable British troops were left at Kings Bridge. Lee promised nevertheless that some of his troops would leave the next day.[30]

From Washington in Newark on November 27th: "My former letters were so full and explicit, as to the necessity of your marching as early as possible, that it is unnecessary to add more on that head."[31] Lee responded on the 30th that "I have done all in my power, and shall explain my difficulties when we have both leisure." Lee claimed that he had 4,000 men but would have had substantially fewer had he already left New York.[32]

From Washington in "Brunswick" on December 1st: "I must entreat you to hasten your march as much as possible, or your arrival may be too late to answer any valuable purpose."[33] Again from Washington, now in Trenton on December 3rd: "You will readily agree that I have sufficient cause for my anxiety, and to wish for your arrival as early as possible. . . . This has been the language of all of my letters since I had occasion to call for your aid. The sooner you can join me with your division, the sooner the service will be benefitted."[34] Lee responded, but he obviously did not consider the situation to be as dire as Washington did. First of all, Lee suggested that "I should not be able to join you at all" now that Washington had left New Brunswick. Second, Lee saw himself as leading the greater part of the army, bolstered with the troops returning from Canada and now near Morristown. ("Shall put myself at their head tomorrow.") Lee supposed that he would have 5,000 men at his command once reaching New Jersey and that he could serve as a frightening force "hanging on" the flanks or rear of the British army chasing Washington. As if this cavalier response was not enough, Lee blithely asked Washington "to order some of your suite to take out of the way of danger my favourite mare, which is at Hunt Wilson's, three miles the other side of Princeton."[35]

Days later, Lee wrote again to Washington, having successfully crossed over into New Jersey and now leading, as he estimated it, just under 4,000 troops altogether. He claimed that he heard that Washington had recently been "considerably reinforced" and so he had no plans to rush to a combination. Rather, he felt comfortable in his position and proposed to hang on the British rear at Chatham.[36] And later that day, having learned Washington's true position, Lee stated that it would be difficult for him to join Washington and asked, "[C]annot I do you more service by attacking their rear?" In any event, Lee said, "I shall look about me tomorrow, and inform you further."[37]

Needless to say, an exasperated Washington by this time must have had doubts about his ability to command Charles Lee, but he exhibited extraordinary patience. He wrote letters on December 10, 11, and 14, all to the same effect. He believed that the British aim was the capture of Philadelphia, and he needed Lee's troops to put up an effective resistance. The last of these letters included detailed information on the route that Lee should take, along with the exclamation that "I am much surprised that you should be in any doubt respecting the route."[38] Alas, his instructions were too late for Charles Lee to follow.

It is difficult to read these exchanges indifferently after the fact, knowing the calamity that befell Charles Lee on December 13, Washington's masterful military stroke on Christmas Day at Trenton after the two armies had combined, and Lee's subsequent life history. In the light of those events, Lee's actions appear insubordinate if not foolish. Was Lee acting in his personal best interest? Was he leaving Washington to the agony of his indecisiveness? Was he willing to see Washington and his division defeated in order to rise immediately to the top command? In hindsight, these all look like plausible explanations of Lee's motives. But ambition and self-aggrandizement figure into the actions of many military leaders at key moments. Bold strokes are rewarded by history. Lee could have simply been following his own military instincts.

Howe had his troops spread out from Princeton to Trenton and exposed to Lee in his rear. Whether Howe respected Lee as a general or not, he had to be concerned about such a sizable force behind him. Lee's troops had captured stragglers and small parties of British troops and some supplies since entering New Jersey. Indeed, Howe's Hessian aide-de-camp remarked more than once in his daily transmittals that the "support lines behind us become more and more unsafe because of General Lee, who is audacious."[39] Lee may have had the opportunity he was looking for. Washington's smaller army could have been overtaken a number of times if Howe had been more aggressive. Lee's larger force was safely ensconced in New York at first, and then behind the British once Lee crossed into in New Jersey. Did it make sense to combine with Washington and present a stronger but still inferior force to the British in an all-out fight? Would it not make more sense for Lee's army, safe behind the Watchung Mountains, to aid Washington by launching raids on the flanks and rear of Howe's troop lines? Lee disagreed with Washington that Howe's aim was Philadelphia.[40] Even if it were, perhaps Howe would bed down in New Jersey for the winter and pick up the fight in the spring. As it turned out, after the Battles of Trenton and Princeton, Washington moved his troops back to Morristown and behind the Watchung Mountains where he was able to spend the winter in relative safety.

Had Lee not been captured on December 13, American history might have unfolded in a dramatically different manner.

CAPTURE

Charles Lee's fortunes changed irreparably on the morning of December 13, 1776. Carelessly, Lee exposed himself to the British military in New Jersey, and they seized the opportunity to capture Britain's most notorious traitor. It could be that Lee did not understand the state's geography or the whereabouts of the British troops or their interest in his person. Whatever the cause, the result was devastating for Lee and disheartening for the American troops in the field, already crestfallen by their failures and retreat over the previous three months.

Lee had crossed over to New Jersey with his troops by December 6, moving east to west across the northern third of the state to Morristown, where he expected to meet up with some of the troops returning from Canada under the leadership of Horatio Gates. After a week, his troops had only advanced as far forward as Vealtown (now Bernardsville). At this point, Lee detached himself from the main body of his command to spend the night of December 12 at an inn maintained by a widow at Basking Ridge, just a few miles to the southeast. The British Army had stopped in its chase of George Washington, posting garrisons of Hessians at Trenton and Bordentown and regulars at Princeton and New Brunswick, to Lee's south and west. Lee neglected to take any sizable force with him to Basking Ridge, apparently believing that the British were too far from his theater of activity to be of any concern. He was wrong.

The capture of Charles Lee had a certain drama, but it was over in just minutes. Lee arrived in Basking Ridge on the 12th, intending to spend the night at the inn. The several officers and foreigners with him included two Frenchman, Jean Louis de Virnejoux, recently commissioned, and M. de Gaiault, recently arrived from overseas. Also in the house was Major William Bradford. A small guard detachment was housed in a nearby outbuilding. Throughout the afternoon and evening, a number of visitors came and went, including a Tory complaining that his horse had been confiscated. Lee gave him little regard. Late in the evening, James Wilkinson, a young aide of Horatio Gates, arrived with a letter for Lee, with orders to wait for a response. The letter expressed veiled concerns about George Washington's military abilities and leadership. Wilkinson joined the crowded group at the inn, and his account serves as one of the bases for the events of that night and the next morning, notwithstanding his checkered career after this point and doubts about his general veracity.

In any event, it appears that Lee, his companions, and apparently his guards, welcomed the dawn reluctantly. Lee, according to the accounts, was not fully dressed by 10 A.M. and was just sitting down to respond to Gates's letter. Wilkinson was eager to leave. It does not appear, however, that Lee was in any hurry or that he had plans to return quickly to his troops in Vealtown for a fast dash to the Delaware, as his commander, camped across the Delaware River, would have preferred.

The situation was totally different to the south, in the British encampment at Trenton. Howe and his generals were mindful of Lee's forces in their rear and along their flanks. Several small skirmishes had resulted in losses, and, along with their futile attempts to find boats to cross the Delaware River to confront Washington, these officers were concerned with Lee's threat. Some accounts suggest that the British were always concerned about Lee's where-abouts, out of respect for his military abilities; other accounts see the British dismissing Lee as an adventurer with a reputation considerably greater than his abilities. Whichever the case, Lee himself represented a thorn in the side for the British, an officer recently on half pay leading a respectable force against the Crown. His capture had already been reported with much elation in the British press in June, only to be found false later.[41]

One officer keenly aware of Lee's proximity was Colonel William Harcourt of His Majesty's Sixteenth Light Dragoons, a unit that had supported Lee in his victory at Vila Velha fourteen years earlier in Portugal. On the morning of December 13, Harcourt had his horsemen up early in the hope that Lee was not so far distant that a rapid strike might bring him home. Among Colonel Harcourt's lieutenants was Cornet Guy Tarleton, who had served with Lee in Portugal and who envisioned Lee's capture as a personal achievement. Starting off in the early morning from Pennington, near Trenton, this force of 30 horsemen traveled the thirty miles to Basking Ridge in just several hours, stopping at various points along the way to confer with Loyalists about Lee's forces and his whereabouts and picking up rebel troops whose questioning was not quite as polite. According to British accounts, a rebel soldier gave up the general when a noose was dangled before him. Other accounts attribute the betrayal to a local Loyalist, perhaps the same man who had complained the evening before about his horse. Whatever the case, once Harcourt had Lee within his reach, he would not be denied.

Somewhere between 10:00 A.M. and noon, Harcourt's forces approached the Widow White's Inn. According to Wilkinson, he gazed out the front window while waiting for Lee to finish his letter to Gates and saw the dragoons approaching. He sounded the alarm, but it was already too late. One of the guards noticed their advance, also too late, and sacrificed his life for the delay. The inn's guests quickly realized their predicament. A small exchange of fire brought threats to burn the house down. Lee saw the futility of a fight and negotiated a surrender through Major William Bradford. Lee came out of the house peacefully. Some reports have Lee in his pajamas, but this may be too theatrical. No doubt Lee did not have a great coat and had to have a blanket thrown around him when he was bound and placed on Wilkinson's horse, which was tied at the front of the house. Wilkinson, according to his own account, hid himself inside the house "with a pistol in each hand" ready "to shoot the first and the second person who might appear, and then appeal to my sword."[42] One report says that Bradford appeared outside the last time dressed as a servant so that he could slip back into the house without incident. The British were not interested in Bradford. Taking just one of the Frenchmen, they left Bradford to report Lee's capture and made a fast retreat. Wilkinson emerged from his hiding place once the dragoons were gone, "mounted the first horse I could find, and rode full speed to General Sullivan." Harcourt beat a path to Pennington with his prisoner. General John Sullivan at Vealtown, on hearing of Lee's capture, sent a detail after Harcourt, but to no avail. The Light Horse made their escape easily with their treasure in tow, losing only one cornet to a farmer's bullet during the ride.[43]

On this morning of Friday, December 13, Charles Lee fell from a great height. Just days before, Washington's adjutant had praised him in a private letter in stark comparison to their commander. Lee commanded the better half of the Continental Army and was about to add in Gates's troops from Canada. He was far enough away from Washington to operate independently with both personal and military rationale. And Wilkinson had Lee's freshly written and scurrilous letter to General Horatio Gates:

> The ingenious manœuvre of Fort Washington has unhing'd the goodly fabrick We had been building—there never was so damn'd a stroke—*entre nous,* a certain great man is most damnably deficient—He has thrown me into a situation where I have my choice of difficulties—if I stay in this Province I risk myself and Army and if I do not stay the Province is lost for ever—I have neither guides Calvary Medicines Money Shoes or

Stockings—I must act with the greatest circumspection—Tories are in my front rear and on my flanks—the Mass of the People is strangely contaminated—in short unless something which I do not expect turns up—We are lost—our Counsels have been weak to the last degree—as to what relates to yourself if you think you can be in time to aid the General I wou'd have you, by all means go. You will at least save your army—it is said that the Whigs are determin'd to set fire to Philadelphia if They strike this decisive stroke the day will be our own—but unless it is done all chance of Liberty in any part of the Globe is forever vanish'd—Adieu, my Dr Friend—God Bless You.

Charles Lee[44]

As always, if you can ignore the invective, Lee sums up the political and military situation concisely. The cavalier willingness to sacrifice the City of Philadelphia to jump-start the cause may appear shocking, but it is typical Charles Lee—using hyperbole to make his case.[45]

The several weeks following Lee's capture overshadow his relevance in the war and subsequently, to history. Washington, distraught at the capture of his second in command, consoled himself with the combination of his forces on the west side of the Delaware River. General Sullivan, assuming command at Vealtown upon the loss of Lee, immediately followed orders to move, crossed the Delaware River, and joined Washington on December 20 with the 2,000 troops left in the command. Washington also received Gates's 800 men at about the same time. In the following days, with all of his troops available to him, Washington would hatch his plan for a daring raid on Trenton on Christmas Day. This masterstroke, beautifully executed, led to a victory at Princeton on January 3 and eventually to safety behind the Watchung Mountains for the remainder of the winter. It also saved Washington politically, forcing his doubters and critics to reevaluate or at least to remain silent for a period. Washington had breathed new life into the Revolution and transformed the military situation from one of desperation to a contest that could possibly be won by the rebels.

Charles Lee, on the other hand, must have feared for his life. To some in Great Britain, Lee was a traitor who should be dealt with as a traitor and hanged in London. The British Cabinet ordered Howe to ship Lee back to England immediately.[46] But Lee's status was not that simple, and although Howe may have preferred this resolution, he hesitated. Before the fighting started Lee had indeed been in His Majesty's service, albeit on half pay. But Lee had adroitly finessed this issue by publicly renouncing his position and the salary that went with it. Could he now be considered a traitor even if he commanded an army against the king? To the Americans, Lee was a prisoner of war to be treated with the gentlemen's code of honor that applied to all officers captured in battle. Congress recognized the issue immediately and sought to protect Lee by declaring that Lee be treated as an officer, threatening retaliation against British prisoners if Lee were to be maltreated, and discontinuing prisoner exchanges until the matter was settled. Washington did not want to act so precipitously. He urged restraint in his letters to Congress and worried that exchanges in the works would be abandoned. At the same time, he carried on a correspondence with Lord Howe, urging fair treatment of Lee. But Congress held to its initial reaction in a second vote, and its actions proved effective. Howe moved slowly and eventually adopted the prisoner of war position.[47]

While his immediate fate was being debated, Lee had to content himself with whatever comforts he could inveigle.[48] After Washington's triumphs at Trenton and Princeton and the turn of the new year, Lee was removed to New York, where he was able to dine and converse with British officers, notwithstanding his confinement. George Washington, concerned about Lee's welfare, almost immediately passed on a draft for funds arranged by Lee's financier, Robert Morris, asked about Lee's "health and situation" and promised to send additional supplies as soon as possible. Lee wrote to Robert Morris from New York on January 28, 1777, and asked for his servant Giuseppe and his dogs. Several days later he wrote to Washington asking for help in securing his dogs—"I never stood in greater need of their Company than at present"—and an aide-de-camp. Initially, Lee was not treated badly, and, in fact, some observers wondered at the courtesies he was given by General Howe and his officers. Although confined to the city and under guard, Lee had decent quarters, including, eventually, a room in City Hall. He dined with British officers and kept close to officers and friends from earlier days who were stationed in the city. It must have become clear to Lee and all other observers after several months that a trial for treason would not take place and he would not be sent to England.[49]

Sometime shortly after his capture, however, Lee appeared to envision a new role for himself in the war. He offered himself as a negotiator of a peace accord. In the letter to Washington asking for his dogs, Lee enclosed a letter to the president of Congress, urging the immediate dispatch of "two or three gentlemen" under a flag of truce to discuss issues that impact the "Interests of the Public." Failing a response, Lee sent another letter to John Hancock to the same effect. Keep in mind that just weeks earlier, on his return to the North after his victory at Charleston, Lee had advised Congress to beware of the overtures of Lord Howe for reconciliation and even for a conference. He had counseled Congress to send only some patriotic citizens to satisfy public opinion, as nothing of value could come from such a meeting. The tables now turned, most members of Congress did not share Lee's optimism or urgency. Washington's victories at the end of the year raised their expectations, and Lee's coziness with British officers had always offended some of the more skeptical. Lee misjudged his position. In his letters he suggested that Congress would take any action necessary for his *personal* concerns and that his requests now rise above the personal and must be answered. Although Washington told his confidantes that such a conference could not cause much harm, he advised Lee in a letter dated April 1 that Congress could not agree to such a summit. John Adams adopted Lee's earlier reasoning in an exchange of letters with General Nathanael Greene, saying that it "appears to be an artful stratagem of the two grateful brothers [Lord and General Howe] to hold up to the public view the phantom of a negotiation." Adams was also concerned that a conference would send the wrong message to the French court, which the Americans were lobbying for more pronounced support.[50] Apparently, some members of Congress also did not trust General Howe and feared that they would be taken captive and maybe tried for treason. Lee's good friend, Richard Henry Lee, responded directly to Lee, distraught that he could not accommodate his request and to assure Charles that his own personal safety was not an issue that impacted his decision: "I have not the smallest idea of personal danger, nor does this affect the present question."[51]

We can only conjecture what motivated Charles Lee at this point in his life. Through a volatile combination of personal pique, political beliefs, ambition, and self-interest he had abandoned his loyalty to the British Crown, given up his commission in the British Army, and risked all that he had in life on the American cause. After only eighteen months that gamble had paid enormous dividends. He held a vaulted position in the Continental Army, could boast of victory at Charleston, and was untouched by the criticism that hung over the leadership of George Washington. He stood at the head of the greater part of the army. It had appeared, just days earlier, that he was destined for greatness. But by his own carelessness he had thrown this advantage away and was now an observer, owing to the British military again for his bed and board. Adding to this indignity, he watched Washington execute the masterstroke at Trenton that could have been his own and wondered now whether the war might not end quickly without him.

At this point in his life, Charles Lee made his gravest error.

CHAPTER 9

CAPTIVITY, BETRAYAL, EXCHANGE

Congress rejected Charles Lee's demands for an audience in the first months of 1777. His reaction reflected the frustrations of a person who does not understand the rationale and a desperation at becoming marginalized. Unless he could return to the Continental Army quickly, the war might end without him in a leadership position, preferably on the winning side. Exchange was a possibility but not a viable option at the moment; the British were still working through their legal position relative to Charles Lee (traitor or prisoner of war?), and Washington did not have a comparable British officer to offer.

"Mr. Lee's Plan"

Lee, now reacquainted with most of the British officers, must have examined his position and come to the conclusion that his greatest value was as a go-between. He knew the leaders on both sides and counted them all among his friends. If he could not win the war in the field, perhaps he could become the catalyst in resolving it. His star would rise on the world stage, and any threat of hanging would be eliminated. The obstinacy of his American friends frustrated this plan, however. A man of cool temperament or controlled ego might have bided his time and waited for a better opportunity. And so it appeared for Charles Lee. He remained in captivity for another twelve months, and the limited correspondence available during this period reflects only the frustrations of an energetic man with little to occupy himself.

The war continued without him. At first, it must have appeared that the Americans had turned the tide with Washington's victories at Trenton and Princeton. But as the year wore on, Lee received news of the British victory at Brandywine on September 11, the capture of Philadelphia weeks later, and another British triumph at Germantown in early October. The last British success, however, was followed fast by a brilliant American victory at Saratoga, with laurels goings to Lee's good friend and Virginian neighbor, Horatio Gates. Lee was strictly an observer from afar. After having a relatively comfortable situation in New York City—a room, British friends and officers to dine and converse with, and good food—Lee was moved to the *Centurion*, which was lying in the New York Harbor in June. He endured these cramped and confining quarters until December. But neither the tide of the war nor the relative comforts of his quarters were important. Charles Lee had cast his fate early in his captivity, and the rest of his wartime activity, whether with the British or the Americans, could not overcome that decision. Finally, in December 1777, after extended negotiations, Lee was granted parole as a preliminary to a prisoner exchange and allowed to return to the American lines. As was his routine, one of his first stops was at the Congress, evacuated from Philadelphia and now convened in York, Pennsylvania. He renewed his appeals to use him as a go-between to broker a resolution of the war. Congress continued to ignore these pleas. Eventually, in April 1778, he returned to George Washington, who was encamped with his army at Valley Forge, Pennsylvania. Lee received a hero's welcome.

Unfortunately, Charles Lee carried a secret with him that affected every action he took. In March 1777, just a few months after his capture on December 13, 1776, Charles Lee authored a document that puts into question his loyalty to the American cause. "Mr. Lee's Plan—March 29, 1777," as it has become known, provided a blueprint for British victory over the Americans.[1] A brief summary of the plan tells all.

Lee begins by expressing his opinion that America has "no chance of obtaining the ends She proposes to herself," and that a continuation of the war will only "put the Mother Country to very serious expence both in blood and Money." The result will be harsh on both sides. He proposes to bring the war to a quick end by cutting the colonies in half. He acknowledges that General Howe will move against Philadelphia in the spring but dismisses this as of little consequence. Congress, he predicts, will abandon the city for safer ground and continue the war in the hope that a foreign power will intervene. Victory will come only if Howe can take control of Maryland, Virginia, and Pennsylvania. If Maryland is "reduc'd or submits," Virginia will not be able to reinforce Pennsylvania, so that "the whole machine is dissolv'd and a period put to the War." New Englanders will stay at home rather than cross the North River. Lee is "so confident of the event" that he asserts "with the penalty of my life" that the war will end within two months of the adoption of his plan.

The Plan contains detail and commentary enough to demonstrate that it was not a momentary exercise in military strategy. Lee clearly utilized his knowledge of the geography south of Philadelphia to emphasize his points:

> On the supposition then, that General Howe's Army (including every species of Troops) amounts to twenty or even eighteen thoushand men at liberty to move to any part of the Continent; as fourteen thoushand will be more than sufficient to clear the Jersey's and take possession of Philadelphia, I wou'd propose that four thoushand be immediately embark'd in transports, one half of which shou'd proceed up the Patomac and take post at Alexandria, the other half up Chesepeak Bay and possess themselves of Annapolis. They will most probably meet with no opposition in taking possession of these Posts, and when possess'd they are so very strong by nature that a few hours work and some trifling artillery will secure them against the attacks of a much greater force than can possibly be brought down against them—their communication with the shipping will be constant and sure—for at Alexandria Vessels of a very considerable burthen (of five or six hundred Tons for instance) can lie in close to shore, and at Annapolis within musket shot.

From these posts, "proclamations of pardon shou'd be issued to all those who come in at a given day," and all of the inhabitants within reach will "lay down their arms" rather than allow their countryside to become the seat of war.

Both the identity and the intent of the writer of "Mr. Lee's Plan" have been challenged since it came to light in 1858. Those questioning the authenticity have little to stand on other than their belief that Charles Lee would not have written such a document. The manuscript was found among the papers of Henry Strachey, the secretary for the Royal Commissioners (the brothers Sir William Howe and Lord Admiral Richard Howe) in New York in 1777, commanding His Majesty's land and naval forces and assigned to negotiate a resolution of the war. It contains Strachey's legend, "Mr. Lee's Plan—March 29, 1777," and is most assuredly written in Charles Lee's hand. And, reading Lee's correspondence closely over the remaining years of his life, one can find allusions to the plan. Most historians have reluctantly come to the conclusion that Charles Lee did indeed author this document.[2]

Lee's intent, however, remains an issue of contention. At least two biographers ascribe good motives to Lee in an ill-advised venture. Samuel White Patterson reviews "Mr. Lee's Plan" "in the cool light of sweet reasonableness" and characterizes it as "a fictionalized guidebook" to trick the Howe brothers into dividing their forces. He describes Lee as a strong patriot, skilled at extracting information from unsuspecting guests. John Richard Alden dismisses the plan as a misguided attempt to help the American cause. He argues that Lee gave no information about the Continental Army to Howe and that the strategy most assuredly would have resulted in disaster for Howe, again by separating his forces in North America. He accepts Lee's suggestion in a letter, written years after the fact, that Lee "saved" the American Revolution by clandestine efforts during his capture, relying almost exclusively on his conclusion that Lee never lied. And he makes the technical legal argument that Lee could not be guilty of treason because he had never taken an oath of loyalty to the United States.[3] Neither argument retains any viability after a reading of the plan in the context in which it was written.

A recent doctoral dissertation offers yet another explanation:

> While the true reason(s) for "Lee's Plan" will probably never be known, I see Lee's scheme as being symptomatic of paranoia. Given his propensity for viewing his military and civil authorities as inept, it is entirely possible that Lee lacked better judgment than sending a premature opinion about gentlemen who made him feel expendable. Believing this to be true, "Lee's Plan" was an "I'll show you!" response, a protective barrier for a man whose social and professional inadequacies were magnified by his sensitivities. If Lee felt slighted by King George III for not helping him regain a position in the British army, is it not possible that he felt just as slighted in not being taken seriously by the Continental Congress?[4]

In other words, Lee wrote the plan to spite the Continental Congress for not sending representatives and allowing him to broker a settlement of the war.

Notwithstanding these apologies, an officer in captivity who puts in writing a plan to defeat his own troops knows the consequences of such a document and knows that it will never be interpreted as a ruse if discovered. Charles Lee was not so foolish as to think that he could persuade the Americans of his loyalty after the fact, given that he was an officer recently on half pay to the British and was now wining and dining with old friends in the safety of New York City. Or, even if he was so foolish, why did he not mention the plan to Washington or anyone else as soon as he was paroled? He knew the consequences if he could not persuade—banishment at best and execution as a traitor at the worst. He may have been playing a dangerous game, but which side was he on? If, as he stated in the plan, he did not believe the Americans could win the war, Charles Lee may have believed that turning back to the British was his smartest play in March 1777. Exchange did not appear certain or imminent. Collapse of the American army and the American government would surely leave Charles Lee with no support. His position as a prisoner of war was tenuous. His continued income, as well as his freedom, depended on the generosity of the British government. Lee was back with friends on what appeared to be the winning side, and perhaps his attempt was to make the most of it.[5]

Did Lee lose his faith in the American cause in March 1777, or did he choose the wrong side in 1775? Did he overestimate the fervor of the Revolution or the ability of Americans to face the British in an extended fight? Did the bickering and micromanaging of the Congress cause him to rethink his original observations and doubt the outcome? Did he lose confidence in George Washington or simply see, in the reality of his situation in March 1777, that he would never now replace the hero of Trenton? Or did his personal courage merely fail him? But Charles Lee was no coward. He surely had faced life-threatening episodes—in the French and Indian War, in Portugal, in Hungary, and in personal duels. And although most of the accounts of these events come from Lee himself, the episodes surely happened. Except for the suggestion of cowardice from third-party accounts of his capture at Basking Ridge, no one had occasion to label him a coward.[6] Indeed, while it may be true that awaiting a hangman's noose presents a greater psychological burden than marching into battle with a trained force of men, nothing suggests that Lee so feared for his life in the opening months of 1777 that he cracked under the pressure. The accounts of his captivity at this time paint a picture of an officer well cared for and composed.

Perhaps Lee feared that in captivity he would become irrelevant just when he was reaching the height of his ambition. Why, otherwise, would he completely change his position on the usefulness and immediacy of a conference? He had dismissed such a conference out of hand weeks earlier on his return to New York from the South, but shortly after his capture he proposed just such a meeting. Why the change of heart? It could be that in early 1777, Charles Lee felt marginalized. Captivity could not have suited him. His ego required him to be the center of attention, someone who commanded respect for his opinions. His eccentric and flamboyant style forced his audience to listen; his stories of European courts and armies, personal duels and military exploits held listeners close; his passionate diatribes against King George and his glorious calls for personal freedoms echoed the political backing of the Revolution and made him a leader of men. As a prisoner in New York City in the winter of 1777, however, Charles Lee lost the power of his persona. An eccentric personality and flamboyant style needs the freedom to move from place to place to captivate new audiences. These traits wear thin after a while. Stories of European sights and sounds or military exploits sell best to audiences unfamiliar with them. His captors would not have been impressed. And passion for a political cause is difficult to maintain if you are surrounded by only those who do not care to debate the issue. Charles Lee, by all accounts, did not dazzle his captors as he had the American rebels. If the Americans glorified Lee's military history, the British military establishment did not. He was simply another officer with limited leadership abilities and questionable European experience. His capture itself diminished his military stature and raised anew questions about his ability. His failure to gain traction with the Congress may have convinced him to try to gain some respect from the other side.

Examining "Mr. Lee's Plan" in this context provides some explanation. He is clearly trying to demonstrate his knowledge of the possible theaters of activity and his strategic prowess to the Howes. Disturbingly, he also offers valuable insight (as he sees it) into the minds of the Americans, suggesting that "all the Inhabitants of that great tract southward of the Patapsico and lying betwixt the Patomac and Chesepeak Bay and those on the eastern Shore of Maryland" will surrender if Alexandria and Annapolis are taken, as will the "potent and populous German districts, Frederic County in Maryland and York in Pennsylvania." If the Howes were to receive his plan as he presented it, Lee would once again be a player in the great drama unfolding on the North American continent rather than an insignificant officer languishing in captivity.

We do not know, and we will never fully understand, Charles Lee's calculation in writing the plan. We can only speculate. To give Lee all benefits of the doubt, he explains that his proposal demonstrates concern for those he is betraying: he comments that his strategy "will be attended with no bloodshed or desolation to the Colonies." Also, no credible stories about the exchange of money can be found. Whatever Lee's motives and misgivings, however, the plan cannot be read as anything other than a betrayal. Lee was not mistreated by his captors. Although at first he faced the possibility of a trial for treason, the immediate demands of Congress and Washington, and the reaction of the Howes, made it clear that any threat to his life was not likely. The plan does not appear to have been prompted by a request for valuable information by the Howes. By most accounts, General Howe avoided Lee during his captivity. If the plan was a plea by Lee for attention, he failed his purpose. Simply put, Charles Lee—who had railed for independence just six months prior and had chastised Congress just weeks earlier for even considering a reconciliation conference—gave up the cause and the men he had stood with.

For those who suggest that Charles Lee sought to mislead the Howes, consider what would have occurred if "Mr. Lee's Plan" had made its way out of New York City to a revolutionary pamphleteer *at any time* after it was written. If it surfaced during Lee's captivity, while he dined regularly with British officers and enjoyed the comforts of New York City, he would be vilified. Could he possibly explain then that it was a ruse? Would Washington have worked so hard to find a suitable exchange and welcomed him to Valley Forge as a hero? Of course not. And what if the Howes had exposed the document on Lee's arrival at Valley Forge? In February 1778, the Continental Congress decided, for its own reasons, that a loyalty oath should be administered to all officers in the army, disavowing King George and acknowledging allegiance to the United States.[7] Washington obliged, and had the oath formally recited by all officers in camp at Valley Forge in May. Lee and the Marquis de Lafayette were not in camp that day. Washington assembled Lee and the Marquis several weeks later on June 9 to take the oath, which he himself administered. According to the Marquis (albeit fifty years after the fact) Lee twice removed his hand from the Bible. This sleight of hand did not go unnoticed by Washington, who asked for an explanation. Lee, who had been a forceful proponent of loyalty oaths during his short time in command in Rhode Island and New York City in the winter of 1775–1776, responded: "As to King George, I am ready to absolve myself from all allegiance to him, but I have some scruples about the Prince of Wales." Charles Lee then placed his hand on the Bible and swore the oath.[8] Anyone hearing this story surely connects the two events—the betrayal contained in the plan and the oath—even though the events can be construed as separate and unrelated. The officers gathered that day, not aware of the plan, laughed off the incident as another eccentricity of Charles Lee. Nevertheless, had Lee's plan become known within days of this event, Lee would have found himself only days from the gallows.

Similarly, what would have happened if the plan had been exposed just days after Lee's performance at the Battle of Monmouth in June 1778? As we will see, many doubted Lee's loyalty at this time *without* knowledge of the plan. It would have sealed his fate. All argument over his motives and his actions during that battle would have been preempted by an immediate march to the gallows.

The most amazing aspect of this story is that the plan never saw the light of day during the war, during Charles Lee's remaining life, or during the lives of anyone associated with the Revolution. It surfaced in 1858, when found by clerks rummaging through Henry Strachey's papers in England. The original was quickly purchased by George H. Moore, the librarian of the New-York Historical Society, who immediately wrote "The Treason of Charles Lee," a paper read before the Society on June 22, 1858. Moore was not kind to Lee, and his paper effectively closed the book on Lee's life. The apologists come much later and with little effect, notwithstanding that Lee's biographer

Samuel White Patterson dismissed Moore's book as part of a "chain reaction of patriotism" that arose after the fiftieth anniversary of the Revolution.

Why is it that the Howes did not expose Charles Lee? They never expressed any particular affection for him. Perhaps they preferred to have a compromised officer as second in command of their enemy. Lee's actions at Monmouth surely can be interpreted as the efficacy of such a strategy. Another explanation comes from a review of Moore's book in the *New York Times* in 1860. As the reviewer sees it, the Howes definitely altered their upcoming strategy to adapt to Lee's suggestion. The subsequent failure of their half-hearted attempts left them embarrassed to acknowledge the source of their change in plans:

> Now, as this plan was the very reverse of the one agreed upon by Sir WILLIAM HOWE and the English ministry, discussed and digested during the Winter, and suddenly changed within three days after the receipt of Mr. LEE's communication, are we not justified in concluding that it was that communication which produced the change? The English General had made his preparations to act by the Hudson River, and in conjunction with the army of Canada. He did act by the Chesapeake Bay, attacking Pennsylvania from the south, and leaving the army of Canada to its own resources. That he did not adopt the whole of LEE's plan may have proceeded from a natural and even unconscious distrust of the source from whence it came. Its outline, its fundamental idea of a separation between South and North, by acting from the centre, was adopted; and when it failed, what more natural than that Sir WILLIAM HOWE should have hesitated to tell the world that he had been led into the capital error of his career by listening to the counsels of a traitor? . . . We can see, too, why a document of so much interest remained so long concealed, and why in the discussions and animadversions which the blunders of the war called forth, no allusion should have been made to the real cause of the greatest blunder of all.[9]

George Moore goes out of his way to demonstrate that General Howe not only read the plan, but executed it—albeit poorly and half-heartedly. Moore discusses the apparently quick and unexplained shift in British strategy after April 1, 1777—from the combining of the British armies in New York and Canada to the transporting of the New York troops by sea to the Chesapeake. Moore points out that the northern strategy had been accepted by the officers under General Howe and by the ministry in London, all of whom were flabbergasted when it was abandoned. Sir Henry Clinton, soon to relieve Howe, argued against taking troops south by sea and felt short-handed and unable to act decisively when Howe sailed off on July 30, leaving him in

New York.[10] Moore, like his reviewers in the *New York Times* quoted above, suggests that Howe's silence and excuses about this strategy came from embarrassment, not by the strategy's ultimate failure, but for taking "the suggestions of one who was personally so obnoxious to the king and ministry."

Lee's biographer John Richard Alden, on the other hand, dismisses the thought that General Howe accepted Lee's plan except, perhaps, as a confirmation of his preconceived strategy: "It is unlikely that he altered his projects for the coming campaign in the slightest because of [Lee's plan]. Conceivably it influenced him to move against Philadelphia by way of the Chesapeake rather than directly by land across New Jersey, as he had earlier intended. If he took Lee's suggestion seriously, he certainly gave Lee no credit for his assistance, for he was determined even as late as June to do what he could toward punishing him for serving in the American army."[11] The resolution of this controversy would surely have military and historical significance, but Howe's acting on or rejecting of the plan does not absolve Charles Lee from the ignominy of writing it in the first place.[12]

Whatever Lee's purpose in writing the plan and whatever its impact on General Howe, every action taken by Charles Lee after his return to the American side in 1778 must be viewed in the context of the plan's existence. And this concept must serve as the basis for any examination of the remainder of Lee's life. Lee had compromised his position as a military leader in the Revolution and had placed his life in immediate peril. From this time forward, he had to weigh every move he made against the knowledge that the British military could easily end his career and, most assuredly, his life—not on the battlefield but in the press. And he could share this personal agony with no one.

The pressure on Charles Lee in 1778 must have been enormous. He was a man without a country.

EXCHANGE

Once it became clear that the British would not treat Lee as a traitor, but rather as any other captured enemy officer, an exchange became a possibility. Unfortunately, in the early months of 1777, Washington did not have a British officer of equal rank in captivity. Several entreaties were made about the exchange of numerous lower-ranking officers for Lee, but to no immediate avail. Congress had offered a British officer of mid-rank and eight Hessian officers immediately upon Lee's capture, but the offer was rejected out of hand.[13]

While at first he had fine quarters in Manhattan, Lee spent the months from June to December confined to a ship in the harbor. The British used many ships to house the thousands of American prisoners captured in 1776 and 1777, and many Americans died on these leaky, unseaworthy vessels from malnutrition or disease. Lee's confinement on the active vessel *Centurion* may have been much less disagreeable—it was a top-of-the-line vessel, and Lee had his manservant Giuseppe Minghini and his dogs as company, as well as the occasional visitor. But the confinement had to be difficult. In August, Lee wrote to Henry Clinton, asking for relief. These were cramped quarters for Lee, who was allowed only limited time on the quarter deck. It appears that Clinton intervened with the captain of the ship to ease the terms of Lee's confinement.[14]

Charles Lee, the firebrand British officer who turned on the king, was not forgotten by the Americans, however, and some action needed to be taken if Lee was to be returned to them. As it turns out, several New Englanders saw a remedy. On the night of July 9, Colonel William Barton and thirty-six brave, or foolhardy, men set out in boats from Tiverton, Rhode Island, to the British encampment at Newport. Their target was Major General Richard Prescott, the British officer in command at Newport, notable only for having been once before captured by the Americans—and exchanged. Three men found their way in the dark to Prescott's quarters, entered, subdued him, tied him up, and dragged him to their boat. Within hours of having left, the raiding party returned, essentially unscathed, with their prize in hand. Now Washington had an officer of equal rank with Lee.[15]

Negotiations took another six months, while Lee languished most of the time on the *Centurion*. On December 30, 1777, Charles Lee wrote to Washington advising him that he had been placed back on parole in New York and that his condition was "much better'd":

> [I] have the full liberty of the City and its limits, have horses at my com-
> mand furnished by sir Henry Clinton and General Robinson—am lodg'd
> with two of the oldest and warmest friends I have in the world—Colonel
> Butler and Major Disney of the 38th Regt with the former I was bred up
> from the age of nine years from school—the latter is a Commilito from the
> time I enter'd the service in the 44th Regmt. —in short my situation is
> rendered as easy, comfortable and pleasant as possible for a man who is in
> any sort of a Prisoner—.[16]

Washington did not receive this letter for several weeks but in his reply acknowledged that Lee's fate was tied to that of General Prescott. In January 1778, Elias Boudinot, assigned by George Washington to negotiate the exchange, visited with Lee in New York City. Boudinot came away horrified. He later related that Lee doubted the ability of the Americans to win the war and urged that "Congress would immediately have a strong fortress built at Pittsburgh" to safeguard the "Riches of the Country" as well as the "old Men, Women and Children." Congress should also consider building boats to flee to the safety of the "Spanish Territory." Lee also related information to Boudinot about British strategy, in direct violation of the terms of the meeting, offering several papers that Boudinot rejected.[17] By March 15, Boudinot had arranged for Lee to be picked up in Philadelphia on parole. Lee's affidavit of parole is signed April 5, 1778, acknowledging that he remained a prisoner of war for the time being but the parole allowed him to return to the American lines.

During this period of time, as Charles Lee passed from prisoner of war to prisoner on parole to fully exchanged, his actions and his words appear incredible. He maintained a dialogue with the highest-ranking British officers, lectured Washington and Congress on the organization of the army (from which he had been absent for more than a year), lobbied for higher rank, and offered himself as the intermediary who could bring the war to a close satisfactorily to both sides. Surely, by this time, Charles Lee had regained his confidence in himself if, indeed, he had ever lost it. It may be difficult to ascertain the true mind of a man from the cold pages of a few letters, but it surely appears that from January to June 1778, Charles Lee was a mangle of self-contradictions and divided loyalties.

On April 3, Lee met with General William Howe in Philadelphia. Howe had arranged this unnecessary trip to Philadelphia ostensibly to take Lee's parole personally. Apparently, Howe wanted to discuss the state of affairs with Lee to see if a negotiated peace was still possible. According to Lee, the two men discussed the foolishness (as Howe saw it) and the efficacy (as Lee saw it) of the Declaration of Independence at this meeting. After the conference, Howe acknowledged Lee's time by sending wine and spirits to his quarters.[18]

Days later, Charles Lee arrived at Valley Forge. Although Lee was still on parole and not fully exchanged, Washington had an escort ride out four miles to meet him, and officers and men lined the route for two miles as the two top-ranking officers in the army rode into the camp.[19] That night, Washington gave Lee a room in his house, an honor not ordinarily bestowed. In addition, we know that officers' quarters were rearranged to accommodate Lee's arrival.[20] Yet another strange story accompanies Lee's arrival at Valley Forge. Elias Boudinot, no admirer of Lee, wrote after the fact that Lee brought a "miserable, dirty Hussy with him from Philadelphia (a british Sergeant's wife) and had actually taken her into his Room by a back door, and she slept with him that night."[21]

Lee stayed only a few days at Valley Forge before leaving for York, Pennsylvania, to meet with the Continental Congress. In a letter dated April 13, 1778, Lee chides Washington to get Congress to move more quickly on completing his exchange, adding that "we cannot expect expedition from democratic councils—it is a curse annexed to the blessing." Accompanying the letter is a "Plan of an Army" that "has long been the object of my studies," based on his studies of "Machiavel" and Marshal Saxe, whose works he claimed to understand "better than almost any man living." The plan is "a hobby horse of my own training and it runs away with me indeed I am so infatuated with it that I cannot forbear boasting its excellencies."[22] When Washington replied just days later to acknowledge his full exchange, he jokes about Lee's enthusiasm for the multipage document: "The contents shall be the subject of conversation, when I have the pleasure of seeing you in circumstances to mount your hobby-horse, which will not, I hope on trial be found quite so limping a jade, as the one on which you set out for York."[23]

At the same time Lee wrote directly to Congress, telling the president of the body that he deserved to be exchanged for General John Burgoyne (captured on October 17, 1777, at the Battle of Saratoga) rather than Prescott, because Burgoyne was the highest-ranking British general now in captivity and because the British did not "set the least value upon" Prescott. Besides, Lee added, Washington "cannot do without me." With Lee, ego always surfaced.[24] Next, Lee wrote to Congress demanding a promotion now that he was returning to the Continental Army. His letter of recommendation (for himself), considering the details of his capture and his absence from the army for more than one year, is fantastic: "Since the first establishment of the American army a very great and rapid promotion has been made of General Officers, All the Brigadiers, a multitude of Colonels, and some even below that rank are now in the same rank with myself, in short, whilst others are advanced several steps, I remain stationary—I hope I shall not be thought to speak invidiously when I remark that there is no officer in your service of any degree whatever, who held the same rank in Europe that I did, and that had I chosen to have remained in the Polish or Portuguese service or entered into the Russian, I should at this day have been a Lieut. General."[25] Congress was not moved to action.

Lee's hubris at this moment cannot be denied. Did he forget the plan he had left behind with the Howe brothers? Apparently not. In May 1778, Lee wrote out a "Memorandum" that he passed on to George Washington, discussing strategy: "I have the strongest reason to think (my reason shall be given hereafter) that it is not General Howe's intention to direct his operations against Boston, but that his views are to establish himself in the Middle Colonies. I may be mistaken but the reasons for my surmise are very strong . . . I have likewise the strongest reason to think that they flatter themselves that by establishing themselves about Annapolis, Baltimore, or even Alexandria—They shall be able to augment considerably their army with convicts and indented servants."[26] In this oblique reference that Washington could not be expected to understand, Charles Lee acknowledges for historians the existence and content of his plan left with the Howes. He tried, a month later, to give Washington his "reason" for believing that the British would move to the Middle Colonies. In a letter dated June 15, Lee discusses several possible movements by the British, including the prospect that they will "pass through the Jerseys to N. York." He rejects this alternative (although this is what the British ultimately did do) and repeats his warning: "I have particular reasons to think that They have cast their eyes for this purpose, on the lower Counties of Delawar and some of the Maryland Counties of the Eastern Shore, that They have had thoughts of adopting this measure some time ago I learnt from Mr Willin when They entertain'd an idea of offering or assenting to, if proposed, a cessation of hostilities."[27]

And in this state of renewed or continuing self esteem, Lee writes to his confidante Benjamin Rush a long letter with a blushing defense of General William Howe! Lee throws aside his earlier "prejudices" but still finds it difficult to make his praise palatable. He has always found Howe "friendly candid good natur'd brave and rather sensible than the reverse" and assigns Howe's actions in North America to his blind and lazy acceptance of his position. Even Lee realizes his attempt to argue his position leads to an absurd conclusion, and though logic fails him, his pen, as always, does not. Here's the *praise* that Lee bestows:

> You will say that I am drawing my Friend Howe in more ridiculous colours than He has yet been represented in—but this is his real character—He is naturally good humour'd and complacent, but illiterate and indolent to the last degree unless as an executive soldier, in which capacity He is all fire and activity, brave and cool as Julius Cœsar—his understanding is, as I observ'd before rather good than otherwise, but was totally confounded and stupefy'd by the immensity of the task impos'd upon him—He shut his eyes, fought his battles, drank his bottle, had his little Whore, advis'd with his counselors, receiv'd his orders from North and Germain, one more absurd than the other, took Galoways opinion, fought again, and is now I suppos'd to be called to Account for acting according to instructions; but I believe his eyes are now open'd.[28]

According to Lee, Howe should be excused because he never really paid attention to what he was doing or saying up to this point. The letter was prompted apparently by the stir caused when Lee visited with Howe in Philadelphia on April 3 to get his parole.

Lee did not write to only Washington and his congressional allies during this period after his exchange. He wrote as well to Sir Henry Clinton. It remains unclear whether Washington or Lee's friends in the Continental Congress knew of this correspondence, but most likely not, as no mention is made by any of them in their writings. Lee went out of his way to congratulate Clinton on his appointment to the command of Britain's American forces.[29] This correspondence was facilitated through Major General James Robertson. Aside from pleasantries, the letters deal with Lee's continuing efforts to serve as an intermediary to bring the war to a close. Some historians have suggested that the correspondence by itself is an act of treason—communicating with the officers of the enemy without the knowledge or sanction of his superiors.[30] However one views this correspondence, Lee's bravado cannot be disputed. Did he see himself as someone above all of the rules that applied to others? Was he so sure of his position with the Americans that he could risk being discovered in a secret correspondence with the commander of the enemy's army? Or was he simply hedging his bets, reminding Clinton subtly that he might be counted on if circumstances allowed him to be of use as an intermediary or reminding Clinton that he might need a safe harbor if circumstances otherwise required?

Lee received a full exchange and freedom on April 21, 1778. And so it was that he found himself at Valley Forge in June 1778, again George Washington's second in command, as the Americans readied themselves to cross the Delaware River once again, this time to shadow Sir Henry Clinton's troops on their march across New Jersey. The two armies would meet at Monmouth Courthouse on June 28, 1778.

CHAPTER 10

MONMOUTH

As spring arrived in 1778, the war between Great Britain and its American colonies was about to enter a new phase. The Americans had suffered harsh cold and depravations in winter camp at Valley Forge but spent the time training and drilling to prepare for the spring campaign. The British, safely ensconced in Philadelphia during the winter, learned with the spring thaw that they now faced a new and more dangerous foe: France recognized the fledgling United States on February 6 and entered the war against its longtime enemy, Great Britain.

The British high command in Philadelphia had hoped to forestall this inevitability by inflicting a major blow on the Continental Army. Although they did not challenge the Americans at Valley Forge, the British hoped that Washington would expose himself at some point so that they could crush his ragtag army and bring the war to an end. Washington almost obliged them in May. When news of the French alliance reached Valley Forge, Washington allowed the exuberant Marquis de Lafayette to take 2,000 troops in a foolish attempt to reconnoiter and harass the British. Sir Henry Clinton, now in command at Philadelphia, learned of the Marquis's movements while hosting a ball in honor of the departing General Howe on May 18. He hurriedly moved 8,000 men to encircle Lafayette, certain that he would capture the Frenchman and be able to send him to London as a prize. He took General Howe along for the show and arranged a banquet for the night of the 20th to display his trophy. The Marquis, now at Barren Hill, eleven miles from Valley Forge and across the Schuylkill River, had almost no warning before he saw the vanguard of the British columns and quickly realized that his avenue of escape back over the Schuylkill had been cut off. A single road remained to a secondary ford. The Marquis made dispositions of some of his troops to divert the British while the main force scurried to and across the ford to safety. A cool head, luck, and grittiness saved his command from capture.[1] A quick victory to crush the rebellion eluded the British, who now faced an extended war on multiple fronts.

The French government had secretly aided the Americans from the beginning of hostilities. The failure of the British to inflict a crushing blow in the first two years of the conflict, Horatio Gates's stunning victory at Saratoga in the fall of 1777, and the amazing resiliency of the Continental Army under George Washington had finally convinced the French that their active participation in the war would serve their national interests by defeating the British. The French alliance brought not only the possibility of French troops but a threat to British navigation at sea and its interests in the Caribbean and Canada. British strategy had to change to meet these new threats.

The British had entered Philadelphia on September 27, 1777, and they enjoyed their stay over the winter of 1777–1778. The officers had been well housed and well fed, and the ladies of the city offered more than a visual distraction from the war during the quiet months of the winter. Balls and parties provided considerable solace. But Philadelphia's military usefulness was negligible, as Charles Lee had pointed out on several occasions. The British discovered throughout the war that holding cities offered few advantages against an army that came from and lived off of the farmlands in between. Lee had predicted that France would join the fight to advance its own national interests, and, with France in the war, the British altered their strategy. Ships and troops were now needed in the West Indies and elsewhere to protect the valuable British assets in North America. The cost, in men and money, of holding Philadelphia was not worth the small gains that taking the rebel capital had provided.

The Continental Congress, meanwhile, having abandoned the city in advance of the British army, took up temporary quarters in York (again as Charles Lee had predicted in his plan). George Washington found the safety of Valley Forge, and the winter his army spent there has become a symbol of the worst of times suffered by the American fighting men during the war, even though several winters (especially at Morristown in 1779–1780) may have, indeed, been harsher on the troops. Nevertheless, Washington used the time to advantage. General Friedrich Wilhelm von Steuben, a Prussian officer who was able to find a rank in the American army, drilled the men throughout the winter months in an attempt to create a fighting force with disciple and stamina. His efforts proved worthwhile as the months unfolded. The army that Washington had at his command in the spring of 1778 differed considerably from the army that he had raced across New Jersey just eighteen months earlier to avoid a head-on confrontation with the advancing British.

And, as we have seen, Washington used the time to work out an exchange for his second in command, Charles Lee.

THE ROAD TO MONMOUTH

The Battle of Monmouth, and Charles Lee's role in it, has been the subject of debate since the fighting stopped at about six o'clock on that brutally hot day of June 28, 1778. Lee had left the field several hours earlier, sometime after a confrontation with General George Washington. Later that day, Lee sulked in his tent away from the battle listening to the officers and men originally under his control praising the heroics of Washington to save the day. The British, undefeated but badly battered by the day-long affair, were already preparing to leave the field quietly during the night to keep a date with the transports awaiting them at Sandy Hook for the short sail to Manhattan. The Americans, exhausted, were congratulating themselves on their ability to stand man to man with the "flower of the British Army" and glowing as they recalled George Washington astride his white horse leading the troops in the fight, oblivious to the fire and personal danger.

One of the most fascinating aspects of the Battle of Monmouth was the array of officers and men who fought on the field. Washington and Lee represented the main actors in the drama, but many other recognizable names also played major roles in the fighting and the controversy that day and thereafter.[2] First and foremost was the Marquis de Lafayette, the officer originally given the command of the vanguard units sent to attack the British. Next were Generals "Mad" Anthony Wayne and William Maxwell, each in command of one of those units. Traveling with Washington's troops were Lord Stirling (William Alexander), Nathanael Greene, Henry Knox, and Friedrich von Steuben. Daniel Morgan and his 600 rifleman were separated from the main forces but expected to be called into action. Similarly, General Philemon Dickinson was nearby with the New Jersey militia. Lieutenant Colonel Alexander Hamilton played a key role by transmitting orders and information between the American forces; his archrival later in life, Aaron Burr, served with one of the units on the field and courageously led a counterassault on British forces late in the fight. Both Hamilton and Burr were injured during the battle. Hamilton's horse stumbled, and the fall injured his shoulder sufficiently to take him off the field; Burr's horse was hit by a cannonball, throwing Burr to the ground, and by the end of the day he was suffering from sunstroke as well.[3] These men faced General Henry Clinton, in command of the British forces, with Major General Earl Charles Cornwallis as his second in command and Hessian Lieutenant General Baron Wilhelm von Knyphausen, who was guarding the extensive baggage train. Much has been made of the gallant death on the field of Lieutenant Colonel Henry Monckton, commander of the Forty-fifth Regiment of Foot, Second Battalion of Grenadiers, a renowned soldier in Clinton's forces, who was cut down while leading a charge against well-protected American forces.

It is not the role of this book to detail the strategy and movements of the Americans at Monmouth. Much has already been written by military scholars and others about what happened and what should have been done, all without any definitive conclusion. Some steadfastly stand with Lee and hold that he was scapegoated by those who wished to see all the glory for the day placed upon their favored commander, General George Washington. Others hold that Lee's actions that morning were no less than traitorous and that his punishment, meted out months later, too light. Within just a few days of the battle, Charles Lee faced a court-martial, by his own demand, to determine whether he failed to follow Washington's order to attack the British, whether he called an unnecessary and "shameful" retreat, and whether his comments after the fight insulted the commander in chief. I will review Lee's actions in the field and his outrage, but of course, a more intriguing question lingers. What was Lee's state of mind on June 28, 1778?

When the fighting ceased at dusk, Charles Lee was damaged but not ruined. He could have kept his thoughts to himself and joined in the warm feelings that pervaded the American camp. Immediately after the battle he received criticism for his actions, or inaction, by some of the other officers on the field, but the dust would have settled after a few days and before any serious recriminations might arise. Perhaps a court of inquiry or a court-martial would have been convened in any event, but Lee did not have the personal discipline to hold his tongue or the political skills to deflect the criticisms. Instead, he initiated the call for an inquiry by immediately raising the issue of his role in the battle and did so in a way that was personally insulting to George Washington and could not be ignored. As a result, all subsequent discussions of the Battle of Monmouth have revolved around the actions of Charles Lee. It must be remembered that at the time of Lee's court-martial no one involved knew of "Mr. Lee's Plan" except Charles Lee himself. This remained true for all persons offering opinions of Lee and the events at Monmouth, right through 1858. But, surprisingly, very little discussion of Lee's state of mind has surfaced since then. Shouldn't the existence of the plan be considered in trying to understand Lee's actions? Let's start with the departure of Washington's army from Valley Forge in June 1778.

Once the British command determined sometime in early 1778, after the entry of France into the war, that holding Philadelphia served no military or strategic purpose, events began to unfold. General Howe was recalled in February, and the command was left to Sir Henry Clinton with instructions from home—abandon Philadelphia for New York so that some of his forces could be diverted to protect the substantial British economic interests elsewhere. If "Mr. Lee's Plan" had ever appealed to General Howe, it could not withstand the pressure from London or the instructions sent to Clinton. Lee's suggestion that the British move into the Middle Colonies to split the states apart was not pursued.

The British could leave Philadelphia by land or by sea, but a sufficient number of ships were not available to move all of the stores, baggage, Tories, camp followers, and troops. In addition, word was received that the French were sailing a significant fleet from Toulon. The British did not want to risk being bottled up in the Delaware River if the French fleet, under the Comte d'Estaing, should arrive before they could sail out to the Atlantic. The sick and wounded, Tories, equipment, and supplies would take the sea route. General Clinton would lead the remaining troops and an enormous baggage train across New Jersey to a point either directly north of the Raritan River, or further northeast, to Sandy Hook and the Raritan Bay. From either spot British ships could meet them and transport them to Manhattan. The British began their march on June 18. Washington kept a close watch on the British through his network of spies and decamped from Valley Forge as soon as the British crossed into New Jersey. Washington was already developing plans to attack the British, slowed by their heavy baggage train, somewhere along the route, and orders were issued to all the officers to prepare for a crossing of the Delaware. Clinton, concerned about the possibility of Horatio Gates's return from upstate New York, kept his options open, but he ultimately decided to take the eastern option, toward Sandy Hook, once he reached Allentown on June 24.

After the British left, American forces entered Philadelphia. Washington assigned Benedict Arnold, still recuperating from his wounds at Saratoga, to this task. Washington then began moving his army north and east from Valley Forge to shadow Clinton's movement north through New Jersey, with the intention of placing his troops within striking distance of Clinton somewhere in the middle of the state. Before crossing the Delaware River, Washington solicited written advice from his senior officers on the course to follow once they closed on the British. He received their tentative responses on June 18. Only Nathanael Greene argued for a confrontation and was willing to engage the entire army if necessary; Anthony Wayne and John Cadwalader wanted to harass the British but were reluctant to gamble on a general engagement; Charles Lee, Friedrich von Steuben, and Louis Duportail argued against engaging such a strong and disciplined force.

Six days later, after the crossing at Coryell's Ferry (now Lambertville in Hunterdon County), Washington called a second council of war in Hopewell, New Jersey. At this point, the British were twenty miles away to the southeast at Allentown. Washington's officers suggested that they "should keep a comfortable distance from the enemy, and keep up a vain parade of annoying them by detachment." In a letter after the fact, Alexander Hamilton derisively dismissed the actions of the council on June 24: "the result would have done honor to the most honorable society of midwives, and to them only." One of the strongest advocates of this wishy-washy strategy, "the primum mobile of this sage plan," as Hamilton saw it, was General Charles Lee.[4] Lee argued that a general engagement would serve no purpose other than to put the Continental Army at risk at a point when the tide was turning in favor of the Americans with the entry of France into the war. Better to build a "bridge of gold" for the British to cross the Jerseys rather than risk everything by forcing a battle in the open field.[5]

Despite Hamilton's observations after the fact, Lee's approach had merit, and Washington must have recognized its wisdom. Washington, as was his style, reserved his decision but took some action to achieve his goal once he was better situated to persuade his officers to follow his plan. Washington was a man of bold strokes, and he knew that he had an opportunity in the next few days that might not come his way again. He listened to the skeptics, but also to Greene, who wanted a fight. Greene wrote to Washington with his opinion that more men should be added to the vanguard force to bring on an engagement:

> I am not for hazarding a general action unnecessarily, but I am clearly of opinion for making a serious impression with the light troops and for having the Army in supporting distance. . . . The attack should be made on the English flank and rear. If we suffer the enemy to pass through the Jerseys without attacking, I think we shall ever regret it. . . . We are now in the most awkward situation in the world and have come to our grief repeatedly—marching until we get near the enemy and then our courage fails and we halt without attempting to do the enemy the least injury. . . . People expect something from us and our strength demands it. I am by no means for rash measures but we must preserve our reputations and I think we can make a very serious impression without any great risk and if it should amount to a general action I think the chance is greatly in our favor. However, I think we can make a partial attack without suffering them to bring us to a general action.[6]

A strategy of harassment was already in place. Washington had three units engaged in hit-and-run tactics against the moving British Army. Eight hundred New Jersey militia under Philemon Dickinson, 900 New Jersey Continentals under the command of General William Maxwell, and 600 men from Virginia under the command of Colonel Daniel Morgan (who was born in Hunterdon County, New Jersey) kept close to the British in New Jersey and did everything they could to slow them down by burning bridges, spiking wells, and felling trees. The British baggage train lengthened to twelve miles long and offered an appealing target. Several skirmishes along the road reinforced Clinton's concern about his vulnerability and the possibility that Washington's main force might be nearby looking for a broader engagement. Desertions throughout the march, especially by the Hessians, were weakening his force as well.

Washington planned for an engagement. He must have had his own doubts about risking his entire army, so, taking Greene's advice and to hedge his bets, he settled on a compromise that would leave him options. On June 25, after the Hopewell council, Washington created a vanguard force under the command of the Marquis de Lafayette of about 1,500 men from his total force of 12,000 to march ahead and close on Clinton's left flank. A limited engagement would be better than letting Clinton cross the Jerseys unscathed, and, if given the opportunity, he could bring up more troops and, perhaps, his entire force. Washington would augment this force to 2,500 men several days later and then again to 5,000 men. The New Jersey militia was also on alert on Clinton's left with 600 men.

As the armies came in close contact, however, the advisability of an attack remained uncertain. Notwithstanding his belligerence after the fact, Hamilton's letters just prior to the battle reveal his doubts as well about bringing on a general engagement. Circumstances would need to be ideal. On June 26, 1778, Hamilton was with the Marquis's troops surveying the situation for his commander. Even though eager for the fight, Hamilton twice wrote to Washington with doubts. At first Hamilton expressed concerns about logistics: "We are intirely at a loss where the [British] army is, which is no considerable check to our enterprise; if [Washington's] army is wholly out of supporting distance, we risk the total loss of the detachment in making an attack." He reiterated his concern in the second letter: "To attack them in this situation, without being supported by the whole army would be folly in the extreme."[7] Several days later, and again at Lee's court-martial, these reservations must have been forgotten.

With the Marquis moving to within striking distance of Clinton, Charles Lee's actions befuddled Washington, just as they had in December 1776. Eighteen months earlier, Lee had delayed crossing the Hudson River into New Jersey to join Washington. Lee had legitimate military reasons at that time, but in June 1778, his strange behavior brooks no strategic purpose. For some reason, it appeared that Lee could not make up his mind whether he wanted to take part in a battle if it unfolded over the next week. He declined leadership of the vanguard force, allowing the command to fall to the Marquis de Lafayette, who eagerly accepted the honor. Several days later, when Lord Stirling demanded the command if Lee would not, Lee agreed to take the spot that rightfully belonged to him as second in command. But Lee then reversed himself and declined the command a second time. By this point, Lafayette had rushed his men forward to find himself precariously ahead of the remainder of Washington's force and only one mile from Clinton's much superior force. When Washington increased the troops to 5,000 on what appeared the eve of the battle, Lee demanded the command once again. Washington, now embarrassed to approach Lafayette, agreed that Lee could take the lead if he paid attention to whatever plans for battle Lafayette had already devised. Lafayette, for his part, graciously stood aside but ached for the fight to begin.

This charade plays out in the letters exchanged by both Lafayette and Charles Lee with Washington in the few days before the battle. In a letter of "instructions" dated June 25, Washington directs Lafayette to harass Clinton's force and "for these purposes you will attack them as occasion may require . . . and if a proper opening should be given, by operating against them with the whole force of your command." Sometime on that same day, Lee lets Washington know of his change of heart: "When I first assented to the Marquis de Lafayette's taking the command of the present detachment, I confess I viewed it in a different light from that in which I view it at present. I considered it as a more proper business of a young, volunteering general, than of the second in command in the army; but I find it is considered in a different manner. They say that a corps consisting of six thousand men, the greater part chosen, is undoubtedly the most honorable command next to the Commander-in-chief."[8] Lafayette writes the next day (the same day that Hamilton was expressing his concerns about a "total loss") to let Washington know that he will "cheerfully obey and serve" Lee if Washington decides "to send him down with a couple of thousand men."[9] And that is just what Washington did in an open attempt to assuage everyone's honor and feelings. The extra men would also relieve some of Hamilton's angst.

What was Lee thinking? Some suggest that he had legitimate concerns about forcing a fight in an open field and did not want to be associated with the disaster that might ensue. Following along this theory, allowing the impulsive Lafayette to blunder into a morass with a small force was then little price to pay to be proven correct, even if it meant embarrassment for

Washington. But Lee could not refuse the command of a force as large as 5,000 men or remove himself from the field of a major battle because he disagreed with Washington's approach. Those who see Lee as a traitor, of course, assign sinister motives to his actions, suggesting that he was intentionally trying to bring on an American loss. But Lee may have had other, more personal reasons, for his indecisiveness, without wishing to assist the British. Could he lead a major force against Clinton given his actions just months earlier in New York, when he appeared to be willing to help the British win the war without major bloodshed? Could he lead a major force against Clinton knowing that in victory or defeat his position in the American army would immediately unravel with the revelation of his plan by a disgruntled or glorious Clinton? Just weeks before, Lee had written a letter of congratulations to Clinton on his elevation to the command of all the British troops.[10] We do not know if Clinton was aware of Lee's offer to help General Howe, but either way, Lee found himself in an untenable position. Perhaps Lee had hoped that the entry of the French into the war would bring about a reconciliation before he needed to take up arms again and that he could mediate an end to hostilities because he was on favorable terms with both sides. His insistence to both sides on such an approach in the weeks leading up to Monmouth suggests as much. The quick events unfolding in June, however, made this waiting game impossible. Lee eventually decided that his best approach was to act the part he was playing.

Another observation about Charles Lee's perspective must be considered. In opposing the engagement, Lee argued that the Americans were no match for British troops, notwithstanding his compelling arguments in 1774 and 1775 to the contrary. In April 1778, on the way to exchange, Lee submitted a "Plan of an Army, etc." to Washington and the Congress with this decidedly different opinion: "There is little Probability of America being so superior in Force with their Manifest Inferiority in other Respects as to make an Offensive War: to say that the Americans are so equal to the British in Discipline Officers, and even Ardor or Numbers, as that a Decisive Action in fair Ground may be risqued is talking Nonsense—to hold this Language to the common Soldiers may be prudent enough; but to try the Experiment would be Insanity: a plan of Defense, harassing and impeding can alone Succeed."[11] To accept this argument forces the conclusion that Lee's stirring declaration of superiority in 1774 was just a ruse to goad the Americans into a fight. Lee was now arguing for a guerrilla type of conflict to avoid the loss of the Continental Army, but he could not be a good judge of the fighting ability of the Continental Army in June 1778. His captivity had kept him from Washington's victories at Trenton and Princeton and from the engagements at Germantown and

Brandywine. His late arrival at Valley Forge provided little opportunity to gauge the transformation of Washington's ragtag soldiers into disciplined fighting men. Does it make sense to believe that Lee's change of heart about the relative qualities of the troops was based on observations, even though he had been out of the fight for the past eighteen months? Does it make sense that Lee's indecision to take the command at this crucial moment and his about-face on the eve of battle rested on the idea that the size of the vanguard force was now better suited to his stature? These explanations take the existence of the "Mr. Lee's Plan" out of consideration altogether. But in Lee's mind the existence of the plan must have been paramount—unless you believe that he did not understand the ramifications of his actions in New York or was deftly able to erase the plan's existence from his mind.

On June 28, 1778, Lee found himself in the undesirable position of leading an army against a foe he had just recently embraced, if not wholeheartedly, at least sufficiently to put his life at risk with his compatriots. His extraordinary and futile attempts upon his release from captivity to broker a settlement of the conflict reflected his need for the war to conclude immediately, before he was asked to take sides once again on the open field. Every day that passed made the exposure of his treachery more likely. June 28, 1778, came too soon for Charles Lee.

The Battle of Monmouth

The confrontation between General George Washington and General Charles Lee at midday on June 28 defines the Battle of Monmouth and ended Charles Lee's career. No one knows exactly what words were exchanged. Lee took offense and demanded an apology. Washington refused to apologize and never offered any hint of what he said. General Charles Scott, well after the fact, claimed that Washington "swore on that day till the leaves shook on the trees," but others who may have been close enough to overhear denied Scott's claim.[12] The charge that Lee heard and that so irked him, by his own account, was Washington's suggestion that Lee should not have taken the command if he did not intend to fight.

The military story of the Battle of Monmouth begins on the afternoon of June 27, when George Washington rode to Charles Lee's encampment at Englishtown to discuss plans for the next day. The American advance corps was within several miles of the British Army at Freehold, and despite the wariness expressed about a "general engagement" at the councils of war leading up to this point, all of the generals, including Charles Lee, understood that Washington did not want the British to march through New Jersey unmolested. The meeting confirmed Washington's desire to confront the British, and he reinforced that desire with a directive to Charles Lee to call together his officers later that afternoon to prepare a plan for battle. The meeting was also intended to smooth over any lingering bad feelings caused by the last-minute replacement of the Marquis de Lafayette with Charles Lee as commanding officer of the advance corps. That corps now numbered almost 5,000 men, slightly less than one-half of the Continental Army that had left Valley Forge just days before. General Philemon Dickinson was also camped nearby with 800 Jersey militiamen, and General Daniel Morgan was somewhere to the southeast with 600 riflemen and infantry.

Charles Lee had less than twelve hours to prepare. He set the meeting of officers for 5:00 P.M. at his tent at Englishtown. Generals William Maxwell, Anthony Wayne, and the Marquis de Lafayette arrived on time, but they received no directions. The meeting lasted less than thirty minutes, because the generals were clearly gone when General Charles Scott arrived at 5:30 P.M., mistaken about the time of the meeting. Scott received the same message as the others, perhaps more succinctly stated, that no benefits would come from making plans if the Americans were unfamiliar with the ground on which the battle was to be fought and did not know the exact location of the enemy. Lee satisfied himself by repeating to his generals the admonition given earlier by George Washington that they should avoid bickering over rank and order during the day. The purpose of the warning was to deal with the fact that the divisions had recently been reformed with a mix of veterans and recruits under generals without familiarity with their subordinates and to soothe any bad feelings that may still have been extant concerning Lee's late acceptance of the command over Lafayette.

Lee was right to be concerned about the terrain. The ground that he needed to maneuver was not inviting for advancing troops. Moving from west to east required that Lee cross several depressions, or morasses. High ground stood on the northwestern side of the first morass. Once across this morass, Lee's troops would find open fields in front of them, woods to their left and the village of Freehold about two miles to the southeast. The village could boast no more than a few houses. Slightly further to the east was the Monmouth Courthouse. About one mile after passing the western morass, Lee would need to cross another morass and, one mile further, cross the road that led to the Amboys and then the eastern morass. The British troops had entered Freehold on June 26 and set up camp just to the east of this morass. The distance from Lee's camp at Englishtown on the northwest to the edge of the British camp on the southeast was seven and a half miles. The two days the British spent in Freehold were not easy on the locals, who suffered indignities and depravations from the troops looking to restock their stores. Dickinson's men were encamped to the northwest of Freehold, and Morgan's men were thought to be somewhere to the south.[13]

Charles Lee later argued that his lack of knowledge of the terrain, along with no intelligence on the strength of the British troops to be faced, justified his failure to make any plans for the movement of his troops the next morning. But it does not appear that Lee took any action to overcome either obstacle. Surely, some of the men in the ranks were New Jersey men familiar with the area and could have been called on to enlighten him on the terrain. Similarly, Lee could have called on them for knowledge of the strength of the British force that had encamped on their homestead for the past forty-eight hours, or he could have called on Morgan and Dickinson, whose forces had shadowed the British for days. Lee did not pursue these sources of intelligence. Just as curious, he did not discuss with his generals the time for movement, the order of the divisions on the march, the availability of guides, or how the artillery or light horse might be used. He intended to improvise as the action unfolded. He would wait for the light of the next morning to reconnoiter.

The accounts of the twelve hours from five o'clock on the evening of the 27th to five o'clock on the morning of the 28th, demonstrate no extensive or careful preparations, even as recalled by those assigned to the duty. No evidence exists that Lee or his aides—Captains Mercer and Edwards and Lieutenant Colonel Brooks—were up all night coordinating events for the next day. George Washington, on the other hand, had concerns during the night. He worried that the British troops would disappear and foil his plans. Sometime around 1:00 A.M., Washington directed Alexander Hamilton to contact Lee with orders to move 600 to 800 men closer to the British to assess their movements and to strike if they moved.[14] He wanted Dickinson and Morgan contacted to the same purpose and to prepare them for the morning's events. Captain Edwards had ridden out to General Dickinson at about 5:00 P.M. on the 27th, shortly after George Washington's departure, to tell Dickinson that Lee would be counting on him for intelligence the next morning, but Lee and his aides were uncertain about the whereabouts of Morgan. It would seem that Lee had time to fix Morgan's location and to coordinate the time and place of attack with both Dickinson and Morgan, but Lee had already decided that all plans would be fruitless. Captain Mercer recalled the one o'clock orders from Washington to move some troops closer to the enemy and the directive that Morgan should attack the enemy's right flank in the morning.[15] Other than that, Mercer could "remember nothing further of consequence, except orders being given to the troops to hold themselves in readiness to march at any hour of the night." Captain Edwards confirmed that this message from Washington awoke him at some point after one o'clock, prompting him to get up to send word to Colonel Morgan. Even though Morgan's exact whereabouts were unknown to Lee, this message reached Morgan, but it may have been misleading. The message to Morgan, dated June *28th*, advised him to be ready for action "tomorrow morning."[16]

No hour-by-hour record of the activities of Lee and his aides exists for this twelve-hour period, but why did Lee wait until 1:30 in the morning and need the goading of Washington to contact Dickinson and Morgan, especially if Morgan's whereabouts were uncertain? Was this a deliberate failure to prepare or just poor leadership? The answer cannot be known, but the resulting confusion on June 28 can be assigned in large part to the incomplete and unclear messages coming from Lee's camp and his dereliction in coordinating the actions of Dickinson and Morgan with his own.

Just a mile or two away, Henry Clinton, in command of the 10,000 British troops encamped at Freehold, was busy throughout the night, establishing marching orders for his troops. After staying two days at Freehold to rest his men and horses and to scavenge provisions, Clinton wanted to get back on the move to Sandy Hook. But he knew Washington was close, and he expected an attack. He placed his baggage wagons at the front of the train, guarded by the Hessian troops under General Knyphausen, with orders to march at 3:00 A.M. Knyphausen left late, at 4:00, but was on the move early enough. Behind Knyphausen would be Cornwallis, leaving just hours later, and 1,500 troops would remain behind with Clinton to deal with the expected attack. It appears from his reports that Clinton feared most for his baggage train, convinced that this was the target for Washington's movements.

Lee roused his troops at about 5:00 A.M. Captains Mercer and Edwards were to have secured guides, but for some reason unexplained, the guides failed to appear. Colonel William Grayson would not move his men without guides, so a call went out again to procure some willing locals. Grayson waited at least one hour before he was satisfied that he could start out.[17] Why was this detail left to the morning of the intended battle? If guides were identified on the afternoon of June 27, why were they not stationed with the troops who were scheduled to step off at first light? Lee had made the point at the meeting of his generals that he and they were not familiar with the terrain. Did he deliberately leave this detail unattended to, or were his aides just incompetent? Wouldn't Dickinson have had some men in his Jersey militia who could have served this purpose if locals could not be found or were unreliable? The next day, in the heat of the battle, Lee encountered local Peter Wyckoff, who offered aid. Later in the day, George Washington brushed into

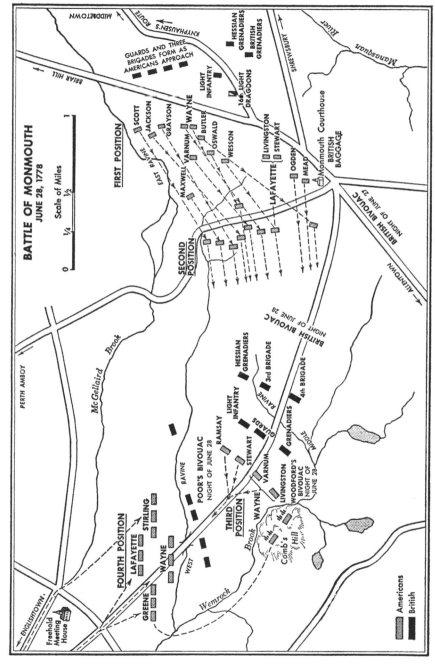

From Alfred Hoyt Bill, *Valley Forge: The Making of an Army* (New York: Harper, 1952). Reprinted with permission from HarperCollins.

Lieutenant Colonel David Rhea of the Fourth New Jersey Regiment, whose family owned the Carr farm located on the battlefield. Washington immediately recognized Rhea's value and urged him to supply intelligence on the placement of troops. Why did Lee not send out word to the New Jersey militia and the New Jersey Continental troops on the 27th in search of men familiar with the terrain?

As Lee prepared his troops to march toward the British, he was waiting for General Dickinson, in command of the New Jersey militia, to provide him intelligence about the size and location of the British troops. Lee did not want to march into a waiting army twice his size. He would prefer to chase a moving force and attack a detachment in the rear. Early morning intelligence (around 4:30 A.M.) from Dickinson provided the news to Lee *and* to Washington that the British were already moving on the road to Sandy Hook. Having secured guides, Grayson's troops began to move at about 6:30 A.M. Lee's troops—Wayne's unit, Scott's unit, Maxwell's brigade, and Colonel Jackson's unit, all under the command of Lafayette—began their march toward the British at about seven o'clock, but it took more than an hour to get them all on the road. Washington, about three miles to the north at Ponolopon Bridge (Manalapan), saw the morning unfolding as he had hoped and began to move his troops toward Englishtown at about 8:30, sending word to Lee to bring on an engagement as soon as possible "unless some very powerful circumstance forbid it."[18]

But Lee's troops had traveled only about one hour when Lee ordered a halt. General Dickinson now appeared in person to retract his earlier report and to warn Lee that Clinton had not left but was instead massing his troops to attack. Worse, Dickinson animatedly alerted Lee to the dangers he faced if he crossed the eastern morass in front of the British. Lee let Dickinson know that his information on the British troop movements was inconsistent and confusing but could see for himself that Dickinson's advice on the terrain was accurate. His view of the field must have chilled him. Lee's troops had already passed over the western morass. Forward movement was difficult (requiring a shift from line to column) and retrograde movements almost impossible. Once across the eastern morass, any retreat would be stalled by the single causeway crossing back over the morass. A superior British army could destroy the American force easily. Lee would not risk his advance troops. They waited about an hour while Lee reconnoitered himself and sought other sources to confirm or deny Dickinson's report on the whereabouts of the British troops. Clearly, Lee was receiving conflicting reports, but he hesitated to deny Dickinson's report for fear of the difficult terrain. Finally, he convinced himself to march off again. But—after some time, and more

conflicting reports—Lee stopped a second time. In fact, each observer reporting to Lee saw the British activity that morning differently, although all of the
reports had some truth to them. Clinton moved the Hessians and his baggage
train out of Freehold at first light, and Cornwallis followed just hours later,
confirming the reports that the British were on the move. But Clinton
remained in place with 1,500 men, confirming reports that the British had not
left Freehold. And, sometime before noon, Clinton called back a portion of
Cornwallis's detachment, substantially increasing the strength of the force
directly in front of the Americans.

June 28, 1778, was one of the hottest days of the year. The temperature
reached ninety degrees well before noon on this day, and the Americans were
standing or marching, often at a rapid pace, in the open sun. The heat and the
blazing sun played a crucial role throughout the day as men became parched
and exhausted, and scores of men and horses died from the elements. Even
though the Americans had not seen any action as of yet, they had been
exposed and on the road for more than four hours.

Sometime before noon, those units in the American front could hear
artillery and skirmishing on their right near Monmouth Courthouse.
Apparently a small number of Dickinson's militia had encountered some
British light horse. The result was insignificant for either side but delayed
Lee's advance further. Charles Lee then spread his troops across the field. He
moved two experienced units under Colonel Richard Butler and Jackson to
the front and asked General Wayne to come forward to take command of this
advance corps. He placed the Marquis de Lafayette on the right near the
Courthouse with the majority of the force. General Maxwell commanded the
troops in the rear. Another delay occurred at this point when it was discovered that Jackson's men had insufficient cartridges. Collections had to be
taken from troops in their rear. Again, why was this detail left to the morning
of the battle and until after the unit was placed in the advance? These
advanced troops now crossed the eastern morass with Butler on the far left.
Lieutenant Colonel Eleazer Oswald brought two cannon across the eastern
morass in support, but his ammunition wagon had to stay behind because of
the terrain. At about this time, Lee rushed some of his troops further back
down the road they had just traveled to meet the possibility that Clinton
would try to envelop him along an intersecting road. Dickinson had raised
this concern, but it proved to be a false alarm.

Butler's men and Jackson's men could now see the British in front of them.
They estimated the force at about 1,500 light horse and infantry and saw that
they were in motion. A small force of American light horse appeared before
the British and prompted a direct assault from the much larger force of

British light horse. This was the start of the Battle of Monmouth. The American light horse retreated behind Butler's men who stood firm and waited for the British to get close before unleashing a barrage of fire. The British light horse broke before the fire and retreated back to their lines. Their chaotic run broke the British infantry to their rear as well. Wayne, in command of the advanced forces, wanted more men brought up so that he could pursue the fleeing British. But Lee hesitated.

Lee was still uncertain about the strength of British force in front of him, but he sensed that one part of that force was separated from the main body, off to the American left. In addition, one of his aides, Captain Edwards, had just come back from a review of the road leading off to the left—by Forman's Mills—and advised Lee that the road was clear, passable, and led behind the detachment of the enemy that Lee could see on the British right. Lee saw an opportunity to sweep around and take the separated British force by surprise. He immediately began to move the bulk of his men to the far left and up this road. He sent word to the Marquis de Lafayette to prepare to move his men up the road to the left and to Wayne to hold back. Lee wanted to avoid pushing the British in front of Wayne into the detachment he sought to capture or to solicit a British charge on Wayne's small force. He sent word to Brigadier General Scott, to take up a position on the American left in a woods, and to hold firm. Lee went to the front of his troops and began marching them to the left of Scott's unit, up the road to victory. He lingered just long enough to send a message to George Washington that a stunning victory might soon be in his grasp.

But unfortunately for Charles Lee, his plans soon fell apart. His movement was not as swift as he intended, and the element of surprise was passing him by. He marched his force one and a half miles and arrived near to the British position at about one o'clock. Lee arrayed his troops defensively and rode forward with the Marquis de Lafayette to assess the situation. Although Clinton began the morning with about 1,500 troops immediately in front of the oncoming Americans and some of them slightly separated to his right, he realized that he needed a larger force and, sometime before noon, called back General Cornwallis from his march up the road leading away from the action. Three brigades of Guards and a unit of Knyphausen's light dragoons were returning as Lee approached. Rather than facing a rear guard of 500 to 1,000 men, Lee could see the combined force gathering at Briar Hill to his east. At about the same time, Clinton recognized that the American right was unprotected and began moving a portion of his men from Briar Hill to Monmouth Courthouse. Lee knew immediately that his pincer movement would not now work and that he faced a possible disaster if Clinton could flank his troops on the opposite side of the field. Lee took the main body of the troops with him back around and behind the eastern morass, but sent Lafayette with three regiments across the front of the eastern morass to the American right.

As Lee repositioned back to the American center, he could see men on the far side of the eastern morass moving back over the morass in retreat. He could not determine who, if anyone, gave an order to retreat. Oswald was also moving his two cannon back over the morass. His shot was finished, and he found his guns and his men unprotected on both sides. At about this time, Lee learned as well that Scott was no longer on the American left. Lee's aides could not find and never reached Scott with orders to stand firm. He had disappeared. Scott had advised General Maxwell to retreat as well. Wayne, frustrated that he could not follow up the recoil of the British light horse, saw the movement on his left and decided that his position in the front was no longer tenable. The American right, which could have been supported by Morgan's men, had been exposed most of the morning because Morgan never arrived for the fight. At about this point, a messenger from Colonel Morgan reached Wayne, now west of the morass but still east of Lee. Morgan could hear the fighting and wanted to know if he was needed. Wayne, disgruntled with Lee's inaction, apparently thought that Morgan would be of little help in the retreat of Lee's troops and left Morgan to his own counsel. By this time Wayne had stopped communicating with Lee and did not send Morgan's messenger to Lee. Morgan never entered the fight. With the departure of Scott's, Maxwell's, and Wayne's men, the Marquis found his left uncovered. He could see men moving back on his left and Clinton advancing on his right. Although Lafayette could find no source for the order to retreat, he soon determined that he had no choice but to retreat as well. Exposed on both sides, he risked being enveloped. When the Marquis fell upon Charles Lee as his troops moved back, he explained his decision, and Lee concurred that he made the right move.

Charles Lee now found himself in between the several morasses that crisscrossed the field, unclear of the whereabouts of General Scott and his men, and watching the mass of his force move backward onto an untenable position. He could not know that some of the retreating forces were already behind him, over the bridge and behind the western morass, making their way back to Englishtown. Lee began a review of the area to find a suitable geography to protect his men. At first he thought he could make a stand at the village of Freehold, but the few houses offered little or no protection. A local militia man, Peter Wyckoff, appeared on the battlefield at this point to offer his help with the terrain. He spoke with Lee and pointed out several possible locations, none of which appealed to Lee. Instead, Lee concluded that his best defense could be made by moving his men further back and eventually to the heights on the other side of the western morass at his rear. He was attempting to make dispositions to achieve this end with the British troops now coming upon him on the American right.

WASHINGTON APPEARS ON THE FIELD

George Washington began the morning secure that his orders to attack the British at first chance would be carried out. Shortly after dawn he received the intelligence from Dickinson that he wanted—that the British were beginning to move from their encampment, justifying an attack on their rear guard. Later in the morning, Washington wrote to Congress announcing Lee's position and his orders to "attack their rear if possible." About noon he received word from Charles Lee that he expected to capture a British detachment without delay. Washington had roused his 6,000 men at about 5:00 A.M. and began the three-mile march to Englishtown to support Lee in whatever way he could. As Washington approached the action at about midday, therefore, he must have been in good spirits, expecting to find Lee's troops engaged. Instead, he came on a stream of men moving to the rear. His first encounter was with a young fifer who told him that the American force was in full retreat. Washington ordered the man arrested to stop the spread of such a story. But as he continued to move forward, he found more men falling back, and many in disarray. Obviously, his temperament must have changed as he now began looking for the general in command. Lee, in between the morasses regrouping his troops, did not see the stream of men behind him. His attention was to the east, as his own troops retreated in front of him with the British advancing behind them. His view of the retreat was decidedly different from Washington's view. He did not know the extent of the retreat and confessed at his court-martial that he was unaware that men in his command were streaming back to Englishtown across the *western* morass. Washington came upon Charles Lee as the general was trying to decide where to post his troops. Here was the making of the most dramatic confrontation of the war.

Washington crossed the rearward morass and rode up to Lee. Washington's appearance and evident bad temper clearly ruffled Lee. If the contemporaneous accounts of the event can be credited, Washington immediately demanded the meaning of the retreat. Lee stammered ("Sir, sir . . ."), either not hearing Washington or unable to fashion a quick response. According to two witnesses, and Lee himself, Washington said something to the effect of "if you had no intention of carrying out the attack, why did you take the command?"[19] Regaining some composure, Lee claimed that he had acted as necessary, owing to poor intelligence and the failure of subordinates to obey his orders. Nevertheless, he claimed he was in full command of his forces and that he was about to move his troops behind the rearward morass. Washington countermanded him. Lord Stirling and his troops, marching with Washington, were already falling into position on the knoll behind Lee. Washington wanted Wayne and Maxwell to remain in front to secure Stirling's movement. He then rode forward to reconnoiter for himself.

Charles Lee remained on the field and continued to give orders to the generals and subordinates around him. He understood that Washington's presence on the field relieved him of overall command, but he retained his rank and acted the part. Even so, one of his aides reminded him to be careful not to countermand the orders that Washington was giving to the same officers on the field. Washington returned to Lee after just a short interim, and it appears that his temper had cooled once he had a chance to see the situation at the front. The British were advancing fast. At this meeting, Washington specifically asked Lee to resume command and to secure the causeway over the rearward morass until the remainder of Washington's men came up and Wayne and Maxwell's men could make their way back across. Lee promised that he would be the last man across the bridge and, riding up at this moment, Alexander Hamilton declared that he would stand with Lee to the death.[20] Lee fulfilled his promise to Washington and eventually fell back after the last of the troops. At this point, Lee met Washington again, and Washington ordered him to move back to Englishtown to reassemble his troops. A short time later, Washington sent General von Steuben to perform this task and to relieve Lee for the day.

Lee's day on the field ended at this point, at about three o'clock. He had been up since early in the morning, moving about in the intense heat. The remainder of the battle proceeded without him.

Washington remained on the field for the rest of the day, moving from point to point, arranging and exhorting his men, often exposing himself to personal danger. The officers and men around him saw him clearly on the field, and appreciated his presence. Lafayette, a Washington devotee, exclaimed afterward that this was Washington's finest moment: "His presence stopped the retreat; his dispositions fixed the victory; his fine appearance on horseback, his calm courage roused to animation by the vexations of the morning, gave him the air best calculated to excite enthusiasm."[21] Washington ordered General Nathanael Greene, commanding the right wing of his forces, to move south from the Tennent Meeting House to cover the army's right flank. On executing this order, Greene noticed Comb's Hill on the southeast, one of the several places suggested by local resident Wyckoff to Lee at their meeting in the field earlier in the day. Comb's Hill was not easily accessible, and Lee had rejected it for that reason, but given some time and the cooperation of fresh troops, General Greene was able to lay down rails and moved four cannon to this eminence. From this height, he could severely harass the advancing British troops in front of the American line for the rest of the day. This battery, and another commanded by Lord Stirling on the north, proved crucial for the Americans as the fight unfolded.[22]

At this point, the British took the offensive and attempted to break the American lines, at one point crossing the west morass but without major success. The fighting and the artillery barrages, from both sides, were intense throughout the afternoon, with the two forces in continuous close contact all across the line, with the effort shifting from one point to another as the British attempted to break through. The Americans held firm, aided substantially by the batteries established by Greene and Stirling, and eventually Clinton moved his troops back to save them from the crossfire they faced with the morass in their front.

The heat of the day proved as devastating as cannon and musket shot, as many men and horses fell from heat stroke. By 6:00 P.M. both sides were exhausted, and the fighting ceased before daylight faded. The British withdrew from directly in front of the American position, and a counterattack ordered by Washington late in the day fizzled owing to the exhaustion of his troops. The opposing sides ended the fighting in place just yards apart from each other. By formal reporting, the Americans lost 72 dead and 161 wounded in the day's action; British losses were significantly greater, 207 dead (from battle injuries and heatstroke) and 170 wounded. Actual British losses were surely substantially higher than reported by Clinton (based simply on the numbers buried by the Americans the next day), and the British lost several hundred Hessians through desertion. The Hessians deserting during and after the battle joined the hundreds who had slipped away on the way to Monmouth, seeking to return to Philadelphia. But by all other measures, the fight had been at best a draw. Washington fully expected the action to pick up again at morning's light, and the Americans were ordered to sleep on their muskets. As Washington surveyed the situation at the end of the day, he believed that the Americans had held their own against the "flower of the British Army." He was proud of his troops and must have been satisfied that the days of training at Valley Forge over the winter had truly transformed the ragtag mass of men that had been the Continental Army into a dangerous fighting force. Washington expected that the next day would confirm his confidence in his army.

But Washington did not get the chance to continue the battle. Clinton wanted no more. His primary mission was to move his army and his baggage across New Jersey safely. He entertained the fight on the morning of June 28 because he had no choice if he was to protect his baggage train lumbering toward Sandy Hook. If he had obliged Washington for a fight in the hope that he could crush the Continental Army, the opportunity was lost. He would not be distracted further and refused Washington's invitation to resume the battle now that his baggage train was safely on its way. Over the course of the night, Clinton steadily and quietly withdrew his men from the field. Fires were maintained to deceive the Americans, and his withdrawal was efficiently and effectively carried out. When the Americans awoke on June 29, the British were gone. In his eagerness to complete his primary mission, Clinton left behind his dead on the field and the wounded who could not move with the rest of the troops.

Understandably, the two sides had different perspectives on the day's events. The Americans considered the ultimate outcome a victory. They alone remained on the field of battle, their losses substantially fewer than the British. Washington issued an order to his troops the day after the battle congratulating them on "the victory obtained over the arms of his Britannic Majesty."[23] The British, on the other hand, saw the action as relatively insignificant and a draw. The American army had not succeeded in routing the British and had not taken any ground from the British. As Clinton saw it, his men "took the position from which the enemy had been first driven, after they had quitted the plain . . . [and] I took advantage of the moonlight to rejoin Lieut. Gen. Knyphausen."[24] Indeed, the Americans ended the fighting in the same position where they started, behind the rearward morass in a defensive position. Clinton's baggage train was never in danger, and the vast majority of his fighting men reached New York City.

In addition to undercounting his dead and wounded, Clinton made an additional lapse in his formal report. Even though the general states that his retreat was conducted by the light of the moon, it was quickly noted that the moon set early that night and before the movement began. One patriot composed a ditty to commemorate the error:

> He forms his camp with great parade,
> While evening spreads the world in shade,
> Then still, like some endangered spark,
> Steals off on tiptoe in the dark,
> Yet writes his king in boasting tone.
> How grand he marched by light of moon.[25]

Some supporters of Charles Lee argue that all of Lee's actions on June 28 were defensible and, in fact, that his quick thinking saved the vanguard of Washington's army from annihilation and, perhaps, the main body of the army as well. Theodore Thayer based his 1976 book about Charles Lee—*The Making of a Scapegoat*—on this premise.[26] These advocates begin with the assumption that Clinton's forces would have overwhelmed the Americans given the opportunity and that only an effective withdrawal from a precarious position not of Lee's choosing prevented the disaster that Washington's flawed strategy had set in motion. Without question, the terrain favored the British on defense and presented the possibility of entrapment of the Americans between the morasses. And, without question, several of the American officers failed to follow orders or effectively control their units, ordering or allowing a retreat that Charles Lee did not order. But this analysis accepts the theory that Clinton's troops would have bested Lee's or Washington's troops and ignores the reality that the Americans were able to stand against the British as the advance troops did in the early fighting and as all of the Americans did, once organized, later in the day.

The alternative can also be argued, that had Lee attacked early in the morning, when Clinton did not have Cornwallis's returning troops in support, the Americans might have been able to destroy or capture the smaller British force. The defense of Lee as the commander in the field who saved the day also ignores Lee's failure to plan adequately and his inability to communicate with his officers once battlefield maneuvers began. Clearly, Lee suffered from poor intelligence and leadership among his subordinates, and he made the most of a deteriorating position by accepting the retreat and regrouping behind the eastern morass. But Lee's preparations for the day were inadequate and his initial movements haltingly slow and indecisive. Had he been prepared with a plan for action with advance units on the ready, he might have been able to catch Clinton without a strong enough force to respond vigorously. As with all discussions of the Battle of Monmouth, the end result becomes speculation. But by the early afternoon, Lee found himself in an untenable position between two morasses and his men in retreat. Lee could not prevent or slow the retreat—he simply accommodated the situation, hardly the actions of a commander responsible for saving the day.

As events unfolded, the Americans were able to make a formidable stand behind the western morass and stalled the British advance until dusk. Perhaps this was as much as the Americans could have expected on June 28, and surely the outcome fulfilled Washington's original gamble and game plan to prevent the British from passing through New Jersey unmolested. But as to Lee's claim that his decisive actions saved the day, it hardly stands up when what he did was accommodate a retreat that he did not order and could not control.

As the Americans awoke on the 29th to find the British gone from the field, good feelings began to spread throughout in the realization that the British had abandoned their position without a further fight. As the field commanders counted the wounded and the dead, the Americans realized that they had inflicted much greater losses than they incurred. As they recalled the events of the previous day, the officers and men felt a confidence in themselves and in their commander, George Washington, who came onto the battlefield to find his forces in disarray. Washington's courage and his ability to rally the troops turned the tide. All involved had to feel good about the battle, with the single exception of Charles Lee. Lee resented Washington's remarks on the field, especially the questioning of his taking command if he had no intention to fight. Late in the afternoon of the 28th, before he retired, Lee had confronted Washington on this point, but Washington was too busy and in no mood to engage Lee. He simply rode away.

On the 29th, Lee had a choice. He could ignore Washington's upbraiding, keep his own counsel, and ride out the questions about his leadership in the good feelings that pervaded the aftermath of the battle. This would be difficult. Some of the officers, particularly Wayne and Scott, complained to Washington about Lee's lack of aggressiveness, and the comparisons with Washington's performance on the same field must have been galling to Lee as well.[27] Lee could have gone to meet with Washington. Perhaps he could explain the difficulties he faced from poor intelligence and officers who disobeyed his orders; perhaps he could offer a compliment to Washington on "their" victory; perhaps he could complain as well about the officers who failed *him*. Lee, instead, chose a different approach. He would express no humility and would seek no understanding or forgiveness. He would offer no congratulations to Washington or the men who fought under either of them the day before. No, Lee would attack his critics as always—with a scathing pen.

Immediately after the battle, Lee wrote the following letter to his commander in chief:

> Sir,—From the knowledge I have of your Excellency's character, I must conclude that nothing but the misinformation of some very stupid person, or misrepresentation of some very wicked person, could have occasioned you making use of so very singular expressions as you did on my coming up to the ground where you had taken post; they imply'd that I was guilty either of disobedience of orders, of want of conduct, or want of courage; your Excellency will, therefore, infinitely oblige me by letting me know on

which of these articles you ground your charge, that I may prepare for my justification, which, I have the happiness to be confident, I can do to the army, to the Congress, to America, and to the world in general. Your Excellency must give me leave to observe that neither yourself nor those about your person cou'd, from your situation, be in the least judges of the merits or demerits of our manoeuvres; and, to speak with a becoming pride, I can assert, that to these manoeuvres, the success of the day was entirely owing. I can boldly say, that had we remained on the first ground, or had we advanc'd, or had the retreat been conducted in a manner different from what it was, this whole army, and the interest of America, would have risk'd being sacrificed. I ever had, (and hope shall ever have) the greatest respect and veneration for General Washington; I think him endow'd with many great and good qualities; but in this instance, I must pronounce that he has been guilty of an act of cruel injustice towards a man who certainly has some pretensions to the regard of every servant of this country; and, I think, Sir, I have a right to demand some reparation for the injury committed, and, unless I can obtain it, I must, in justice to myself, when this campaign is closed (which I believe will close the war), retire from a service at the head of which is placed a man capable of offering such injuries; but, at the same time, in justice to you, I must repeat, that I from my soul believe, that it was not a motion of your breast, but instigated by some of those dirty earwigs who will forever insinuate themselves near persons of high office; for I really am convinced, that when General Washington acts for himself no man in his army will have reason to complain of injustice or indecorum.

I am, Sir, and hope I ever shall have reason to continue, Your most sincerely devoted, humble servant,

Charles Lee[28]

Charles Lee misdated the letter as "July 1, 1778" and sent a second letter apologizing for the error. As if his condemnation of "those dirty earwigs who will forever insinuate themselves near persons of high office" was not enough, this second letter contains this fascinating sentence: "I trust the temporary power of office, and the tinsel dignity attending it, will not be able, by all the mists that they can raise, to offiscate the bright rays of truth; in the meantime, your Excellency can have no objection to my retiring from the army."[29]

Washington replied three days later, more succinctly, less floridly, but in kind:

Sir:

I received your letter (dated, through mistake, the 1st of July) expressed, as I conceive, in terms highly improper. I am not conscious of having made use of any very singular expressions at the time of my meeting you, as you intimate. What I recollect to have said, was dictated by duty, and warranted by the occasion. As soon as circumstances will permit, you shall have an opportunity either of justifying yourself to the army, to Congress, to America, and to the world in general; or of convincing them that you were guilty of a breach of orders, and of misbehaviour before the enemy, on the 28th inst., in not attacking them as you had been directed, and in making an unnecessary, disorderly, and shameful retreat.

I am Sir, your most obedient Servant,

G° WASHINGTON[30]

Lee could not let Washington have the last word, however, and responded immediately:

Sir,

Since I had the honour of addressing my letter by Colonel Fitzgerald to your Excellency, I have reflected on both your situation and mine; and beg leave to observe, that it will be for our mutual convenience, that a Court of Enquiry should be immediately ordered; but I could wish it might be a Court Martial: for, if the affair is drawn into length, it may be difficult to collect the necessary evidences, and perhaps might bring on a paper war betwixt the adherents to both parties, which may occasion some disagreeable feuds on the Continent; for all are not my friends, nor all your admirers. I must entreat, therefore, from your love of justice, that you immediately exhibit your charge; and that on the first halt, I may be brought to a tryal, and am, Sir,

Your most obedient Humble Servant

CHARLES LEE[31]

This exchange of letters at the end of June 1778 sealed Lee's fate.

CHAPTER 11

COURT-MARTIAL

Washington, still glowing from the events of June 28 and engaged in writing to the Congress to announce his victory, had to take time to deal with this sticky personnel issue. Charles Lee would not sit quietly and wait for Washington to assess the situation. His impertinent letter demanded a response. Nor would Washington's other officers stand by.

Generals Wayne and Scott barely waited for the dust to settle on the field before writing to Washington to explain their actions that morning and to excoriate Lee: "We have taken the liberty of stating these facts, in order to convince the world that our retreat from the Court House was not occasioned by the want of numbers, position, or wishes of both officers and men to maintain that post. We also beg leave to mention, that no plan of attack was ever communicated to us, or notice of a retreat, until it had taken place in our rear, as we supposed by General Lee's order."[1] Washington may have preferred, now that his temper had cooled, to let the issues of conduct on the field settle for some time before he had to take any action. But his subordinates would not let the issue lie for that long. Lee forced Washington's hand and gave Washington an easy solution. In his July 1 report of the battle to the Congress, Washington deftly walked away from the controversy: "The peculiar situation of Gen. Lee at this time, requires that I should say nothing of his conduct. He is now in arrest. The charges against him, with such sentence as the court-martial may decree in his case, shall be transmitted, for the approbation of disapprobation of congress, as soon as it shall have passed."[2]

THE COURT-MARTIAL OF MAJOR GENERAL CHARLES LEE

Charles Lee got what he sought from Washington—a court-martial to determine whether his conduct on June 28 was appropriate. But the language of the charges must have stunned him:

> First: For disobedience of orders, in not attacking the enemy on the 28th
> of June, agreeable to repeated instructions.
> Secondly: For misbehaviour before the enemy on the same day, by
> making an *unnecessary, disorderly, and shameful retreat.*
> Thirdly: For disrespect to the Commander-in-Chief, in two letters dated
> the 1st of July and the 28th of June.[3]

The proceedings started almost immediately, on July 1. The first entry is made at Spotswood, New Jersey, but testimony did not begin until July 4 at New Brunswick. The court met on and off over the next two months at various locations, moving with the army as necessary. By accepting Lee's demand, Washington was able to dissociate himself from any further discussion of the events of that day. Washington's only comment prior to the proceedings can be found in a letter to his brother John Augustine, characterizing Lee's actions as "strange" and expressing a noncommittal attitude as to whether the retreat was "by his order, or from other causes."[4]

Washington appointed Lord Stirling as presiding officer and twelve officers—four brigadier generals and eight colonels—as the judges.[5] Lord Stirling, a major general, was a respected officer in the Continental Army. He began the war by recruiting a company of New Jersey militia and serving as colonel of the unit. Congress commissioned Lord Stirling as a brigadier general in the Continental Army in March 1776, and he fought alongside Washington at Long Island, Trenton, Brandywine, and Germantown before Monmouth. His appellation came from a disputed claim to a Scottish title, the Earl of Stirling. He based his claim to the title on the fact that he was the senior male descendant of the last holder of this vacant knighthood. The House of Lords rejected his claim, and the land grants in America that would have gone with it, but Stirling refused to accept their judgment and kept the title for the rest of his life. Born in New York City in 1726 as William Alexander, his title belied his allegiance. He had an estate at Basking Ridge in New Jersey and was connected to the first governor of the state, William Livingston, by marriage to his sister. Lord Stirling committed himself to the American cause early in the dispute and stepped up immediately once the fighting began. He served through the end of the war with distinction as one of several serviceable generals that George Washington knew he could rely on. Unfortunately, he died in 1783, just before the end of the war.

Lord Stirling may have been the perfect choice for this task. Although he fought at Monmouth, he was traveling with Washington and did not appear on the field until after the events leading to the court-martial had occurred, so he was close to the action but not part of the controversies in question. Another advantage was his loyalty to Washington, which never came into question throughout the war. He held the respect of all of the officers in the army, as demonstrated by their willingness to address him as "Lord Stirling" even as they joined in fighting the British. Coincidentally, Lord Stirling had been captured by the British on Long Island (on the battlefield) in 1776 and later exchanged. And perhaps Washington saw a political advantage, or irony, in placing the British-titled officer as presiding officer at the trial of a former British officer.

Once the proceedings started, testimony was taken over twenty-nine days in six different locations as the army moved from place to place, but mostly in New Brunswick, New Jersey, and North Castle, New York. More than thirty witnesses were called, including all of the major players in the drama of June 28, with the notable exceptions of General Philemon Dickinson of the New Jersey militia and Colonel Daniel Morgan. Much of the testimony is repetitious, some contradictory, or confusing, and much more is irrelevant to the charges. Reading through the transcript generates the feeling that Charles Lee reveled in the opportunity to present his case and to demonstrate his military knowledge, his perceptions, and the certainty of his position. He appears to have accepted the proceedings as drama and saw himself not only as the center of the action but as the smartest man in the play. Only at the end, when Lee provided a summary of his defense, can a reader of the transcript detect the slightest self-doubt or regret. That defense runs thirty-three printed pages, delivered on August 9, 1778, at North Castle. As in most such proceedings, some obvious questions are left unasked and others, if asked, are left without satisfactory answers. But much of the writing about the Battle of Monmouth and the actions of Charles Lee has been gleaned from the transcript of the testimony and Lee's impassioned defense at the end.

On the first charge, the court and Lee spent considerable effort trying to demonstrate whether Washington's orders to attack were positive or preemptory. Lee fell back on the claim that no order to attack can be preemptory when the terrain is uncertain, the location of the enemy is uncertain, and the enemy's strength is uncertain. But Lee's defense sounds hollow as one officer after another testified that they understood Washington clearly, starting with the first witness on the first day of testimony. Lee asked Brigadier General Scott directly whether the orders were to attack "at all events, whatever might be their situation or their force, whether, for instance, it consisted of such a body as General's Washington's intelligence announced, that is, a slight covering party, or whether of the greater part of the flower of their troops, as it turned out, or whether of the whole body of the British army?" Scott did not flinch: "I do not know what intelligence General Washington had, but I understood that we were to have attacked the enemy at all events." Lee asked if he [Lee] was "absolutely enjoined, by my instructions, to march forward?" Scott responded, "I conceived you were to proceed on, and wherever you met the enemy to take the earliest opportunity to attack them."[6]

Lee pressed the same argument with the other officers on the ground: Was he lacking in all maneuverability and enjoined to attack? Asked the same question as Scott, Anthony Wayne gave the same answer, with an elaboration that could not help Lee: "I understood that we were to attack the enemy on their march, at all events, and that General Washington would be near us to support us with the main army."[7] Neither Scott nor Wayne testified that Washington gave a "positive" order to attack, but the court may have had difficulty distinguishing a positive order from the understanding that Lee should attack "at all events."

Considerable effort was also spent by Lee in eliciting the perception of the various officers on the strength of the enemy. He apparently wanted to demonstrate that the British force was substantially larger than most of the officers perceived, but his questioning on this subject just demonstrated a consensus among the officers that the British force, at first sight, was between 1,500 and 2,000 men, including cavalry. In fact, in his summary, he agrees that these early observations were correct. One witness, "Doctor M'Henry," testified that Lee told him to inform General Washington that "the rear of the enemy was composed of fifteen hundred to two thousand" as Lee was beginning to make his movement to the left to cut off a separated unit. Only when Lee appeared on the left and had "a full view of the ground" did he see greater numbers: "The plain was extensive, and to me appeared unembarrassed; their force was considerably larger than I had been taught to expect; a column of artillery, with a strong covering party, both horse and foot, presented themselves in the centre of the plain, another much larger appear'd directing their course toward the Court-house on our right."[8] Surely, Lee was viewing the return of Cornwallis with his troops close to midday. Even so, he offers no numbers himself. Instead, he moves on immediately to the concern, legitimately felt, that the British were attempting to turn the American right.

Some third-party testimony suggests that Lee discovered the British cavalry to be so numerous as to make his position untenable, but Lee fails to make this claim through testimony or in his summary. He comes back to the issue of numbers a second time and again fails to give specifics, stating only his conviction later in the day of "their whole army, at least their whole flying army, being in the field."[9] We now know that both the initial reports to Lee and Lee's own observations may have been correct: although General Clinton had only 1,500 troops at the early part of the day aligned against Lee, his numbers increased considerably when Cornwallis returned from his movement up the road. But the members of the court-martial did not have this information, only the consensus testimony that the British numbered just 1,500 to 2,000 at the beginning of the fight.[10] All of Lee's efforts on this subject could not have helped his case and may have hurt him. Lee claimed that he had only 1,500 effective men under his command, but the court knew well that he started the day with 5,000 men at his disposal.

The issue of command on the field also arose in the proceedings. Without question, the testimony reveals a clear lack of lines of communication between Lee and his officers and units. Despite his dilatory tactics on the 28th, Lee did put several units in a position to attack. Butler's unit and Jackson's unit, under the leadership of Wayne, were directly across from the British, but not until close to noon and with no specific orders from Lee to attack. The fighting started only when the British light horse charged the Americans. Rather than follow up the repulse of the light horse by charging the retreating British, as Wayne wanted, Lee directed Wayne to hold back while Lee pursued a flanking movement on the left. Wayne's impulse might have resulted in disaster, because of the large force opposing him, but Lee's alternative maneuver proved fruitless.

Lee never disputed his failure to attack. He defended the charge by claiming his orders were not preemptory and by listing the reasons why an attack was not advisable. He maneuvered some units into position to attack, he marched a major part of the command to the left with the intention to attack, and troops under his command fought once attacked by the British light horse, but Charles Lee never gave an order to attack. If the members of the court-martial panel believed Washington's orders to be preemptory, Lee was guilty of failing to obey those orders. If they accepted Charles Lee's claim that his orders were not preemptory, they would have to accept his reasons for not attacking a force that all agreed was no larger than his own force and, perhaps, smaller.

Throughout the trial, Lee returned to a singular line of defense, that the unknown terrain and the unknown location and the unknown strength of the enemy hampered his movements and limited his options. He used this argument to support his contention that an attack would have been foolhardy and to demonstrate that his orders must have been discretionary. And yet, this approach placed Lee in the untenable position of needing to explain why he failed to prepare for the battle the night before and failed to develop a plan for attack. He never addressed these issues, even though his critics did. In their letter, cited above, Generals Scott and Wayne make the claim that "no plan of attack was ever communicated to us," putting this issue directly in contention. Were Lee's actions excusable because of his lack of intelligence, or were his actions condemnable because of his failure to overcome this lack of intelligence? Months later, Lee realized the vulnerability that this conundrum imparted to his argument and argued in the press that he was placed in this position by *Washington's* failure to prepare adequately.

The testimony on the second charge—that Lee made "an unnecessary, disorderly, and shameful retreat"—favors Lee. No one disputed that Lee's troops retreated, and some of the testimony suggested that the retreat was, indeed, disorderly. No one testified, however, that Charles Lee ordered the retreat. Lee admitted that he did not have the ability to stop the retreat once it began and instead used his powers to regroup his troops in a better and defensible position. It appears from the transcript that some of the men and their officers simply were spent from marching, countermarching, and sitting in the sun on this one hundred–degree day and had had enough by noon. Parched and exhausted, men started to move to the rear, and the poor lines of communication could not stop the movement before it became too late. It appears that Lee was genuinely horrified by the retreat, once he recognized what was happening. He simply lacked the leadership authority or ability to do anything about it. Lee accepted the event because he understood that the troops left on the front were vulnerable and, lacking the numbers to hold their ground, would become ensnarled in the morass behind them. Better to let them move back to a safer and more defensible position than leave them to be lost. What Lee did not know, however, was that some of the troops were already over the morass and were well behind him on their way to Englishtown, miles away. Ironically, some of those men were under the command of Brigadier General Scott, who may have been the person responsible for the retreat in the first instance. The testimony clearly demonstrated that Scott abandoned the vanguard position on the left of the American line when he perceived that the troops to his right were retreating (or when Oswald moved his spent and unprotected artillery and men to the rear) and then convinced General Maxwell to join him. The troops on his right may have been moving, but no other witness testified that these troops were moving to the rear.

On the third charge, no testimony was taken. The letters Lee wrote speak for themselves. Lee offered no credible defense for these shameful missives other than his pique at being criticized for what he saw as a brilliant series of actions on his part. He defended his words as no more or no less than what would be written by any military man slandered when he expected to be praised. He awaited Washington's apology after his first letter, and when it did not arrive, he felt the need to express his outrage: "but when, instead of the apology I had flattered myself with, these thundering charges were brought against me, comprehending the blackest military crimes of the whole black catalogue, I was more than confounded, I was thrown into a stupor, my whole faculties were for a time benumm'd."[11] Lee makes an important point at the end of this defense, however, and a point often overlooked: his perception and Washington's perception just prior to their fateful meeting on the Monmouth battlefield, were entirely different:

> But here I must, in justice to His Excellency, observe, that when I imputed his conduct towards me, to misrepresentation and misinformation, I was ignorant of a third circumstance. I was ignorant of it at the time I wrote those letters, and I protest solemnly, I was ignorant or it till long after this Court-Martial sat; I mean the filing off of part of the troops of my detachment beyond the eminence proposed for my position; these the General met in his march from English-Town, and hastily concluded, I must be void of all attention; but that this was contrary to my intention and orders has been repeatedly observed, and is what I think myself by no means responsible, for the reasons already given.[12]

It appears from these remarks that even Charles Lee himself understood his letters to be ill-conceived and disrespectful, given all the circumstances.

On August 12, the court issued its opinion: Guilty on all three counts. The only deference given to Charles Lee was the rewording of the second charge from the original—"For misbehaviour before the enemy on the same day, by making an unnecessary, disorderly, and *shameful* retreat"—to "by making an unnecessary, *and in some few instances*, a disorderly retreat." The sentence: suspension from command for a term of twelve months.

The judgment of the court-martial itself created a controversy. Did the punishment fit the crime? If, indeed, Charles Lee was guilty of disobeying direct orders, ordering a disorderly retreat, and disrespecting his commanding officer, would a twelve-month suspension be a sufficient penalty? Most observers see the result as unbalanced and suspect that the officers sitting in judgment felt obliged to find Lee guilty but understood that the evidence adduced at the trial did not support the charges. If all three charges were sustained by the evidence, the sentence appears extraordinarily light. The officers on the panel surely understood this contradiction. But Lee made a critical error in challenging George Washington in such a direct and brutal manner. Washington picked the officers to sit on the court-martial board, and they could not allow the insult to their commander, who they all believed had saved the day and the army at Monmouth, go unpunished. Perhaps they understood the respect that many inside and outside of the army held for Lee's military experience and that his friends in the Congress would continue to support him. Their judgment on Lee's actions saved face for George Washington; the sentence provided Lee with the chance for redemption, but only after a cooling-off period.

Charles Lee wanted nothing to do with redemption. He exploded in vitriol at the verdict and his fate, but he was spitting in the wind. Even his friends felt uncomfortable in defending him. After all, the Americans had just achieved what all considered a great victory. Did it serve a purpose to denigrate the commander in chief and the person everyone—military and civilian— credited for the victory? Lee chose bad ground for a fight and pursued poor tactics: a direct personal assault on George Washington. He was destined to lose this political battle and could find few allies to stand with him in what everyone could see as a losing effort. Reading between the lines, one can perceive that even his friends wanted time to pass and tempers to cool before moving to his assistance. But not Lee. He would not bide his time and seek redemption. He wanted his vindication, and he wanted it immediately.

Once again, an observer with the knowledge of Lee's dealings in New York City just one year earlier has to wonder at his actions at Monmouth and his response to Washington's rebuke. It could be that Washington's question on the battlefield—"if you had no intention of carrying out the attack, why did you take the command?"—terrified him because it suggested that he had lost his willingness to fight the British and would eventually lead to a discovery of his betrayal. The intensity of his reaction can then be laid to a well-conceived defense of his honor, a high-stakes and dangerous political game that would preclude that question being pursued any further. Or it may just be that Lee misunderstood the precariousness of his position. Could it be that he did not perceive his treacherous actions in New York City in 1777 as harmful to the United States? Or, was his ego so great that he saw himself as someone above the petty need to take sides in the fight? The disclosure of "Mr. Lee's Plan" at any time after the close of the Battle of Monmouth would most surely have led to his trial for treason and, most likely, hanging.

More likely, Lee had made a reasoned determination in early 1777 that England would win the war and that he wanted to be on the winning side in the end. At that point, he also may have perceived his life to be in danger if tried for treason in Great Britain. The military plan that he submitted to the British was an attempt to shift his alliance. Its tepid, if not cold, reception and his removal from comfortable confines in New York City to a prison ship in the harbor in June must have tempered the expectation that his mother country would welcome him home. The negotiations for his exchange late in the year put him in the difficult position of being compromised on both sides. His meeting with Howe in Philadelphia in April may have been an attempt to resolve his conflict, but to no apparent effect. Surely, his frantic efforts in early 1778 to negotiate a peace by personal appeals to Congress reflect an understanding of his tenuous position. Forced back to the American side without any commitment from the British, Lee tried to play the part he was in, albeit poorly. After Monmouth, he had no standing with either side.

The Verdict of Congress

In the immediate aftermath of the court-martial, Lee pinned his hopes for vindication on the Continental Congress. His standing among political men always ranked high, and he had advocates inside and outside of the Congress. A favorable vote rejecting the findings of the court-martial would suffice. Lee may not have desired a quick return to the army, but at least he could rehabilitate his name and choose his time and place for a return, if that would be his desire. But congressional vindication would not be easy to achieve. Most Americans viewed the Battle of Monmouth as an American victory, and politicians understood that hashing over who deserved the day's laurels would only diminish the value of the outcome both domestically and in foreign courts. In addition, most of the officers on the field that day not only believed Washington to be the hero but also understood that Lee had forfeited his usefulness to the army by his conduct on the field and afterward. Lee had difficulty finding advocates.

Among others, Lee turned to his strongest allies, Dr. Benjamin Rush and Richard Henry Lee. Rush was not admirer of Washington, but even he seemed to back away from full support of Lee. On August 13, Lee expressed exasperation in response to a letter from Rush "of no date and sign'd with no name." Lee offered to provide proof of his conduct notwithstanding Rush's reluctance to embrace his cause because "[y]ou tell me gravely that you still believe me honest." At the end of this letter, Lee foretells his approach to this fight with a typical rhetorical flourish: "I shall not trouble you with any detail on this subject—but be assured of this—that G. Washington saw, knew, and was almost as little concern'd in the affair of the 28th as he was in the battle of Philippi."[13] Notwithstanding the impropriety of his own conduct, Lee exhibited either a military or emotional blindness in discounting Washington's exploits that day. This attitude only made his chances of finding advocates more difficult. At the end of his court-martial, with the outcome still uncertain, Charles Lee almost sounded apologetic for his tirade against Washington immediately after the battle. But now, the contest was on, and he set Washington up as the villain of the piece, as was always his approach in a paper fight. A month later, Lee's attacks were full throttle in a letter to Richard Henry Lee: "for what sort of people have I sacrificed every consideration—what a composition of false wickedness and folly! to be ruined for giving victory to a man whose head was never intended for a sprig of laurels!"[14]

One of Lee's aides on the day of the battle, Evan Edwards, was in Philadelphia in August calling on congressmen to tell Lee's version of the events of June 28. And Lee bolstered his case at about this time by producing a letter from Major John Clark, an intermediary that day between the divided American forces. Clark confirmed that Lee's orders from George Washington were discretionary and that some of Lee's subordinates failed to follow orders. Clark had not been called to testify at the court-martial, but even so, his recollections deal with the time frame when Lee had already fallen back behind the easterly morass, sometime after noon, and offered little new to the case.[15] One man who was on the field that day who does appear to have taken up Lee's cause was Colonel Aaron Burr. Lee wrote a letter to Burr in October that starts this way: "As you are so kind as to interest yourself so warmly in my favor, I cannot resist the temptation of writing you a few lines."[16] Tellingly, at about the same time, Lee wrote to Benjamin Rush, who apparently was still not in his camp: "I find you are not thoroughly perswaded of the propriety of my Conduct on the 29th of June."[17]

Without question, Lee's lobbying had some effect. Joseph Reed, the president of Pennsylvania and a delegate to the Congress in 1778, wrote a private letter to General Nathanael Greene to report that Lee "is making his Court, & I believe successfully to the same Interests, at least if we may judge from personal civilities and attention." This is the same Reed who, as adjutant to Washington in 1776 questioned Washington's abilities and solicited Lee as a possible replacement, only to be discovered after the fact by Washington. But Reed doubted Lee's innocence at Monmouth and related that after his discussion with Lee they parted "mutually unconvinced," but not before Reed gave Lee some sound advice that Lee ignored: "I only added one Piece of Advise to him to forbear any Reflections upon the Commander in-chief, of whom for the first time I have heard Slander on his private Character."[18]

Lee's temperament could not keep him from his attacks on Washington, but as the weeks passed, his approach to his defense changed, if not in full, at least in nuance. In a "Vindication to the Public" published in December, Lee moves the question of whether he should have attacked from his movements *early* on the morning of the 28th to his position between the morasses *later* in the day. This shift in timing dovetails nicely with the letter of support Lee received from Major John Clark several months earlier, as mentioned above. In addition, Lee makes the outlandish claim that his movements that day were deliberate and designed to lure the British into a precarious position. In this telling, Lee lured the British westward across the easterly morass: "by drawing them over all the ravines, they were as much in *our* power; besides, it must occur to every man who is not destitute of common reason, that the further they were from their ships and the heights of Middletown, the point of their security, the more they were (to use the military language) in the air."[19] According to Lee, this tactic was all the more brilliant because it neutralized the British advantage of cavalry, useless between the morasses.

By taking this new approach, Lee is able to reconstruct the entire day in lights favorable to his conduct. First, he turns his lack of preparation and reconnaissance on its head by declaring that the failure to obtain "a proper knowledge of the theatre of action" was someone else's fault (the unnamed George Washington). Second, he states that this failure prevented the "decisive blow [that] might have been struck" and dares to suggest that the outcome was a draw. He concludes that Washington failed to achieve the decisive victory that should have been: "Thus, in my opinion, was a most glorious opportunity lost; for what followed on both sides was only a distant, unmeaning, inefficacious cannonade; and what has been so magnificently stiled a pursuit, was no more than taking up the ground which the British troops could not possibly, and were not (their principle being retreat) interested to maintain."[20]

Lee answered one more criticism in this newly formed, and brilliant, exposition of his conduct at Monmouth. He denies wholeheartedly that he ever doubted the valor or the fighting ability of the American soldier. This is an important issue because it harkens back to Lee's initial bond with the American patriots in 1774. At that time, he bolstered the confidence of the Americans by denigrating the fighting ability of the British regulars and glorifying the effectiveness of Americans in the use of firearms and in standing up during the French and Indian War. In early 1778, however, Lee expressed doubts in conversations with members of Congress that the American soldier could challenge British regulars in open battle and suggested a defensive strategy to avoid the destruction of the army.[21] By December 1778, Lee must have realized that these comments were hurting his cause:

> P.S. A thousand wicked and low artifices, during my trial, were used to render me unpopular. One of the principal was, to throw out that I had endeavoured, on every occasion, to depreciate the American valour, and the character of their troops. There never was a more impudent falsehood; I appeal to my letters addressed to Mr. Burgoyne—to the whole tenor of

my conversation, both previous and subsequent to the commencement of the present war, and to all my publications. It is true, I have often lamented, as to me it appears, the defective constitution of the army; but I have ever had the highest opinion of the courage and other good qualities of the Americans as soldiers; and the proofs that my opinion was just, are numerous and substantial.[22]

But another matter appears to have eluded Lee. In a letter to the president of the Continental Congress dated October 16, Lee went to pains to establish the correct dates for his letters to Washington after the Battle of Monmouth. He obviously did not recognize that the most damning charges against him—the reason why even his friends were reluctant to return him to the army—were his own words. The politicians in Philadelphia surely understood that a vindication could put Lee back in the chain of command under the officer he had vilified on June 29 and continued to disparage to everyone he spoke with since that day.

Unfortunately for Lee, his revised defense fell on deaf ears. Congress confirmed the findings of the court-martial on December 5, 1778. Lee's continued efforts in person, in letters and in the press, replete with subtle and not-so-subtle criticisms of George Washington, did, however, finally prompt a personal response from George Washington, who had studiously avoided any public discussion of Lee's case. In a letter to Joseph Reed, his former adjutant, on December 12—*after* the confirmation of the court-martial verdict— Washington refers specifically to Lee's printed defense and exclaims that Lee has "most barefacedly misrepresented the facts in some places, and thrown out insinuations in others that have not the smallest foundation in truth."[23] Washington's exasperation with Lee's antics cannot be denied:

> It became a part of General Lee's plan, from the moment of his arrest (though it was an event solicited by himself,) to have the world believe that he was a persecuted man, and that party was at the bottom of it. But however convenient for his purpose to establish this doctrine, I defy him or the most zealous partisans to adduce a simple instance in proof of it, unless bringing him to trial at his own request is considered in this light. I can do no more; I will defy any man out of my own family to say that I ever mentioned his name after his trial commenced, if it was be avoided; and, when it was not, if I have not studiously declined expressing any sentiment of him or his behaviour. . . . His temper and plans were too versatile and violent to attract my admiration: and that I have escaped the venom of his tongue and pen so long, is more to be wondered at than applauded; as it is a favour, that no officer under whose immediate commands he ever served has the happiness (if happiness can thus be denominated) of boasting.[24]

It appears from the last sentence quoted above that Washington had a good take on Charles Lee's temperament and modus operandi.

Lee's December 1778 diatribe and, perhaps, the vote by Congress, also unleashed those who admired George Washington to take action. Lee received at least three personal challenges within the next thirty days: first from Baron von Steuben (in French: "Vous m'avez offense—je vous en demande Raison") who objected to Lee's characterization of him as a spectator to the events at Monmouth;[25] second, from John Laurens, an aide-de-camp of Washington, bristling at the charges raised by Lee against his revered commander; and third, from General Anthony Wayne. Alexander Hamilton, whose life would be ended by a duel twenty-five years later, figured in two of these encounters. He corresponded with Steuben after Lee was able to deflect the baron by a letter of apology, and he sneered at Lee's facility to avoid the encounter. Hamilton also served as Laurens's second in a duel that did take place on December 23, 1778, just on the outskirts of Philadelphia. After the first discharge of pistols, Lee declared himself wounded but wished to continue the affair. Considerable discussion took place between the combatants and their seconds (Evan Edwards for Lee), and the matter resolved without a second pacing. Lee's wound in the right side was not life-threatening, and a written "Narrative" signed by Hamilton and Edwards described the affair and the exchange between Lee and Laurens on the character and disparagement of George Washington. Lee stated that despite his comments about Washington's "military character" he "always esteemed General Washington as a man" and the two departed "with all the politeness, generosity, coolness and firmness that ought to characterize a transaction of this nature."[26]

Wayne's challenge came just after the new year. As with Steuben, Lee was able to avoid the confrontation with Wayne through artful correspondence. Lee dismissed any idea that he ever intended to criticize Wayne's actions, either in his testimony at the court-martial or in his "Vindication" published in *Dunlap's Press*. Lee was willing to fight Wayne, but asked that Wayne wait to read his further explanations, soon to be published. He added that he was befuddled that he was being persecuted even though he had "twice saved" the country from destruction.[27] In August 1779, Lee made sure to congratulate Wayne on his assault at Stony Point, New York, calling it "brilliant" not only "throughout the course of this war," but "one of the most brilliant I am acquainted with in history."[28]

CHAPTER 12

BITTERNESS, DESPAIR, AND DEATH

From the verdict of his court-martial on August 12, 1778, to his death on October 2, 1782, Charles Lee lived a lonely and bitter life. He devoted the totality of his being to two goals: proving himself innocent of the charges against him for his conduct at Monmouth and attempting to tear down the man he held responsible for his ignominy, George Washington. Lee failed on both counts.

"Queries"

After the Continental Congress confirmed the verdict of the court-martial in December 1778, Charles Lee spent much of his time and energy developing an elaborate exposition of his view of events, not just in June 1778, but from his first collaborations with the Americans: his rationale for entering the discourse over American freedom, his value to the Continental Army, and the wrongful prosecution for his actions at Monmouth. He developed his ideas as a sequence of "Queries" and urged his supporters, obviously beleaguered by his constant entreaties, to get these pieces into various newspapers around the country. He wanted his vindication, and he pursued it tirelessly. In the course of this pursuit, he found common ground with the "Tories" he persecuted in New York and elsewhere in 1776.

One of these efforts saw print in the *Maryland Journal and Baltimore Advertiser* on July 6, 1779, and starts philosophically: "1st. Whether George the First did not, on his accession to the throne of Great Britain, by making himself king of a party, instead of the whole nation, sow the seeds not only of the subversion of the liberties of the people, but of the ruin of the whole empire?" Titled "Some Queries, Political and Military, Humbly Offered to the Consideration of the Public," Lee's piece goes on for twenty-five articles and moves quickly to his new claim that the political establishment in America had devolved into the same form of tyranny as existed in Great Britain: "4th. Whether the present men in power, in this state, do not tread exactly in the steps of this pernicious ministry, by prescribing and disfranchising so large a proportion of citizens as those men whom they find in their interest to brand with the denomination of Tories?" He compares a "disfranshised citizen of Pennsylvania" to a subject of Morocco and declares the latter the better off because he is no worse than all about him whereas the Pennsylvanian is "a slave in the specious bosom of liberty."[1]

Lee then turns to George Washington and asks if he, indeed, is a great man. He raises Horatio Gates and Benedict Arnold above Washington in military success. Queries 14 and 15 suggest that Congress recalled Lee from Georgia in 1776 to salvage the Continental Army from the disasters that befell the army under Washington on Long Island, and Queries 15 to 19 question Washington's failure to abandon Fort Washington and his loss of Fort Lee shortly thereafter. Lee questioned the wisdom of maintaining the camp at Valley Forge: "22d. Whether our position at Valley Forge was not such, that if General Howe, or afterwards General Clinton, had been well informed of its circumstances, defects, and vices, they might not at the head of ten, or even eight thousand men, have reduced the American army to the same fatal necessity as the Americans did General Burgoyne?" Then comes the meat of the argument. Why was hearsay testimony allowed at the trial of General Lee (Query 23); and, would not Generals Philip Schuyler and Arthur St. Clair have been found guilty in a court-martial conducted by George Washington on the same grounds as General Lee (Query 24)? Schuyler and St. Clair were the commanding officers at Fort Ticonderoga in July 1777 who were faced with a superior British force advancing quickly and abandoned the fort to save the men under their command. Both were found innocent of the charges against them.[2] All of this leads up to Query 25:

> 25th. Whether it must not appear to every man who has read General Washington's letter to Congress, on the affairs at Monmouth, and the proceedings of the Court-Martial, by which General Lee was tried, that if the contents of the former are facts, not only General Lee's defence must be a tissue of the abominable audacious lies, but the whole string of evidences, both on the part of the prosecution and prosecuted, must be guilty of rank perjury, as the testimonies of those gentlemen, near forty in number, delivered on oath, scarcely in one article coincide with the detail given in his Excellency's letter?

Lee's printed vindications, letters, and "Queries" garnered him no greater support and may have contributed to the disaffection of the public to his cause. His friend Joseph Nourse complained to a correspondent specifically that Lee's "Queries" hurt his cause rather than helped it

Lee's efforts did succeed in generating letters pro and con in the newspapers after each printing, and some of the disaffected did not hold back in proclaiming Lee a "Mercenary," a "Daemon of Discord," and worse. One of Lee's letters prompted Joseph Reed, attempting to protect his own reputation and his improved standing with George Washington, to have his version of events printed in regard to his relations with Lee. The underpinning of this discourse goes back to Reed's letter to Lee dated November 21, 1776, after the fall of Fort Washington and Fort Lee, questioning Washington's abilities and praising Lee. Perhaps Lee reveled in this back-and-forth. Surely, as he proclaimed in several letters, he believed himself to get the better of all of these printed conflicts. He may have been the only person on the continent to see it that way, however.

RELENTLESS ATTACKS

From this point on, Lee left the main stage, except in his own mind. His letters and printed explanations served no real purpose other than to feed his own despair. His attacks on George Washington, although filled with bile and vitriol, went largely unanswered. Eventually, the frenzy of his attack led him to rebuke the Congress and resulted in his dismissal from the Continental Army, not just for one year, but permanently. He moved his center of operations to his estate, Prato Rio, in Virginia and, in these unfamiliar and uncomfortable surroundings, Lee appeared to lose direction and physical strength. He had neither the temperament nor the talents to be a country farmer, and disaster befell him in that role such that he ultimately undertook the frenzied actions that lead to his death in Philadelphia, alone and untethered to man or country.

In some letters, Charles Lee appears totally oblivious to the futility of his actions and his standing in the opinion of the country and its leaders. He repeats the claim that everyone, including *all* members of Congress save two agree with him that he was railroaded by the officers hearing his court-martial. In writing to Horatio Gates in March 1779, after the Congress had rejected his appeal, Lee provides a colorful description of the success of his writings in persuading all but these two of the merits of his case: "—to speak plainly, the Members of the Congress are become extremely civil in their words and actions to the Man whom They so lately affected to shun as the Plague—indeed I do not find that there is a single man so devoid of grace as to insinuate that the charges brought against me had the shadow of support—two notorious Idiots perhaps excepted—one Penn of North Carolina, a broken Attorney, and a Scudder of the Jerseys, a gossiping pragmatical Presbyterian Doctor or Apothecary."[3]

Yet his friends, in letters to him and others, saw it much differently. A Doctor Browne wrote to Horatio Gates in April 1779 wondering about both sides of this conundrum ("Gen.1 Lee is moving to Virginia—He tells me he never stood higher in the opinion of Congress than at present; I wish he may not be deceived");[4] as mentioned above, Joseph Nourse, a former secretary for Lee and a continued confidante, comments in a letter to Gates several months later that Lee should have avoided the publication of some of his diatribes ("on the subject of a number of Queries which were presented to [a printer] by General Lee, I shall only observe that they have only tended to render him more unpopular");[5] later in August, Major John Eustace begs Lee's indulgence for his inability to bring some of the leading lights in Philadelphia to Lee's side ("I cannot eradicate the prejudices that have taken root against you in this city");[6] and, in October, friend Benjamin Rush sought to console Lee's anger that his response to Joseph Reed was refused by the printers ("It was best for you they did so. Have patience. Time, and prosperity will do you justice.").[7]

On the other hand, Lee's failure in the Continental Congress in 1778 was not necessarily a foregone conclusion. His supporters included, among others, William Paca of Maryland, Edward Langworthy of Georgia, and Samuel Adams of Massachusetts. Richard Henry Lee, a longtime friend and confidante, vigorously argued his cause. Nevertheless, once it became apparent early in the deliberations that Lee could not carry the day, few wanted to risk a public denunciation of George Washington, and a number of members noticeably absented themselves from the debates and the votes. Perhaps the crushing the blow was Richard Henry Lee's departure for Virginia in November before the vote, ostensibly to attend to family business. Without the presence and vigor of Richard Henry Lee to plead his case, Charles Lee had no chance. By the count of one biographer, Lee had more supporters than appeared by the ultimate vote of six states in favor of affirmation, two in Lee's favor, three split evenly and two (New Jersey and Delaware) without sufficient members to vote. By individuals, Lee lost 15 to 7.[8]

Lee's exchanges with Congress did not end there, however. His uncontrolled temper led him to send the following letter to Congress in January 1780: "I understand that it is in contemplation of Congress on principles of economy, to strike me out of their service. Congress must know very little of me if they suppose that I would accept of their money since the confirmation of the wicked and infamous sentence was passed upon."[9] Just days before, the

Congress had *rejected* a motion to dismiss Lee from military service at the conclusion of his one year suspension, ostensibly for reasons of economy. When he was informed of the debate, however, Lee's temper got the better of his judgment and he sent off the short letter. Members of Congress took offense, and the vote to dismiss was reintroduced. By a close vote (five states to four) on January 10, 1780, the Congress terminated Lee's commission with the Continental Army permanently.

When he received the notice, now aware that his precipitant action had cost him dearly, Lee sent an uncharacteristic letter of understanding and apology, dated January 30: "I have this day received your letter, with my dismissal from the service of the United States; nor can I complain of it as an act of injustice. The greatest respect is indisputably due to every public body of men, and above all to those who are the representatives of a free people; and I ingenuously confess that the note which I dictated was so far from being dressed in terms properly respectful, that they were highly improper, disrespectful, and even contumacious."[10] One almost has the sense that Lee was relieved that the matter was finally settled, albeit not as he would have liked. He went to explain that he had received erroneous information, that he was pressed for time, and that he was not well. Nevertheless, Lee makes it clear that he is not looking for reinstatement and suggests that he would have shortly resigned "as from obvious reasons, whilst the army is continued in its present circumstances, I could not have served with safety and dignity." Apparently, "present circumstances," meant still under the command of George Washington.

This may have been a period of particular mental distress for Lee. At about this same time, he suggests to Horatio Gates that George Washington is plotting to assassinate the two of them.[11] And, perhaps for this reason, he could not leave it there. After his letter of apology was printed, Lee felt compelled to rehash the entirety of the affair at Monmouth in a lengthy letter dated April 22, 1780. He concludes in full personal glory: "and it is sanguinely hoped by every real enemy to Tyranny, whatever garb it assumes that the present Congress, among their recommendations to the several States, will, above all recommend the restoration and protection of this Palladium both of political and civil liberty."[12]

Having retired to Prato Rio, Lee obviously had time on his hands and used a good part of it writing to friends, openly chiding them for not returning his favors on a regular basis or for not providing the personal support or services he demanded. Indeed, all of Lee's friends start their letters by apologizing or explaining away their failure to write to Lee more regularly. Some of Lee's letters are long, rambling affairs expressing opinions and rants on a number of issues. Those to his sister, Sidney; his friend Benjamin Rush; and his comrade-in-arms Horatio Gates are revealing because they reflect Lee's torment at his situation, his uneasiness with both the United States and Great Britain, and the continued egocentric perception of his actions.

Early in 1779, Lee wrote to Gates from Philadelphia expressing his concern that letters to him and from him had been opened and read in transit. Nonetheless, he says that he has decided to ignore the possibility that his thoughts "shou'd be read by all the Serjeants, Corporals, Committee Men and Waggoners betwixt this place and Boston" and proceeds to refer to George Washington as "our Great Gargantua, or Lama Babak (for I know not which Title is the properest)." He also proclaims his support for Benedict Arnold, recently accused of the misuse of military funds during his tenure in Philadelphia, and for James Wilkinson. The last displays Lee's unlimited ability to exploit his friendships. Wilkinson, a former subordinate officer to Gates, had just recently challenged Gates to a duel. Lee nevertheless describes Wilkinson as "a Man, more sinn'd against than sinning" and lays the blame for his controversy with Gates at the feet of Alexander Hamilton.[13] Wilkinson had been present at Lee's capture in Basking Ridge in 1776, carrying a message from Gates, and he carried back Lee's scurrilous reply criticizing Washington.

Lee wrote to sister Sidney from Prato Rio on September 24, 1779, expressing his despair at the havoc wreaked in the Americas and suggests that had his advice been taken from the first, much of the carnage would have been avoided:

> I feel for the ravages and devastation of this Continent and the ruin of many thousand individuals. I feel for the Empire of Great Britain, for its Glory, Welfare & existence, and I feel for the fortunes of my friends and Relations, which must receive a dreadful shock in this great convulsion. I have been accus'd of making it my Study (from a spirit of revenge,) and exerting all the talents I am Master of, to involve *my Country* in the ruinous situation she is now in. You know—all my acquaintances and correspondents know how false this imputation is. . . . I can safely appeal to the substance & spirits of those letters . . . wherein I propheysed the fatal events that have follow'd.[14] (emphasis added)

Clearly, in this context, "my Country" is Great Britain, not the United States.

But Lee revealed even more in a letter two days later to Benjamin Rush. He agrees with Rush that Great Britain may be on the edge of defeat but warns that the United States has as much to fear from France if the war ends favorably. His advice: "lay the foundation of a formidable Navy" and "establish magazines, docks, &cc," for France and Spain will look after their own

interests and seek to dominate the United States and the seas. He declares that
the American democracy is in peril owing to the "glaring Propensity to
Monarchy" of the "Middle States," Virginia, Maryland, Pennsylvania, and
New Jersey; he rehashes his dispute with Joseph Reed going back to whether
the Americans should have abandoned Fort Washington in Manhattan in
1776; he admits that he is a "wretched Farmer"; he confirms his belief in
Christianity as a salve for society as long as it can relieve itself from the "tedious-
ness and impertinence of the liturgies of the various sects"; and he reiterates
his concern that his letters are regularly opened in transit and read. At the end
of this long letter, however, Lee makes a startling and mysterious revelation:

> America owes me more than she yet knows—the explanation of this I dare
> not trust by common correspondence, but when we meet I will explain it at
> large, in the meantime as Brutus says, my noble Friend, chew upon this that
> if it had not been for my zeal and address [art, zeal when I was a prisoner]
> you had probably been lost—this riddle can only be unfolded to you by
> all the sacred ties [rights] of Friendship [not to] to keep this riddle to
> yourself—there are two men on the Continent to whom I have open'd
> myself and you shall be the third—You have often said that you were sure
> I was an Enthusiast in the glorious cause of the rights of Mankind, when
> I talk to you next, this opinion, I flatter myself, will be more than ever
> strengthened or in fact absolutely confirmed.[15]

Here, again, in his own words, albeit shrouded in intrigue, Charles Lee
admits to the existence of "Mr. Lee's Plan." He suggests, of course, that his
plan was a ruse designed to lure the British into a faulty and fatal military
strategy, artfully constructed and brilliantly executed. Compare this
"defense" of his actions in 1777 to the revised defense of his actions at
Monmouth in June 1778. Several months removed from the action at
Monmouth, Lee defended his actions there as a ruse deigned to lure the
British into a military trap, even though he never raised such a defense in the
summer of 1778 during his court-martial.

Even more intriguing, who are the "two men" in whom Lee had already
confided? Little evidence points to any other of Lee's correspondents or confidantes. Could it be possible that George Washington was one of the two
men? Washington was never a confidante of Lee, but Lee did allude to the
plan in his letters to Washington in May and June 1778, just before the Battle
of Monmouth, by arguing that the British would seek to subjugate the
"Middle Colonies" rather than move to New York. His "Memorandum"
written in May embellishes this opinion by beginning with an explanatory
phrase to support his opinion: "I have the strongest reason to think (my

reason shall be given hereafter) . . . ."[16] It could be that Lee told Washington
of the existence of his plan sometime before June 28 in a personal meeting,
professing his continued loyalty to the United States along with his opinion
that such a plan would be foolhardy for the British and of great benefit to the
Americans if followed. Washington, an accomplished master of espionage,
may have appreciated the information and kept his own counsel about
whether to believe Lee. This might explain the exchange between Washington
and Lee on the battlefield at Monmouth—"if you had no intention of carrying out the attack, why did you take the command?"—and Lee's reaction. It
might also explain the careful distance maintained between the men immediately after the battle. Going further, it could explain Lee's violent turn against
Washington thereafter. As exciting as such a possibility may be, it remains
unlikely. If Washington had such knowledge, why would he allow Lee to take
command of the vanguard troops at Monmouth? Could he have been that
trusting? Or, why would he not have used it (or allowed others to use it) to
defuse the virulent criticism he suffered from Lee's pen after June 1778?
Even a stoic like Washington would be hard pressed to avoid the revelation of
the plan under Lee's constant and withering attack.[17]

AMERICA DISCARDED

In the last years of his life, Lee's writings and correspondence reflect a growing despair. If he had regrets about his choices and decisions since 1773, he did
not express them. His regrets deal with his inability to control events and the
failure of others, people and governments, to take his advice, which in his
mind would have clearly led to a more suitable and acceptable result. He
never second-guessed himself. His actions, his motives, his ideals never came
into question. One must wonder whether this is truly what Charles Lee
believed as his life wound to a close or whether he was trying to convince
himself as well as others of his righteousness.

In September 1779, Lee addressed this issue head-on in a letter to his sister,
Sidney, in England: "until I am conscious of having committed some unworthy action (which I can assure you is not at present the case) the iniquity of
men shall never bear me down." He goes on to express his keen devotion to
"the Empire of Great Britain, for its Glory, Welfare & Existence" but contrasts
that devotion to his "reigning passion," the "liberties of Mankind," "the
purity of the spring of all of my actions."[18] In fact, Charles Lee was rewriting
his history to match his current philosophical and political positions.
He positions himself as a political savant who has remained true to the
principles of human liberty and political rights throughout his life only to be

disappointed that the men and governments he believed in could not live up to his ideals. The American cause was no longer the force for change that he envisioned, and his ardor for it had dissipated. The man so steeped in the Revolution that he hounded Richard Henry Lee repeatedly in the spring of 1776 for a Declaration of Independence now claimed that the call for independence was just a means to achieve greater liberty for the colonies and that he could have reconciled the conflict with Great Britain had he been given the authority to act.[19] The Americans for whom Lee had "conceived the warmest affection from my first acquaintance with them" would be chastened by this observation that they were no longer quite as worthy of his complete respect.

A letter in December to Horatio Gates reveals Lee's posture on the country, the war, and what now is the best route for the United States:

> We have neither money nor credit nor reputation—the failure of the crops aggravates the wretchedness of our prospect—but these considerations, alarming as they are, are still not so hideous as the glaring want of every republican quality and idea maintained through the majority of the States—Of all People on earth the people of America (I mean the Middle States) are the most wretchedly qualify'd for the mode of government adopted . . . —in my judgment there is only one measure which leads to salvation—and this, I care not who knows my sentiments, to propose to the English General (who it is said has full powers) a cessation of arms by sea and land for three, four, or six years—and that during this cessation each Party should hold undisturb'd what at present She is possession of . . . and America will have time to look about her to examine and consider, the state of her resources in men provisions Maritime force and revenue.[20]

It is in this letter that Lee expresses his suspicions that George Washington ("that dark designing sordid ambitious vain proud arrogant and vindictive knave W.") is plotting their assassination. In April 1780, Lee told Benjamin Rush that he was "heartily sick of this country" and had "thoughts of quitting it soon," perhaps for Tuscany or Hungary, the only countries that feature a "well-disposed monarchy," because the possibility of a "wholesome equal republic . . . [is] quite chimerical."[21] And Lee, who was so eager to require loyalty oaths of Tories in New York in 1776, now expressed the opinion that American Tories were subject to persecution and that Whigs were responsible for the adulation of George Washington and the suppression of the press.

In 1780, Charles Lee surely portrayed himself as a disillusioned idealist and a victim. He had risked all that he owned to join the American cause, and it had turned out, in his mind, to have dissolved into petty and personal politics and adulation. Despite his acknowledged and universal reputation as a military strategist, Lee believed himself court-martialed and convicted of military incompetence by men of inferior ability and quality. Notwithstanding his friendships and connections on both sides of this continuing fight, Lee found himself unappreciated by both sides and a useless observer of events. But is this an accurate picture of Lee's state of mind in 1780? Was it the aftermath of the Battle of Monmouth that opened his eyes to the errors of the American cause, or was his fate a direct result of his own actions? It is necessary to move back *before* the Battle of Monmouth to strike the right balance in understanding Charles Lee in 1780.

Something happened between his capture on December 13, 1776, and the Battle of Monmouth on June 28, 1778, that changed Lee's thinking about the American Revolution and his role in it. Apologists can try to explain away "Mr. Lee's Plan" as the musings of a captive or an elaborate ruse, but the context of Lee's writings and actions after 1777 suggest that Lee had a change of heart in that year that ultimately led to his demise and despair. He may have come to regret the plan, but he could not walk away from it in his own mind. He had to justify its existence in order to justify his own. The answer may lie in a letter he wrote in May 1778, before the Battle of Monmouth, that suggests that he had already abandoned the American cause and was trying to find a way home to England.

In May 1778, Charles Lee wrote a long letter to James Robertson, a British officer he had spent time with during his captivity. At this point, Lee had already been paroled from his captivity and was awaiting exchange. He offers his "political Sentiments with Respect to the Situation of Great Britain," and it appears that his intended reader is not Robertson but Henry Clinton, recently appointed the commander of the British troops in North America. The bottom of the letter contains Robertson's handwritten endorsement to Clinton: "You have a copy of a letter wrote by General Lee to me, which he has given me leave to show to you." The letter begins with Lee professing his opinion that the source of all the difficulty between Great Britain and the colonies can be traced to "the Claim of taxing America without her Consent," which had no effect and only gave "greater power to the Ministry already dangerously great." For this reason, Lee opposed the Stamp Act and the Tea Act. He describes himself as "a partial Englishman" and supposes himself "a mere partial American." He then states his purpose: "what I think necessary to be done (if anything can be done) to save the whole Empire from Ruin, and America from the Miseries I foresee if the War is continued." If Great Britain wins the war, it will be ruined by the enormity of the debt incurred; if America wins the war, "I know enough of the Continent to be persuaded that Confusion, Anarchy and civil Wars will be the issue." If only the two sides would have heeded Charles Lee's advice over the past year, he could have brought the war to a better end.

Lee then sets out his proposal. First, Great Britain must provide an "Act of Indemnity" for all players on the American side; second, it must renounce all rights of taxation in the colonies; third it must withdraw all troops from "the thirteen united Colonies at least until the Tempers of both Parties are returned in some measure to their former State of Amity." As for the Americans, they "ought to renounce Independence and give every possible Security for observing the Act of Navigation." *Renounce independence.* Having spent the past fourteen months in British captivity, Charles Lee appears to have lost his ability to read the mood of the American patriots. Here we have Lee, just days before returning to an active command in the Continental Army, addressing the commander of British troops in America and suggesting that the Americans surrender their independence: "I most sincerely wish for Peace, I most sincerely believe that you wish the same, if my Lord and General Howe will empower me to propose Terms liberal, I will at the Risk of my popularity divulge them if an Opposition should be made by any Number."[22] A few weeks later, George Washington would put Charles Lee at the command of a vanguard force to attack Henry Clinton and his British troops encamped at Freehold!

It may appear logical to accept Charles Lee's bitterness in 1780 as a result of his court-martial and ultimate dismissal from the Continental Army. But that cannot be the case. Lee was moving away from the American cause months earlier. Did he intend to make a full break in the spring of 1777 with the writing of "Mr. Lee's Plan," and did he abandon that route when the British failed to embrace him and his strategy? Would he have turned to the British if they had turned to him? We cannot know. But clearly, Charles Lee—who marched with George Washington to Boston in 1775, hunted Tories in New York, coordinated the defense of Charleston, South Carolina, and railed for independence in 1776—had undergone a political, philosophical, or moral transformation by the spring of 1778. According to his written words, he considered the war disastrous for both sides, regardless of the ultimate winner. He saw the Americans (particularly those in the "Middle States") as falling further and further into tyranny, squelching dissent and trampling on the freedom of the press. He feared the influence of France should America win the war and cripple Great Britain. He agonized over the adulation of George Washington by citizens and politicians alike. And he viewed the Declaration of Independence as a bargaining chip.

As always, Lee couched his opinions in the context of his great passion for the rights of man and for a government that could and would sustain his ideals. Lee oftentimes demonstrated uncanny political instincts throughout his life, and his fear in 1780 about the influence of France on the young American republic was not without basis. But he was just as often wrong, as in his prediction that an American victory would surely mean anarchy on the continent. Lee may have sensed the bitterness between patriots and Loyalists (which he surely contributed to), and his concerns about the ability of the states and the federal government to sustain their authorities may have had sound footing. But despite the difficulties the young nation faced, including Shays's Rebellion several years later, he was proved wrong on this score.

Unfortunately, Lee never doubted his own opinions or sought real opposition to them to gauge their value. And he never demonstrated any cleverness or interest in how to transform esoteric political opinions into practical solutions. If he could not conform the will of the government to his purposes, he rebelled and sought another "asylum." So it was that he abandoned Great Britain in the 1760s and now wanted desperately to find another home, as his letter to Benjamin Rush in 1780 suggests, declaring "Tuscany or Hungary" as the only places left on earth the equal of his political values. He acknowledged this fruitless journey through life in one of his last letters to his sister, Sidney, in December 1781: "I remember it was once ask'd, I think it was Mrs. Hinks ask'd me, when I intended to put a period to my peregrinations? My answer, was, that whenever I cou'd find a Country where power was in righteous hands—on this principle, I now find, I may be a pilgrim to all eternity. Great God, what a Dupe and a victim I have been to the talismanic name of Liberty! For I now have reason to believe (from the materials of the Modern World) that this bright Goddess is a Chimera—."[23]

But Charles Lee's ambivalence just as well may have been based on the practical realization that he had placed himself in an untenable position in the war between the colonies and Great Britain. He was not committed fully to either side. He was a "partial Englishman" and a "mere partial American," a dangerous place to be in wartime. Such was already the mindset of Charles Lee as he prepared to face Sir Henry Clinton on June 28, 1778, at the Battle of Monmouth. After the battle, discarded by both sides, he had to make the best of a bad situation, to the public, to his friends and in his own mind. His letter to sister Sidney three years later may reflect Charles Lee's true feelings, or it may simply have been the last version of his story, spun to justify a lifetime of poor decisions.

DEATH

Charles Lee died on October 2, 1782, at the Sign of the Conestoga Inn in the City of Philadelphia. In the last months of his life he was frantic to sell Prato

Rio and rid himself of the financial and day-to-day burdens of farm life. An attempt to sell the estate on his own proved unsuccessful, and he turned to his old friend and financier Robert Morris for help. Morris put the farm on the market and soon found a likely buyer. Lee left the estate in early September with his Italian servant Giuseppe Minghini and his dogs, presumably to complete the transaction in Philadelphia.

Lee was beleaguered by debts. He was cut off from his English sources of funds and no longer drew an officer's salary. He petitioned both his friends and his debtors for money and had to rely on the generosity and financial savvy of Robert Morris more than once to sustain himself. Although Prato Rio had value, Charles Lee had neither the talents nor the patience to extract that value from the land on a continuing basis. The estate house remained unfinished, either from lack of funds or lack of interest. Lee grappled with finances and also struggled to maintain his friends and political contacts. Many people still admired and cared for Lee, but others fell away or were pushed away by his irascible nature. Among the latter were General Horatio Gates, his neighbor in Virginia and confidante during much of the war, who broke off their relationship because of Lee's comments about his wife or perhaps because of doubts about his loyalty, or both. Lee broke with Joseph Nourse and John Eustace as well. Eustace had once been accepted by Lee as an adopted son, but some financial transgressions and his pursuit of Lee's enemies for favors led Lee to believe that he had misjudged the man.[24]

Lee sought help everywhere he could. In 1780, he wrote to Congress recalling his efforts on behalf of the United States and seeking both financial and personal protection from a "distressing state of indigence": "I most humbly request therefore that Congress will when They have call'd to mind the conditions on which they engag'd me in their service devise some method of furnishing me with the means of subsistence in some measure adequate to the fortune I threw into the lap of America."[25] He reminded Congress that he had given up his half-pay commission and risked all of his English property for "my zeal and enthusiasm for America." As a postscript to this letter Lee references a letter printed that day in the *Pennsylvania Packet* suggesting that Lee had conspired with Benedict Arnold (now known to be a traitor) early in the war to "to do everything they should ever have in their power to ruin the Army of the States, and to sacrifice our Illustrious Chief." He notes another from January 1779 in *Flynn's Hibernian Chronicle* that states that he was "touched with *English Guineas* during his captivity." Troubled by these accusations, Lee penned a second letter to Congress just days later asking for *personal* protection from "Assassination" by a "wild fanatick or some collection of 'em" reading these articles. Lee goes out of his way to state his case: "—for

God's sake, Sir, if there is the least ground for suspecting my integrity let me be regularly called before Congress to clear up my character which I am confident I shall do without the least difficulty if I have committed any fault, been guilty of any treason it has been against myself alone, in not once from the beginning of this contest to this day consulting common prudence with respect to my own affairs."[26] Congress offered no solace, either financial or personal, except to enact a resolution acknowledging his loyalty and stating their opinion that "the illiberal insinuations complained of by him are unworthy either of his or the attention of Congress."

By the end of 1781, it had become clear that Great Britain could not win its war with the Colonies. The surrender of Cornwallis to Washington's forces at Yorktown in October 1781 had not ended the war, but even Charles Lee had to recognize the obvious outcome. The ultimate American victory, in which he had played a part, held no solace for him. Indeed, he had broken with the American cause, in his mind and by his actions, even if the break was not known to the public. The Americans had disappointed him and, as he saw it, they did not deserve or could not handle the liberty that they had fought to obtain. His political observations, while still controversial, were more philosophical than useful. With each passing week, Lee's personal observations become more and more embittered. In a long letter to sister Sidney in June 1782, Lee rails against the Americans he had embraced just a few years earlier: "as to these people (who I once to my cost thought quite otherwise) now their characters are developed, They manifestly are not only destitute of the personal good qualities and virtues of their English ancestors, such as truth, honesty, sincerity, frankness and steadiness in friendship" but have not "a single Republican qualification or Idea" save for the New Englanders. As to individuals, Lee saves his most biting comments for George Washington, the "God of the day," infallible and intolerant of dissent, and to whom all must "bow down on pain of political damnation." He goes on at length to describe Washington as a soldier not the equal of a "Corporals Guard" who, after numerous defeats "only stumbled . . . into one successful surprise of a drunken Hessian."[27] His fear of French influence on America led him to suggest to correspondent William Goddard that "royal French gold specifick, has had wonderful operations on public Bodies of men at different times in several parts of Europe, and there is reason to believe that it has operated with not less success on Bodies of men on this side of the Atlantic."[28]

He advised Benjamin Rush that the Americans should "negotiate a cessation of arms by land and by sea for two three four or six years" during which time the country can determine if it has the resources and talents and virtues to be a functioning republic. If not, it can then choose between Great Britain and France as it protector.[29] To Robert Morris he mused that "America had better be conquered: that is, that she had better be reduced to the necessity of accepting the terms which it is said G. Britain means to propose, than to endure any longer such an odious tyranny as the capricious arbitrary government of an unlimited, uncontrollable Assembly."[30] He despaired for "Liberty" without constraint on the legislature and freedom of the press.

Lee appears to have had a premonition of his death. In a letter to Morris on August 15, 1782, he recited his concerns about his outstanding debts and revealed his state of deteriorating health: "I know not what is the cause my dear friend, but of late I find myself much affected in my health—perhaps it is my state of rustication, perhaps the embarrassment of my private affairs, and perhaps in great measure the disagreeable aspect of public affairs, for with submission the prospect is not only disagreeable but hideous, at least to a man of my feelings and sanguine expectations."[31] In anticipation of his fate, he wrote a will dated September 10, 1782, and made his way to Philadelphia. Lee's exact cause of death cannot be determined. He had suffered throughout his life from various ailments, most notably gout and rheumatism; he had nearly died from a virus in the Carpathian Mountains decades earlier and had faced death again just a few years earlier in battle; and he had sustained a wound in his duel with young John Laurens at Christmastime 1778.[32] Clearly, he was suffering from a life-threatening illness by the time he reached Philadelphia, but he was only fifty-one years old.

Despite the lost friendships over his last months and the bitterness of his public life, Charles Lee did not die alone, and his death did not go unremarked. He died in his room at the Conestoga, a second-rate inn that reflected his financial difficulties, with his servant Giuseppe and Colonel Eleazer Oswald nearby, and his dogs in the room with him. Oswald, now a publisher in Philadelphia, had commanded the only artillery aimed at the British early in the day at Monmouth (before the retreat) and remained Lee's friend thereafter, having left the army shortly after the battle. On October 4, Lee's body was taken first to City Tavern and then, with full military honors, to Christ Church for burial. In attendance were a number of friends and dignitaries, including Robert and Gouvernour Morris, John Dickinson of Pennsylvania, John Hanson, president of the Congress, and a number of French diplomats and military officers in the city.

Charles Lee had one last gasp of disrespect, which went, as most, unfulfilled. In his will, he asked a personal favor before stating his religious beliefs:

> I desire most earnestly, that I may not be buried in any church, or church-
> yard, or within a mile of any Presbyterian or Anabaptist meeting-house; for

since I have resided in this country, I have kept so much bad company when living, that I do not chuse to continue it when dead.

I recommend my soul to the Creator of all worlds and all creatures; who must, from his visible attributes, be indifferent to their modes of worship or creeds, whether Christians, Mahometans, or Jews; whether instilled by education, or taken up by reflection; whether more or less absurd; as a weak mortal can no more be answerable for his persuasions, notions, or even skepticism in religion, than for the colour of his skin.[33]

His remains continue to rest in the Christ Church graveyard.

EPILOGUE

A MAN WITHOUT A COUNTRY

In the short period from December 1773 to June 1778, Charles Lee held a prominent place in the hearts and minds of Americans arguing and fighting for their independence from Great Britain. His contributions to the political dialogue that justified the revolution bolstered the spirits and the courage of the patriots; his name figured prominently in every discussion about military readiness and military strategy. Any discussion of Lee's life must begin with his role in the American Revolution. At various times during this period, Lee held center stage: in Congress, in New York City, in Charleston, in the controversy over Washington's fitness for command, and at Monmouth. Had he not become involved in this fight, intellectually or physically, he would have been just one of thousands of middle-ranking officers who served in various theaters in the eighteenth century, forgotten except in the lists kept by the British military. And yet, despite his importance in the early years of the conflict, Charles Lee has always been the forgotten man of the American Revolution, a passing figure in the struggle for the nation's independence.

Why has America chosen to forget, or ignore, Charles Lee?

One reason is that Lee died at the wrong time and at the relatively young age of fifty-one. His death came in October 1782, shortly after George Washington's glorious victory over Cornwallis at Yorktown, Virginia, securing the independence of the United States. Lee's time as a political firebrand and military genius had passed. He had cashiered himself out of the Continental Army in 1778 after the Battle of Monmouth in a spate of arrogance and bad judgment. He blamed Washington; he blamed Congress; he blamed the politically fickle populace of the United States. He then squandered the last years of his life relentlessly attacking Washington. By the time of his death, triumphant patriots would not tolerate criticism of Washington—the country was looking ahead and was about to anoint Washington as its champion.

Lee's early and untimely death facilitated his fall from historical grace, but his lifetime decisions assured it. Lee did not end the struggle for independence as he entered it, a daring critic of the king and advocate for the rights of man, and particularly of American rights. He did not end the war as he entered it, at Washington's side, renowned for his military experience.

Lee failed to see his faults, and he refused to face the consequences of his actions. He had abandoned Great Britain and its military, perhaps the closest "family" he had in his life, for a noble cause that he then betrayed. He carried the knowledge of his betrayal alone to his grave. He must have faced each day with trepidation that his secret would be revealed. Outwardly, he railed against his disgrace at the hand of George Washington; inwardly, he must have feared true disgrace and personal danger from his undisclosed actions. When that disclosure came many years after his death, its impact was anticlimactic, not impacting his life but sealing his legacy as the forgotten revolutionary.

Why then should we be interested in him?

At one point in his life, Lee's timing, judgment, and style conjoined to hurl him into the role of a leading player in the American cause. From December 1773 through December 1776, Charles Lee performed his part with vitality and strength. His decision not only to join in this struggle but also take up its banner as a leading advocate demonstrated courage as well as good judgment. Here was a cause that paralleled his arguments against the king and the king's ministers; here was a fight that could be won. Lee grabbed the opportunity and ran with it, and his voice was heard. For the first time, his loud and caustic tone found an approving audience. He railed against the king, berated the king's ministers, shouted down the Loyalists and the lukewarm. His tongue brooked no restraint. Luckily for Lee, the period for shouting lasted long enough for him to be heard, but it was short enough that he did not become shrill. Soon he had to devote his energies to military matters. But for this one period of time, his characteristic style of personal political assault served him well.

Just a few months later, however, Charles Lee was a man without a country. Captured in Basking Ridge in December 1776, he was suddenly out of the fight. Foolishly, Lee abandoned the American cause that he had so passionately embraced, at least apparently, during the previous thirty-six months. In March 1777, he provided the British with a plan to defeat the Americans. Whether he acted out of fear for his personal safety, an ego so intense that it overwhelmed his reason, or a cold calculation that Great Britain would win the war remains a mystery, but instead of being welcomed back into the British military establishment, if that is what he expected, he found himself just a few weeks later removed from relative comfort in Manhattan to the confines of a prison ship in New York Harbor. Charles Lee became quiet, and his role in the grand conflict declined into insignificance.

Lee resurfaced as a player in December 1777, once the Americans captured an officer of import to effect his exchange. He seized the opportunity to reattach himself to the American side, choosing to ignore his traitorous indiscretion. Lee must have feared that taking an active role in the American military might encourage the British to reveal his recklessness, so he focused his energy on reaching a negotiated settlement between the sides—with himself as the go-between. Only in this way could he extricate himself from the quagmire that he had created. The entry of France into the fight on the side of the Americans in early 1778 offered the possibility that the war might end quickly and before he was revealed. But Washington's insistence on attacking the British as they crossed New Jersey in June 1778 stymied Lee's efforts and forced him to choose sides. His bungling performance at the Battle of Monmouth may have reflected his conflicted position.

What happened to the legacy of Charles Lee after 1858 is perhaps more intriguing. George Moore's presentation to the New-York Historical Society titled "The Treason of Charles Lee" revealed what Lee alone had known at the Battle of Monmouth. Lee was compromised. Moore calls "Mr. Lee's Plan" a "scheme of treason" and a "voluntary offering of cowardice" by Lee for the purpose of securing his personal safety. By Moore's account, at a time when George Washington was struggling to exchange him and Congress was tied in knots over whether he was being treated humanely, Charles Lee calmly betrayed the country whose commission and financial largesse he had accepted just months earlier. Seemingly just as calmly, Lee made a triumphant return to General Washington at Valley Forge, only to bring his service to an end within weeks at Monmouth. Moore's treatise concludes before discussing Monmouth, but the tone and effect of his revelations lead to the conclusion that Lee's actions at Monmouth were deliberate and derived from a decision in 1777 to leave the American cause and rejoin the British.

Nevertheless, Moore's opinion has been challenged. Subsequent biographers have objected to his conclusion that this was treachery almost beyond comprehension. In these apologies, Charles Lee is portrayed as a complex man, a unique mix of idealist political philosophy and personal ego, often blinded by ambition and personal needs. But these apologies cannot explain away his plan. The plan could not have been a ruse. If so, why did Lee not fly to George Washington and with loud laughter disclose the trick he had played out on General Howe? Why would he spend the weeks after his release from captivity chasing the phantom of a negotiated peace? If the plan was not an abandonment of the cause, it can only be explained as a vain effort by a man who saw himself as more important than the countries at war around him.

Lee knew the consequences of his acts. In the first weeks of his captivity, his life hinged on legal niceties and the willingness of the Americans to retaliate life for life. When Lee turned to the British and they failed to embrace him, he faced a dilemma. Revelation of "Mr. Lee's Plan" by the British high command while he remained in captivity would leave him with nowhere to go; after exchange, it could lead to a hangman's noose. Either Lee's life hung by a thread on the decency of the British officers not to reveal him, or he was working for those officers to defeat the Continental Army. As to the latter possibility, no evidence (other than the plan itself) has surfaced that suggests that Lee was actively working for the British upon his return to the Continental Army at Valley Forge in 1778. Perhaps it is the lack of evidence of an *active* collaboration with the British that has led some historians to adopt stilted interpretations of this traitorous act and to give him a pass.

Charles Lee would have liked his legacy to be as a champion of the rights of man, the "Palladium" for the American cause. But his life choices do not support that view. Early biographers, and more recent revisionists, may accept this view of Lee, albeit tempered by his irrational behavior after Monmouth. A true view of his life, however, argues for a more mundane and disturbing assessment. Charles Lee offered no nuanced expression of the Enlightenment theories he espoused, demonstrated no extraordinary military abilities. Although he railed against autocrats, only those who ignored him received his scorn; he willingly embraced those who sought out his opinions. In fact, he dismissed the common man and gravitated throughout his life to those with status and to those in power. For the short period between 1774 and 1776, Charles Lee's voice and persona championed a just cause and rang true to those struggling for the "rights of man"—farmers, merchants, and patriots whose confidence needed to be lifted. Unfortunately, Lee did not understand that following that cause to the end with all of his strength would bring him the respect and glory he so desperately craved.

Charles Lee turned his back on Britain in 1775 to join the American cause and then abandoned the American cause in March 1777.

On the road to Monmouth, Lee could not decide whether he wanted to command the troops to face Sir Henry Clinton or not. No legitimate reason can be fathomed for his rejection of the command or his vacillation. Most likely, he was trying in vain to avoid a confrontation with Clinton. Once committed to the command, he neglected his responsibilities. He failed to properly brief his officers before the battle; he made insufficient attempts to find and coordinate his actions with the militia. Once engaged, he hesitated and hesitated again. Washington demanded that a fight be precipitated early; Lee did not seem to want to risk the effort. Charles Lee's reputation as a military genius may not have been fully warranted, but his actions that morning would not provide credit to any officer in the field. His irrational actions after the battle can be dismissed as the ranting of an egomaniac miffed that Washington would get all the battle's praise, but more clearly they reflect Lee's tenuous position.

As Lee languished at Prato Rio after the Battle of Monmouth, each new day brought the possibility that his transgression in Manhattan in 1777 would be revealed by the British. Lee's prospects looked dim. He might have quietly slipped out of the United States, but he no longer commanded the financial resources necessary. He had lost access to his assets in Great Britain, and Congress cut off his officer's pay in 1780. His only real resource—Prato Rio— was more an encumbrance than a valuable holding. A conclusion of the war offered no allure for Charles Lee. If the Americans won, he would find himself in a colonial society with George Washington the ultimate hero. Return to England would be difficult. Perhaps he could reprise his desultory travels through the capitals of continental Europe, even garnering commissions and praise as a general who had aided the successful American Revolution. But only if he was not revealed. If the British won, a return to England would be even more difficult, as he would be branded a traitor who had chosen the losing side. The ignominy of his condition would be doubled if his treachery against the Americans became public. He would be vilified both in the United States and in Great Britain as a man willing to sell out any side for victory or personal advancement.

It appears that Charles Lee's attempt to aid General Howe in 1777 was received with little appreciation, and his reward amounted to nothing more than a nod of receipt. Lee knew what lay ahead for him. His last letters reveal a state of mind unraveling to some degree. He understood that he no longer could command the respect he required to support his opinions, military and political, and he must have realized as well that his personal safety depended on persons he could not control. Lee's early death in 1782 ended his despair and covered his treachery. It left him forgotten but not disgraced. Unfortunately for Charles Lee, a researcher's thoroughness in 1858 proved his undoing.

APPENDIX A

JAMES WILKINSON, *MEMOIRS OF MY OWN TIMES* (1816): THE CAPTURE OF CHARLES LEE

I was presented to the General as he lay in bed, and delivered into his hands the letter of General Gates. . . . I arose at the dawn, but could not see the General, with whom I had been previously acquainted, before eight o'clock. After some inquiries respecting the conduct of the campaign on the northern frontier, he gave me a brief account of the operations of the grand army, which he condemned in strong terms. He observed, "that our siege of Boston had led us into great errors; that the attempt to defend islands against a superior land and naval force was madness; that Sir William Howe could have given us checkmate at his discretion; and that we owed our salvation to his indolence, or disinclination to terminate the war.—. . ." He had also been opposed to the occupancy of Fort Washington, and the fall of that place enhanced his military reputation, while unavoidable misfortunes, and the unfortunate issue of the campaign, originating in causes beyond the control of the commander-in-chief, had quickened the discontents generated at Cambridge, and raised a party against him in Congress; and it was confidently asserted at the time, but is not worthy of credit, that a motion had been made in that body, tending to supersede him in the command of the army. In this temper of the times, if General Lee had anticipated General Washington in cutting the cordon of the enemy between New York and the Delaware, the commander-in-chief would probably have been superseded, and the man who lived the darling of his country, and died the admiration of the world, might have been consigned to retirement or oblivion. In this case Lee would have succeeded him, whose manifold infirmities would have been obscured by that honest but blind enthusiasm of the public, which never stops to compare causes and effects, much less to analyze motives and measures. This officer's genius, education, military observation, and peculiar talents for war, qualified him to fill with eclat the most distinguished subordinate stations in command; but his disposition and habits were adverse to the preservation of public confidence, or the conciliation of personal feuds and discords; he would therefore soon have been displaced; successor upon successor would have followed him, and the calamities of the country would have kept pace with its impatience and caprice; yet, although the avowal may be more honest than discreet, I owe it to truth to declare, that after the declaration of independence, I could never subscribe to the sentiment, that the cause of the country depended on the life or services of any individual. . . .

General Lee wasted the morning in altercation with certain militia corps who were of his command, particularly the Connecticut light horse, several of whom appeared in large full-bottomed perukes, and were treated very irreverently; the call of the adjutant-general for orders, also occupied some of his time, and we did not sit down to breakfast before ten o'clock. General Lee was engaged in answering General Gates's letter, and I had risen from the table, and was looking out of an end window, down a lane about one hundred yards in length, which led to the house from the main road, when I discovered a party of British dragoons turn a corner of the avenue at a full charge. Startled at this unexpected spectacle, I exclaimed, "Here, sir, are the British cavalry." "*Where?*" replied the General, who had signed his letter in the instant. "Around the house;" for they had opened files, and encompassed the building. General Lee appeared alarmed, yet collected, and his second observation marked his self-possession: "Where is the guard?—damn the guard, why don't they fire?" And after a momentary pause, he turned to me and said, "Do, sir, see what has become of the guard." The women of the house at this moment entered the room, and proposed to him to conceal himself in a bed, which he rejected with evident disgust. I caught up my pistols, which lay on the table, thrust the letter he had been writing into my pocket, and passed into a room at the opposite end of the house, where I had seen the guard in the morning. Here I discovered their arms; but the men were absent. I stepped out of the door, and perceived the dragoons chasing them in different directions, and receiving a very uncivil salutation, I returned into the house.

Too inexperienced immediately to penetrate the motives of this enterprize, I considered the *rencontre* accidental, and from the terrific tales spread over the country of the violence and barbarity of the enemy, I believed it to be a wanton murdering party, and determined not to die without company. I accordingly sought a position where I could not be approached by more than one person at a time, and with a pistol in each hand I awaited the expected search, resolved to shoot the first and the second person who might appear, and then to appeal to my sword. I did not remain long in this unpleasant situation, but was apprised of the object of the incursion by the very audible declaration, "*If the General does not surrender in five minutes, I will set fire to the house*," which, after a short pause, was repeated with a solemn oath; and within two minutes I heard it proclaimed, "*Here is the General, he has surrendered.*" A general shout ensued, the trumpet sounded the assembly, and the unfortunate Lee, mounted on my horse, which stood ready at the door, was hurried off in triumph, bareheaded, in his slippers and blanket coat, his collar open, and his shirt very much soiled from several days use.

. . . Although this misfortune deprived the country of its most experienced chief, I have ever considered the deprivation a public blessing, ministered by the hand of Providence; for if General Lee had not abandoned caution for convenience, and taken quarters two miles from his army, on his exposed flank, he would have been safe; if a domestic traitor who passed his quarters the same morning on private business, had not casually fallen in with Colonel Harcourt, on a reconnoitring party, the General's quarters would not have been discovered; if my visit, and the controversy with the Connecticut light horse had not spun out the morning unseasonably, the General would have been at his camp; if Colonel Harcourt had arrived an hour sooner, he would have found the guard under arms, and would have been repulsed, or resisted until succor could have arrived; if he had arrived half an hour later, the General would have been with his corps; if the guard had paid ordinary atten tion to their duty and had not abandoned their arms, the General's quarters would have been defended; or if he had obeyed the peremptory and reiterated orders of General Washington, he would have been beyond the reach of the enemy.   And shall we impute to blind chance such a chain of rare incidents? I conscientiously reply in the negative; because the combination was too intricate and perplexed for accidental causes, or the agency of man: it must have been designed.

APPENDIX B

"MR. LEE'S PLAN—MARCH 29, 1777"

(From *The Lee Papers*, 2:361–366.)

As on one hand it appears to me that by the continuance of the War America has no chance of obtaining the ends She proposes to herself; that altho by struggling She may put the Mother Country to very serious expence both in blood and Money, yet She must in the end, after great desolation and havock and slaughter, be reduc'd to submit to terms much harder than might probably be granted at present—and as on the other hand Great Britain tho' ultimately victorious, must suffer very heavily even in the process of her victories, evry life lost and evry guinea spent being in fact worse than thrown away: it is only wasting her own property, shedding her own blood and destroying her own strength; and as I am not perswaded from the high opinion I have of humanity and good sense of Lord and General Howe that the terms of accommodation will be as moderate as their powers will admit, but that their powers are more ample than their Successors (shou'd any accident happen) wou'd be vested with, I think myself not only justifiable but bound in conscience to furnish all the lights, I can, to enable 'em to bring matters to a conclusion in the most compendious manner and consequently the least expensive to both Parties—I do this with the more readiness as I know the most generous use will be made of it in all respects—their humanity will incline 'em to have consideration for the Individuals who have acted from Principle and their good sense will tell 'em that the more moderate are the general conditions; the more solid and permanent will be the union, for if the conditions were extremely repugnant to the general way of thinking it wou'd only be a mere patchwork of a day which the first breath of wind will discompose and the first symptoms of a rupture betwixt the Bourbon Powers and Great Britain absolutely overturn—but I really have no apprehensions of this kind whilst Lord and General Howe have the direction of affairs, and flatter myself that under their auspices an accommodation may be built on so solid a foundation as not to be shaken by any such incident—in this perswasion and on these principles I shall most sincerely and zealously contribute all in my power to so desireable an end, and if no untoward accidents fall out which no human foresight can guard against I will answer with my life for the success.

From my present situation and ignorance of certain facts, I am sensible that I hazard proposing things which cannot without difficulties be comply'd with; I can only act from surmise, therefore hope allowances will be made for my circumstances. I suppose then that (exclusive of the Troops requisite for the security of Rhode Island and N. York) General Howe's Army (comprehending every species, British, Hessians and Provincials) amounts to twenty thoushand men capable to take the field and act offensively; by which I mean to move to any part of the Continent which occasion requires—I will suppose that the General's design with his force is to clear the Jersey's and take possession of Philadelphia—but in my opinion the taking possession of Philadelphia will not have any decisive consequences—the Congress and People adhering to the Congress have already made up their minds for the event; already They have turn'd their eyes to other places where They can fix their seat of residence, carry on in some measure their Government; in short expecting this event They have devis'd measures for protracting the War in hopes of some favourable turn of affairs in Europe—the taking possession therefore of Philadelphia or any one or two Towns more, which the General may have in view, will not be decisive—to bring matters to a conclusion, it is necessary to unhinge or dissolve, if I may so express myself, the whole system or machine of resistance, or in other terms, Congress Government—this system or machine, as affairs now stand, depends entirely on the circumstances and disposition of the People of Maryland Virginia and Pennsylvania—if the Province of Maryland or the greater part of it is reduc'd or submits, and the People of Virginia are prevented or intimidated from marching aid to the Pennsylvania Army the whole machine is dissolv'd and a period put to the War, to accomplish which, is, the object of the scheme which I now take the liberty of offering to the consideration of his Lordship and the General, and if it is adopted in full I am so confident of the success that I wou'd stake my life on the issue—I have at the same time the comfort to reflect, that in pointing out measures which I know to be the most effectual I point out those which will be attended with no bloodshed or desolation to the Colonies. As the difficulty of passing and re-passing the North River and the apprehensions from General Carlton's Army will I am confident keep the New

Englanders at home, or at least confine 'em to the East side of the River; and as their Provinces are at present neither the seat of Government strength nor Politicks I cannot see that any offensive operations against these Provinces wou'd answer any sort of Purpose—to secure N. York and Rhode Island against their attacks will be sufficient. On the supposition then, that General Howe's Army (including every species of Troops) amounts to twenty or even eighteen thoushand men at liberty to move to any part of the Continent; as fourteen thoushand will be more than sufficient to clear the Jersey's and take possession of Philadelphia, I would propose that four thoushand be immediately embark'd in transports, one half of which shou'd proceed up the Patomac and take post at Alexandria, the other half up Chesepeak Bay and possess themselves of Annapolis. They will most probably meet with no opposition in taking possession of these Posts, and when possess'd they are so very strong by nature that a few hours work and some trifling artillery will secure them against the attacks of a much greater force than can possibly be brought down against them—their communication with the shipping will be constant and sure for at Alexandria Vessels of a very considerable burthen (of five or six hundred Tons for instance) can lie in close to the shore, and at Annapolis within musket shot—all the necessaries and refreshments for an Army are near at hand, and, in the greatest abundance—Kent Island will supply that of Annapolis and every part on both banks of the Patomac that of Alexandria. These Posts may with ease support each other, as it is but two easy days march from one to the other, and if occasion requires by a single days march. They may join[A] and conjunctly carry on their operations wherever it shall be thought eligible to direct; whether to take possession of Baltimore or post themselves on some spot on the Westward bank of the Susquehanna which is a point of the utmost importance—but here I must beg leave to observe that there is a measure which if the General assents to and adopts will be attended with momentous and the most happy consequences—I mean that from these Posts proclamations of pardon shou'd be issued to all those who come in at a given day, and I will answer for it with my life—that all the Inhabitants of that great tract southward of the Patapsico and lying betwixt the Patomac and Chesepeak Bay and those on the eastern Shore of Maryland will immediately lay down their arms—but this is not all, I am much mistaken if those potent and populous German districts, Frederic County in Maryland and York in Pennsylvania do not follow their example—These

[A] On the Road from Annapolis to Queen Ann there is one considerable River to be pass'd, but as the ships boats can easily be brought round from the Bay to the usual place of passage or Ferry, this is no impediment if the Two Corps chuse to unite They may by a single days march either at Queen Anns or Malbrough.

Germans are extremely numerous, and to a Man have hitherto been the most staunch Assertors of the American cause; but at the same time they are so remarkably tenacious of their property and apprehensive of the least injury being done to their fine farms that I have no doubt when They see a probability of their Country becoming the seat of War They will give up all opposition but if contrary to my expectations a force should be assembled at Alexandria sufficient to prevent the Corps detach'd thither from taking possession immediately of the place, it will make no disadvantageous alteration, but rather the reverse—a variety of spots near Alexandria on either bank of the Patomac may be chosen for Posts equally well calculated for all the great purposes I have mention'd—viz—for the reduction or compulsion to submission of the whole Province of Maryland for the prevention or intimidating Virginia from sending aids to Pennsylvania—for if in fact any force is assembled at Alexandria sufficient to oppose the Troops sent against it, getting possession of it, it must be at the expence of the more Northern Army, as they must be compos'd of those Troops which were otherwise destin'd for Pennsylvania—to say all in a word, it will unhinge and dissolve the whole system of defence. I am so confident of the event that I will venture to assert with the penalty of my life if the plan is fully adopted, and no accidents (such as a rupture betwixt the Powers of Europe) intervenes that in less than two months from the date of the proclamation not a spark of this desolating war remains unextinguished in any part of the Continent.

APPENDIX C

WASHINGTON AND LEE'S
BATTLEFIELD CONFRONTATION

Much of the writing on the Battle of Monmouth deals with the confrontation between George Washington, astride his white horse, and Charles Lee, which occurred somewhere between the morasses on the battlefield shortly after noon on June 28. General Charles Scott (a prolific swearer himself) reported that Washington cursed Lee; the Marquis de Lafayette remembered that Washington called Lee a "damned poltroon."[1] But Scott was probably in the rear with his retreating men, and Lafayette's telling was many years after the fact. The contemporary reports of the confrontation contain less color but remain no less dramatic.

The heat, the intensity of the action, and the limited view of observers also impacts their assessments of this relatively short conversation on a field of battle filled with the sounds and fury of thousands of men and horses moving about to gain advantage or simply to avoid injury and death.

And yet, the several firsthand accounts remain consistent, despite the attempts of historians to make more of this exchange than it was. The context, not the words exchanged, provides enough drama. Lee's aide-de-camp, Captain Mercer, was present and gave a detailed report at Lee's court-martial:

> When we came up to General Washington I was close by General Lee, and heard the conversation that passed between them; General Washington first accosted General Lee, by asking him: What is all this? General Lee not well hearing him, the question was repeated. General Washington in the second question asked: What all that confusion was for, and retreat? General Lee said he saw no confusion but what had arose from his orders not being properly obeyed. General Washington mentioned that he had certain information that it was but a strong covering party of the enemy. General Lee replied that it might be so, but they were rather stronger than

he was, and that he did not think it proper to risk so much, or words to that purport; General Washington replied, then he should not have undertaken it, and passed by him.[2]

Washington's aide-de-camp, Tench Tilghman, recalled the meeting the same way, along with Lee's comment that the action was contrary to his "own opinion."[3] Another of Lee's aides, Lieutenant General Brooks, agreed that Lee expressed doubts about whether the Americans should have sought the fight in the first place:

> Washington asked General Lee what the meaning of all this was: General Lee answered, the contradictory intelligence, and his orders not being obeyed, was the reason for finding him in that situation. *His Excellency showing considerable warmth*, said, he was sorry that General Lee undertook the command unless he meant to fight the enemy or words to that effect. General Lee observed that it was his private opinion that it was not for the interest of the army, or America, I can't say which, to have a general action brought on, but notwithstanding was willing to obey his orders at all times, but in the situation he had been, he thought it by no means warrantable to bring on an action, or words to that effect. (emphasis added)[4]

Brigadier General Knox testified that "his Excellency expressed much displeasure to General Lee at the situation of affairs . . . though I cannot ascertain the precise words."[5]

A private soldier, retreating from the advance position and now near Lee between the morasses, also confirmed the basic details:

> In a few minutes the Commander in Chief and suite crossed the road just where we were sitting. I heard him ask our officers "by whose order the troops were retreating," and being answered, "by General Lee's," he said something, but as he was moving forward all the time this was passing, he was too far off for me to hear it distinctly. Those that were nearer to him said that his words were "d——n him." Whether he did thus express himself or not I do not know. It was certainly very unlike him, but he seemed at the instant to be in a great passion; his looks if not his words seemed to indicate as much.[6]

Charles Lee, in presenting his defense at his court-martial, related the same story, albeit with his own egotistical flourishes:

> When I arrived first in his presence, conscious of having done nothing that could draw on the least censure, but rather flattering myself with his congratulation and applause, I confess I was disconcerted, astonished and confounded by the words and manner in which his Excellency accosted me;

it was so novel and unexpected from a man, whose discretion, humanity and decorum I had from the first of our acquaintance stood in admiration of, that I was for some time incapable of making any coherent answer to questions so abrupt and in a great measure to me unintelligible. The terms, I think, were these—"I desire to know, sir, what is the reason—whence arises this disorder and confusion?" The manner in which he expressed them was much stronger and more severe than the expressions themselves. When I had recovered myself sufficiently, I answered, that I saw or knew of no confusion but what naturally arose from disobedience of orders, contradictory intelligence, and the impertinence and presumptions of individuals, who were vested with no authority intruding themselves in matters above them and out of their sphere. . . .

To which he replied, "All this may be very true, sir, but you ought not to have undertaken it unless you intended to go through with it." Now, what his Excellency meant by saying that I should not have undertaken what I had no intention of going through with, I confess I did not then, nor do I at this day, understand.[7]

APPENDIX D

SHADES OF MONMOUTH

An incredible amount of attention has been drawn to the details of the Battle of Monmouth on June 28, 1778, and the events leading up to it, based on the formal reports written by both sides, the testimony at Charles Lee's court-martial, letters from officers and soldiers in the field, and oral histories given by people claiming to have witnessed the events. Here are some of the stories.

MOLLY PITCHER

The best-known popular story concerns "Molly Pitcher," a woman traveling with an artillery unit of the Continental Army who took up the position of a killed artillery man to keep up the devastating cannon fire in the afternoon fighting that prevented the elite British forces from overrunning the American defensive position behind the west morass. One colorful version of the story is told by J. P. Martin, a soldier on the field that day:

> One little incident happened during the heat of the cannonade, which I was eyewitness to, and which I think would be unpardonable not to mention. A woman whose husband belonged to the artillery and who was then attached to a piece in the engagement, attended with her husband at the piece the whole time. While in the act of reaching a cartridge and having one of her feet as far before the other as she could step, a cannon shot from the enemy passed directly between her legs without doing any other damage than carrying away all the lower part of her petticoat. Looking at it with apparent unconcern, she observed that it was lucky it did not pass a little higher, for in that case it might have carried away something else, and continued her occupation.

Other versions have her carrying water to the artillery detachments, married, unmarried, or a camp follower. This action apparently took place near Comb's Hill, and the woman has been identified as Mary Ludwig Hayes, but she will always be known as "Molly Pitcher."

Washington's Visitors

According to William Stryker in his book *The Battle of Monmouth*, written in 1899, General George Washington had two visitors shortly before the battle.

The first was the governor of New Jersey, William Livingston, who several days before the battle presented Washington with a beautiful white stallion at Kingston, New Jersey, as a gift from the residents of the colony. Washington accepted the horse and rode it through the first half of the battle, making his presence on the field even more remarkable for those who witnessed his magnificent performance. Washington was astride this horse when he confronted Charles Lee between the morasses. As the story goes, the horse succumbed to the heat shortly after their meeting and died.

Washington's second visitor came to his tent in the wee hours of the morning of June 28, just before the troops began their movements. A mysterious "Dr. Griffith," who identified himself as "a chaplain and a surgeon of the Virginian line," talked his way past Washington's guard. Washington is said to have received him, intrigued by what he had to tell him. Dr. Griffith reported that he was privy to knowledge, from sources that he could not reveal, that Charles Lee had agreed to go over to the British and would use the opportunity of his command at first light to hand over the American vanguard to Clinton.

If this man appeared and told Washington this story, Washington apparently did nothing to change his plans.

Notable Men

On the field on June 28, 1778, were two future presidents of the United States, a vice president, numerous governors and senators, secretaries of treasury and war, and various members of Congress in the republic to be constituted twelve years later.

James Monroe	President
George Washington	President
Aaron Burr	Vice President / Governor of New York
Alexander Hamilton	Secretary of the Treasury

Henry Knox	Secretary of War
James McHenry	Secretary of War / delegate to the Constitutional Convention
John Eager Howard	Governor of Maryland
Richard Howell	Governor of New Jersey
John Francis Mercer	Governor of Maryland / delegate to the Constitutional Convention / member of Congress
Joseph Reed	President of Pennsylvania
Charles Scott	Governor of Kentucky
John Hoskins Stone	Governor of Maryland
Joseph Anderson	Senator from Tennessee
Philemon Dickinson	Senator from New Jersey
Frederick Frelinghuysen	Senator from New Jersey
Nicolas Gilman	Senator from New Hampshire / delegate to the Constitutional Convention
William Grayson	Senator from Virginia
William North	Senator from New Jersey
Samuel Smith	Senator from Maryland
Daniel Morgan	Representative from Virginia
Aaron Ogden	Representative from New Jersey
Josiah Parkes	Representative from Virginia
Anthony Wayne	Representative from Georgia
Marinus Willett	Mayor of New York

BATTLEFIELD POSITIONS

The various descriptions of the movements of the American and British forces throughout the day of June 28, 1778, can be both confusing and conflicting. A *New York Times* article on the one hundredth anniversary of the battle gives the best and most understandable description by using one's left hand as a guide and model. It even refers to the Italian gesture "against the effects of the evil eye" to help explain the actions of the British troops late in the day. Here's a part of the guide, describing the early morning disposition of the American forces:

> Extend the little finger of the left hand (palm downward), close to the other three, and stretch out the thumb at a right angle. The nail of the little finger represents Dickinson's division—American extreme advanced left—with the New Jersey militia almost in the right rear of Clinton's first division, (under Cornwallis) facing toward the hand and threatening Clinton's

second division (under Knyphausen) moving off from the hand parallel to the little finger. The thumb-nail indicates the relative position of Morgan with his 600 riflemen, about three miles south of Freehold, at a locality known a century since as "the Richmond Mills; . . . . the four knuckles represent the four (or five, and eventually more numerous) columns or detachments which obliqued to the left, or advanced directly to the front and deployed to support Dickinson in the flanking movement to the left and fill out Lee's line to the right. . . . Freehold or Monmouth Court-house, lay a little back of the knuckle of the index finger, and the severest fighting of the first phase of this battle occurred between the nail of the little finger . . . and the Court-house to the left, where Simcoe's Queen's Rangers made so gallant a charge.

. . .

The operations of the afternoon of this day may be likewise presented by the disposition of the left hand, palm down, pointing west, with the fore and little finger alone extended, as the Italians make the demonstration (*la Gettatura*) against the effects of the evil eye. A coral charm of a hand, thus disposed, is very common. The nail of the forefinger would then indicate the position of the British light infantry and Queen's Rangers, which were repulsed by the American left in their bold attempt at a flanking or turning manoevre.

NOTES

1. Unger, *John Hancock*, 210–211.

2. Throughout this volume, I quote extensively from Lee's letters, in part to demon strate the draw of his writing. Much of what we know of Lee, especially his early life, comes from his own correspondence, and his irascible nature reveals itself over and over again in these letters throughout his life. To some extent, historians have marked Lee's life by his letters: his description of life among the Indians as a young soldier; his veiled comments on George Washington, written minutes before his capture by the British at Basking Ridge in 1776; and his ill-advised letters to General Washington after the Battle of Monmouth, demanding an apology or a court-martial.

3. *Lee Papers*, letter to Edmund Burke, December 16, 1774, 1:145.

4. Ibid., 1:148–149. Less than ten years earlier, Edmund Burke himself faced a simi lar issue and bought an estate to raise his stature in Parliament. See Lock, *Edmund Burke*, 1:250.

5. Butterfield, *Diary and Autobiography of John Adams*, 3:446: "I will add without Vanity, I had read as much on the military Art and much more of the History of War than any American officer of that Army, General Lee excepted."

6. *Lee Papers*, letter to General John Thomas, July 23, 1775, 1:197–198: Thomas relented and resumed his command in Boston. He played an important role in the invasion of Canada in 1776 after the death of General Richard Montgomery and died of smallpox in June of that year during the retreat of the American forces.

George Washington also wrote to Thomas at this time, and his letter contains some of the same arguments and some contrasts with Lee's: "In the usual contests of empire and ambition, the conscience of a soldier has so little share, that he may very properly insist upon his claims of rank, and extend his pretensions even to punctilio;—but such a cause as this, when the object is neither glory nor extent of territory, but a defence of all that is dear and valuable in private and public life, surely every post ought to be deemed honorable in which a man can serve his country.... I admit, Sir, that your just claims and services have not had due respect,—it is by no means a singular case,—worthy men of all nations and countries have had reasons to make the same complaint, but they did not for this abandon the public cause,—they nobly stifled the dictates of resentment, and made their enemies ashamed of their injustice" (Fitzpatrick and Matteson, *Writings of George Washington*, George Washington to General Thomas, July 23, 1775, 3:358–361).

7. Ward resigned his commission within one year of Lee's letter to Thomas, moving Lee up to second in command of the American forces. It was the fresh question of rank after Ward's departure that so irked Lee that he returned to the memory of Artemas Ward's elevation above him. The reasoned deferral of rank addressed to Thomas was forgotten in this letter to Richard Henry Lee, one of Lee's confidantes in Congress (*Lee Papers*, letter to R. H. Lee, July 19, 1776, 2:146–147).

CHAPTER 2 — LEE'S "AMERICAN EXPEDITION"

1. See Alden, *General Charles Lee*, 1–3, for more details on Charles Lee's lineage and family connections.

2. See Anderson, *Crucible of War*, 94–104; Chernow, *Washington*, 52–59; and Crabb, 44th Regiment of Foot, http://44thregiment.itgo.com/history.html.

3. This is the earliest letter extant from Charles Lee written in North America. In *Lee Papers*, this letter is dated "June 18 ye [1756]," which is the earliest it can be. It falls between the Battle of Monongahela in June 1755 and the Battle of Carillon in July 1758. In this letter, Lee seems to apologize to Sidney for not writing more often (probably after receiving a chiding letter from her) and claims to have written from several earlier locations: "I suppose you won't believe me when I tell you that I have wrote several Letters to you from Philadelphia, New York, and this place."

4. *Lee Papers*, letter to Sidney Lee, June 18 [1756], 1:3.

5. See Shy, "Charles Lee: The Soldier as Radical," 24.

6. Not much is known about Lee's Native American wife, and he never mentions her again in his correspondence over the next twenty-four years. One report suggests that his wife bore him twin sons, but Lee's silence on the subject provides no personal confirmation. See Patterson, *Knight Errant of Liberty*, 27–28; and Alden, *General Charles Lee*, 8–9 and notes 32–34.

7. See Pound and Day, *Johnson of the Mohawks*, chap. 13.

8. *Lee Papers*, letter to Sidney Lee, June 18 [1756], 1:5.

9. *Lee Papers*, letter to Sidney Lee, December 7, [1758], 1:18.

10. *Lee Papers*, letter to Sidney Lee, March 1, [1760], 1:28–29.

11. *Lee Papers*, letter to Sidney Lee, June 18, [1756], 1:5–6.

12. *Lee Papers*, letter to Sir William Bunbury, August 9, 1759, 1:20–22.

13. Martyn, *Life of Artemas Ward*, 18–25.

14. Ibid., 27.

15. *Lee Papers*, letter to Sidney Lee, September 16, 1758, 1:6–9.

16. *Lee Papers*, undated letter addressed to "My Dr Lord," 1:15–17; 16.

17. *Lee Papers*, letter to Sidney Lee, July 30, [1759], 1:19–20.

18. *Lee Papers*, letter to Sir William Bunbury, August 9, 1759, 1:20–22. Sir Bunbury responds to Lee in kind with news of the fight in Europe and on the sea. He then turns from such "Publick affairs" and talks of Lee's return to England. He adds that if Lee does not return home soon, "all of our fine young ladies will be disposed of" and proceeds to list those lost already (*Lee Papers*, letter from William Bunbury, November 29, 1759, 1:24–26).

19. *Lee Papers*, letter to Sidney Lee, March 1, [1760], 1:26–28.

20. Lee labels this experience his "American Expedition" in a letter dated March 1, 1766, to his sister, from Constantinople: ". . . had not my frame been harden'd by my American Expedition, I shou'd perhaps have accompany'd them." *Lee Papers*, 1:42–44; 43.

21. This story comes from Grant, *Memoirs of an American Lady*, 25, 32–34. The woman was Margarite Schuyler.

CHAPTER 3 — LEE'S EUROPEAN EXPERIENCE

1. *Lee Papers*, letter from Sir William Bunbury, November 28, 1759, 1:25.

2. Ibid.; see also Alden, *General Charles Lee*, 17–19. See as well, *Lee Papers*, letter to Sidney Lee, July 4, [1761], 1:33: "I yesterday saw a letter from [Lord Pembroke] to Ld Ligonier wherein he says, I cou'd wish to be well with you, but your usage of Lee, in whose interest you know I am so deeply concern'd shocks me; you can have no real objection to him, unless he is too honest."

3. Langworthy, *Memoirs of Major General Lee*, 2–3.

4. Sparks, *Life of Charles Lee*, reprinted in *Lee Papers*, 4:211n.

5. See ibid., 4:214–215.

6. *Papers of Benjamin Franklin*, Benjamin Franklin to William Franklin, March 13, 1768, 15:74–78: The postscript to this long letter discussing the attitudes in England about the American colonies and the questions being raised in the colonies about taxation reads, "I dined yesterday with General Monckton, Major Gates, Colonel Lee, and other officers, who have served in and are friends of America" (78).

7. Patterson, *Horatio Gates*, 33–35; Patterson, *Knight Errant of Liberty*, 15–17.

8. *Lee Papers*, letter to Sidney Lee, May 28, 1766, 1:44.

9. *Lee Papers*, letter to Sir Charles Bunbury, December 7, 1764, 1:44.

10. *Lee Papers*, letter to Sidney Lee [1760–1761], 2:30–31.

11. *Lee Papers*, letter to Sidney Lee, February 19, [1761], 1:31–32.

12. *Lee Papers*, letter to Sidney Lee, July 4, [1761], 1:32–33.

13. See Sparks, *Life of Charles Lee*, reprinted in *Lee Papers*, 4:220–221n.

14. *Lee Papers*, letter from Thomas Wroughton, August 29, 1767, 1:52–54.

15. *Lee Papers*, letter to Sir Charles Bunbury, December 7, 1764, 1:36.

16. Only one other letter remains from this period, a letter to Sir William Johnson, the British Indian Agent in New York, in July 1764, inquiring about the purchase of lands in New York from the Mohawks for Lady Susan Strangway, the daughter of a friend, who had eloped with a "Mr. O'Brien, a Player" to "the great mortification of her family." Her parents decided to provide for the newlyweds by sending them to America. Lee was asked for advice because he "had been some time in America." Lee wanted in on the purchase himself, if enough land could be had from the Mohawks "out of that part lying betwixt Canada & Canajorhie Creeks." Politics intrude into the end of this letter. He hints to Johnson that the British government's ministers are not prepared to deal with America: "By all that is sacred their absurdity is intolerable. Unless they are roused by your remonstrances our acquisitions in that hemisphere will be fruitless" (*Lee Papers*, letter to Sir William Johnson, July 25, 1764, 1:34–36).

17. A short letter on his return displays his lack of concern for family: "I am now five days in England, and write you only these two lines to apprize you of it. I am at present in a Tavern with several of my acquaintances with whom it is as yet the honeymoon. I steal this to you from the side-table. When this honeymoon and the

hurry of my busyness is past you may expect to see me" (*Lee Papers*, letter to Sidney Lee, December 23, 1766, 1:48).

18. Another letter during this stay in England suggests that "the settling of my American affairs" prevents Lee from spending time with his sister (*Lee Papers*, letter to Sidney Lee, May 12, 1767, 1:55; and letter to Sidney Lee, May 28, 1766, 1:44–45).

19. *Lee Papers*, letter to Sidney Lee, April 21, 1768, 1:66–67.

20. Lee never married, except for his Seneca princess during the French and Indian War, but it does appear that he enjoyed the company of women and considered marriage on several occasions. Before leaving England in late 1768, Lee raises the issue with Sidney: "When I have serv'd this campaign I shall perhaps settle; if I had as good an opinion of my own temper and constancy as I have of some women's I shou'd certainly marry—without a thorough confidence in one's self it is a measure not only rash but dishonest; We have seen some dreadful examples but no matter" (*Lee Papers*, letter to Sidney Lee, December 21, 1768, 1:69–71). Of course, he is preaching here to the choir. Sidney Lee did not marry either. See chapter 4 for a broader discussion of Charles Lee's relationships with women.

21. *Lee Papers*, letter to Clotworthy Upton, January 18, [1772], 1:106–108.

22. *Lee Papers*, "Grant of Lands in East Florida, *At the Court of St James's the 3rd Day of December* 1766," 1:46–48.

23. *Lee Papers*, unsigned letter dated January 15, 1767, postmarked New York, 1:49–51.

24. *Lee Papers*, letter to Sidney Lee, November 29, 1768, 1:67–69.

CHAPTER 4 — PERSONALITY AND POLITICAL PHILOSOPHY

1. *Lee Papers*, letter to Lord Thanet, May 4, 1769, 1:76–79.

2. *Lee Papers*, letter to Sidney Lee, March 28, [1772], 1:109–111.

3. *Lee Papers*, letter to Sidney Lee, March 1, 1766, 1:42–44.

4. Lee's introduction to the Prince Hereditary was arranged by Henry Clinton, and Lee thanked Clinton in a letter dated January 28, 1763, written from Berlin: "I must ever think myself indebted to you in the highest degree" (Henry Clinton Collection, Clements Library, University of Michigan). The Prince Hereditary of Prussia was soon to marry, and the sister of his bride must, at one time, have been intended for King George. Lee could not forgo the opportunity to lampoon his own king, who had avoided this match: "What a snare has our gracious bless'd Monarch escaped—had he fallen into it the consequences might have been horrible—a handsome, witty and in every respect accomplish'd wife, might possibly have gained so pernicious an ascendancy over him to have depriv'd us of the salutary and pious counsels of the Earls of Bute and Sandwich" (*Lee Papers*, April 3, [1765], 1:37–39).

5. *Lee Papers*, letter to George Coleman (the Elder), March 16, 1770, 1:92–94.

6. *Lee Papers*, letter to the Earl of Charlemont, June 1, 1765, 1:39–42.

7. *Lee Papers*, letter to Sidney Lee, February 6, 1767, 1:51–52; letter to Sidney Lee, May 12, 1767, 1:55.

8. See Butterwick, *Poland's Last King*.

9. *Lee Papers*, letter to the king of Poland, October 20, 1767, 1:55–59 (emphasis added).

10. *Lee Papers*, letter from the king of Poland, March 20, 1768, 1:63–65.

11. *Lee Papers*, letter to the Earl of Charlemont, June 1, 1765, 1:39–42.

12. *Lee Papers*, letter to George Coleman (the Elder), May 8, 1769, 1:81–84.

13. *Lee Papers*, letter to Lady Blake, May 2, 1769, 1:72.

14. *Lee Papers*, letter to Sidney Lee, December 21, 1768, 1:69–70.

15. *Lee Papers*, letter to Sidney Lee, April 3, 1765, 1:37–39; 38; letter to the Earl of Charlemont, June 1, 1765, 1:39–42; 41; letter to Sidney Lee, March 1, 1766, 1:42–44; 42 and 43.

16. See Sparks, *Life of Charles Lee*, reprinted in *Lee Papers*, 4:214–215.

17. "A Sketch of a Plan for the Formation of a Military Colony," in *Lee Papers*, 3:323–331.

18. See Bunbury, *Memoir of Charles Lee*, 190.

19. Here, again, Lee can see the hypocrisy in his society. He relates eloquently his witness of the torture and execution of a miscreant before a crowd, replete with epithets on the sanctity of life and its consequence loss for misdoings, to be followed shortly thereafter by an officer telling his men that their life's loss in battle is of little consequence for the higher good. "Thus it may be said, we blow hot and cold with the same breath" ("A Sketch of a Plan for the Formation of a Military Colony," in *Lee Papers*, 3:329).

20. *Lee Papers*, 4:81–89.

21. See R. Chernow, *Washington*, 124–125, for a discussion of Washington's love for hunting and a detailed account of the time he spent at this sport. Little evidence exists that Charles Lee ever spent much time hunting, despite his claim that this was the best way to develop the coup d'ocil.

22. *Lee Papers*, 4:91–100; 93.

23. *Lee Papers*, 4:100–108; 104–105.

24. *Lee Papers*, letter to Lady Blake, May 2, 1769, 1:71–75.

25. Letter dated February 1, 1803, from Thomas Rodney printed in the *Wilmington Mirror* in April 1803.

26. Compare Patterson, *Knight Errant of Liberty*, in favor, 48–51; and Alden, *General Charles Lee*, against, 43–44.

27. See Cresswell, *The American Revolution in Drawings*, item nos. 147–151, 47–48, for several renditions of this image, along with the notation: "An idealized portrait with little resemblance to Lee."

28. Butterfield, *Adams Family Correspondence*, letter to John Adams, 1:245–246.

29. Ibid., letter to John Adams, December 10, 1775, 1:335 (and see 1:338n.5); Taylor, *Papers of John Adams*, John Adams to James Warren, July 24, 1775, 3:89; and Butterfield, *Letters of Benjamin Rush*, Benjamin Rush to Thomas Ruston, October 29, 1775, 1: 91–92; 92.

30. Butterfield, *Adams Family Correspondence*, Abigail Adams to John Adams, December 10, 1775, 1:335–338; 335. Edward Langworthy, Lee's earliest biographer, describes his fondness for dogs as a detriment in his attractiveness to the ladies: "The objections to his moral conduct were numerous, and his great fondness for dogs brought on him the dislike and frowns of the fair sex; for the General would permit his canine adherents to follow him to the parlor, the bed-room, and sometimes they might be seen on a chair next his elbow at table" (*Lee Papers*, 4:163).

31. *Lee Papers*, letter to John Adams, October 5, 1775, 1: 208–210; 210.

32. Butterfield, *Adams Family Correspondence*, Abigail Adams to John Adams, March 8, 1777, 2:173–174; 174: "I see from the news papers you sent me that Spado is lost. I mourn for him. If you know any thing of His Master pray Let me hear, what treatment he meets with, where he is confined &c." While he was in captivity, Lee's aides searched for the dog. William Finnie placed an advertisement in the *Virginia Gazette* on March 7, 1777:

> Twenty Dollars Reward LOST or STOLEN, a very remarkable black shaggy dog of the Pomerania breed, called SPADO. He belongs to our brave but unfortunate

general LEE, and was seen in the possession of a person who called himself JOSEPH BLOCK, at Wright's Ferry, on Susquehannah, about the 25th of December last. It is supposed that BLOCK, who pretended to have undertaken to carry him to Berkeley County, Virginia, has parted with him for a trifling consideration, or lost him on the road. Whoever gives information where the said dog may be had, or will bring him to the subscriber in Williamsburg, shall receive the above reward, and no questions asked. WILLIAM FINNIE

33. Patterson, *Horatio Gates*, 50.

34. *Lee Papers*, letter to the president of Congress, February 27, 1779, 3:313–316; 315.

35. *Lee Papers*, letter to Robert Morris, January 28, 1777, 2:357; letter from General Washington, December 29, 1776, 2:356–357; letter from General Washington, April 1, 1776, 2:366.

36. *Lee Papers*, letter to Robert Morris, April 4, 1777, 2:367; letter to Giuseppe Minghini, April 4, 1777, 2:367–368.

37. *Lee Papers*, "Advertisement," June 29, 1782, 4:7–8.

38. *Lee Papers*, letter to Sir Charles Davers, December 24, 1769, 1:88–92.

39. *Lee Papers*, letter to Robert Morris, January 30, 1776, 1:267.

40. See Alden, *General Charles Lee*, 9, 313nn. 31 and 32.

41. *Lee Papers*, letter from Sir William Bunbury, November 28, 1759, 1:25.

42. *Lee Papers*, letter to Sidney Lee, April 21, 1768, 1:66–67.

43. *Lee Papers*, letter to Louisa C., May 4, 1769, 1:75–76; see also a letter "[To Miss Robinson]," December 15, 1775, 1:230–232, of the same tenor.

44. *Lee Papers*, letter to Sidney Lee, August 9, 1771, 1:105; as to those wives with less than admirable qualities, see Lee's comments about the wife of General Horatio Gates, *Lee Papers*, letter to Robert Morris, 3:455–459; 458.

45. Langworthy, *Memoir of Major General Lee*, 63–65. Langworthy perhaps makes the case a little too pointedly.

46. Shy, "Charles Lee: The Soldier as Radical," 22–23, 48n.2.

47. See Alden, *General Charles Lee*, 316n.49. Alden also muses that venereal disease may have been the actual cause of Lee's rheumatism or gout.

48. *Lee Papers*, letter to Miss Rebecca Franks, December 20, 1778, 3:278–281; letter to Miss Rebecca Franks, January 28, 1779, 3:302–303.

CHAPTER 5 — A "LOVE AFFAIR" WITH AMERICA

1. He also had a claim to land on the Ohio or Mississippi Rivers, resulting from his service as an officer in the French and Indian War. As we will see, Lee originally intended to make his way to Florida through the Ohio and Mississippi River Valleys. See Sparks, *Life of Charles Lee*, in *Lee Papers*, 4:252.

2. It has to be a testimony to Lee's truculence that he would write to a friend in a high position, after a long period, asking specific advice and then raising an old claim for sums lent years earlier that Patterson dismisses easily (but not without some indignation). What hold did Lee believe he had on his friends, and why did they tolerate him? The three parts of this letter tell us much about Lee and his friends. The obsequious flattery that Lee employed apparently had its desired effect.

3. *Lee Papers*, letter from Walter Patterson, November 10, 1772, 1:112–116.

4. *Lee Papers*, letter from Thomas Gamble, June 10, 1774, 1:122–123; letter from Thomas Gamble, July 1, 1774, 1:126–127.

5. *Lee Papers*, letter from Thomas Baldwin, September 10, 1774, 1:129–130.

6. Langworthy, *Memoirs of Major General Lee*, reprinted in *Lee Papers*, 4:123–125.

7. Alden, *General Charles Lee*, 50.

8. *Lee Papers*, letters from Thomas Gamble, June 10 and July 1, 1774, 1:122–123 and 126–127.

9. A letter from Thomas Gamble to General Bradstreet quoted in Sparks, *Life of Charles Lee*, in *Lee Papers*, 4:239, suggests that Gamble did see the transformation, but no date is given for the letter.

10. John Adams admitted that the congeniality between Charles Lee and himself "continued, till his Death." Butterfield, *Diary and Autobiography of John Adams*, 3:320–321; see also the comments of L. H. Butterfield in the notes to *Letters of Benjamin Rush*, letter to Thomas Ruston, October 29, 1775, 1:91–93. Lee maintained a strong relationship with Horatio Gates, his neighbor in Virginia. Both generals had suffered from the vagaries of the war and the ascendancy of George Washington and were commiserated. Gates's biographer suggests that Gates may have developed doubts about Lee's commitment to the cause later in the war, after their falling out over the virtues of Gates's wife. Alden concurs in his biography of Lee. See Paul Nelson, *General Horatio Gates*, 256–258; and Alden, *General Charles Lee*, 290.

11. Alden, *General Charles Lee*, 51–52.

12. Ibid., 53–54.

13. As mentioned above in the text, Lee's initial host in New York, Thomas Gamble, made plans to travel to Boston as soon as he heard about Gage's appointment. "I set out in a few days to join our worthy friend General Gage at Boston; he is come out with very extraordinary powers, and has wrote for me: It is very fortunate circumstances, that the power both civil and military hath fallen into the hands of so moderate a man as General Gage." By this time, Lee and Gamble were seeing Gage's appointment in different lights (*Lee Papers*, letter from Thomas Gamble, June 10, 1774, 1:122–123).

14. *Lee Papers*, undated letter to General Gage, 1774, 1:133–135.

15. Ibid., 1:134.

16. John Adams noted meeting with Lee six times in September and October 1774, at dinner or in the evenings, sometimes along with George Washington. Butterfield, *Diary and Autobiography of John Adams*, vol. 2. See the entries for September 18, 22, 28, and October 4, 13, 24.

17. Alden, *General Charles Lee*, 60.

18. *Lee Papers*, September 28, 1774, 1:135–137.

19. *Lee Papers*, December 16, 1774, 1:144–149.

20. Time, however, would turn this issue against Lee. In 1778, before the Battle of Monmouth, Lee would argue the contrary in opposing Washington's desire to attack the British Army in its march across New Jersey. By that time, Lee could argue that experience had taught him otherwise, but the colonials did hold their own in that battle and thereafter in the war. It is possible that Lee had other issues clouding his judgment in 1778.

21. *Lee Papers*, undated letter to General Gage, 1774, 1:133–135. Note Lee's reference that America is the earth's "last asylum."

22. Lee's "Strictures" can be found in *Lee Papers*, 1:150–166. The editor of *Lee Papers*, and others, attribute the "Friendly Address" (New York; repr., London: Richardson and Urquhart, at the Royal Exchange, 1774) to Cooper, but some claim that the writer was Rev. Thomas Bradbury Chandler, the rector of Saint John's Church in

Elizabethtown, New Jersey. It is impossible to know with which clergyman Lee associated the piece, but it is interesting to note that the Reverends Cooper and Chandler were shipmates in May 1775 on the way back to England. See Hoyt, *Sketch of the Life of the Rev. Thomas Bradbury Chandler.* The quote about maritime powers is from Lee's "Strictures" (1:155), and although this and other language is placed in quotation marks, these are not direct quotes from the "Friendly Address," but rather a rhetorical paraphrase of several of Cooper's statements on pages 24–25. The quotes from Lee's "Strictures" are as follows: "single frigate," 156; "Hanoverians," 157; "200,000," 157; "Wolfe," 157; "mercenaries deserting," 158; "Loyalists," 159; "know not how to fight," 162; "pixkaxes," 162–163.

23. Lee's "Strictures" are reprinted in *Lee Papers,* 1:150–166, and he quotes liberally, but not accurately, from Cooper's "Friendly Address" to bolster his arguments.

24. *Lee Papers,* 2:160–161. See Wood, *Battles of the Revolutionary War,* xxvii–xxxii, for a modern discussion of British regulars that echoes Charles Lee's 1774 views. See also Fischer, *Washington's Crossing,* 38–46, for a detailed discussion of the British regulars who fought in the American Revolution.

25. *Lee Papers,* 1:162–163. Of course, as discussed in chapter 2, Lee did not notice these colonial militias when he was in fact fighting as a regular in the French and Indian War.

26. *Lee Papers,* 1:163. In 1778, after his captivity in New York, Lee wrote out a plan of organization for an American force and pressed it upon the delegates to the Continental Congress. Washington asked to see a copy of this plan, and the Maryland militia adopted it for its troops. See "A Plan for the Formation of the American Army in the least Expensive Manner possible and at the same Time for rendering their Manæuvres so little complex that all the essentials may be learnt, and practised in a few Weeks," in *Lee Papers,* 2:383–389.

27. *Lee Papers,* 1:151–166; 153.

28. Ibid., 1:159–160.

CHAPTER 6 — FOREIGN OFFICERS IN SERVICE TO AMERICA

1. *Journals of the Continental Congress,* June 19, 1775.

2. *Lee Papers,* 1:185–186.

3. *Journals of the Continental Congress,* October 7, 1776.

4. See Knollenberg, *Washington and the Revolution,* 38–42. The full excerpt from Richard Henry Lee to George Washington describes this dilemma in detail:

These Adventurers may be divided into three Classes, some who came early and without any recommendation but apparent zeal, with Commissions shewing that they had been in service. Others that brought with them recommendations from our good friend the Count D'Argoud General of Martinique, and from Mr. Bingham the Continental agent in that Island. A third Class includes those who come from France, generally under agreement with our Commissioners, or one of them at least. The strongest obligations rest upon us, (tho' the inconvenience is great) to make good engagements with the latter, and if the second had been disregarded we might have offended a good and powerful Friend in Martinique who has done many good offices there; or have brought our Agent into disrepute. Among the first Class, I realy believe there are many worthless Men, and I heartily wish we were rid of them. . . . I will prevail with the Committee for foreign applications to furnish you with the most explicit views of Congress in ev[ery] appointment, as well as with the recommendations under which each appointment was and is made. We have written both to France and to Martinique to stop the furthe[r] flow of these Gentlemen here, and after the letters arrive I suppose we shall have no more. Many of the last Comers, are, I believe, Men of real merit, and if they will learn to express themselves tolerably in English, may be of service to the Army. The desire to obtain Engineers, and Artillerists was the principal cause of our being so over-burthened. The first that came had sagacity enough quickly to discern our wants, and professing competency in these branches,—they were too quickly believed. And when our Commissioners abroad (in consequence of directions for this purpose) enquired for those Artists, Military Speculation was immediately up, and recommendations were obtained from persons of so much consideration in France, that the success of our applications then made it quite necessary not to neglect them. And at this moment I am apprehensive that the discontent of many may injure our cause abroad when we would wish it to stand well. As you express it Sir, the affair requires great delicacy in its management, as well on the account of our own Officers as on that of these Foreigners.

5. Gottschalk, *Lafayette Comes to America*, 173.

6. George Greene, *The German Element in the War of American Independence*, 106; J. Smith, *Memoir of the Baron de Kalb*.

7. Knollenberg, *Washington and the Revolution*, 40–42.

8. See Russell, "The Conway Cabal"; and Gelb, "Winter of Discontent."

9. Rumors that Gates may have been the illegitimate son of a nobleman have generally been dismissed by his biographers.

10. During this period, Lee and Gates shared the irreverent writer John Hall-Stevenson as a friend in England. See Patterson, *Horatio Gates*, 31.

11. See Knollenberg, *Washington and the Revolution*, 5; and Patterson, *Horatio Gates*.

12. Paul David Nelson, *General Horatio Gates*, 3–44; and see Higginbotham, *The War of American Independence*, 85–86.

13. Chernow, *Washington*, 264–267. And see Lee's bitter exchanges with Joseph Reed after the Battle of Monmouth on the question of Reed's loyalty to Washington, discussed in chapter 8.

14. *Lee Papers*, letter to Patrick Henry, May 7, 1776, 2:1–3.

CHAPTER 7 — AMERICA'S SOLDIER

1. His land purchase in Virginia had yet to be completed, and the details would hector Lee for the next several months while he was attending to the defenses of Boston. Finally, the sale was completed in December (*Lee Papers*, letter to Robert Morris, December 9, 1775, 1:220–221).

2. *Lee Papers*, letter to Dr. Benjamin Rush, July 20, 1775, 1:196–197.

3. "Our miserable defect of Engineers imposes upon me eternal work in a department to which I am a stranger—the undoing what we found done gives us more trouble than doing what was left undone—however we have contrived to make ourselves pretty secure" (*Lee Papers*, letter to Robert Morris, July 27, 1775, 1:199–200).

4. "I think then We might have attack'd 'em long before this and with success, were our Troops differently constituted—but the fatal perswasion has taken deep root in the minds of the Americans from the highest to the lowest order that they are no match for the Regulars, but when cover'd by a wall or breast work. This notion is further strengthen'd by the endless works We are throwing up—in short unless we can remove the idea (and it must be done by degrees) no spirited action can be ventur'd on without the greatest risk" (*Lee Papers*, letter to Benjamin Rush, September 19, 1775, 1:206–207). Lee goes on to suggest "a body of spearmen for each Regiment" as one way to begin the process of changing opinions.

5. *Lee Papers*, letter to Benjamin Rush, November 13, 1775, 1: 216–217; 217.

6. *Lee Papers*, letter to Robert Morris, November 22, 1775, 1:218–220; 219.

7. *Lee Papers*, letter to General Burgoyne, June 7, 1775, 1:180–185; 180, 183.

8. *Lee Papers*, letter to General Burgoyne, June 7, 1775, 1:180–185; 185.

9. *Lee Papers*, letter from General Burgoyne, July 9, 1775, 1:188–193; 191.

10. *Lee Papers*, letter to General Burgoyne, December 1, 1775, 1:222–225; see also Alden's discussion of this exchange of letters, *General Charles Lee*, 84–87.

11. Letter from J. Adams to J. Warren, July 24, 1775. See Butterfield, *Adams Family Correspondence*, 338n5.

12. *Lee Papers*, letter to John Adams, October 5, 1775, 1:208–210.

13. Sparks, *Life of Charles Lee*, in *Lee Papers*, 4:258–260.

14. *Lee Papers*, letter to Benjamin Rush, October 10, 1775, 1:211–212.

15. *Lee Papers*, letter to the President of Congress, January 22, 1776, 1:247–251.

16. *Lee Papers*, letter to Alexander McDougall, October 20, 1775, 1:214–216; 214.

17. *Lee Papers*, letter to Richard Henry Lee, December 12, 1775, 1:228–230; 229. On September 21, 1776, after all the American forces had left New York and the British high command had moved in, the city was engulfed in flames, and a substantial portion burned to the ground. Although the cause of the fire was never discovered, General Howe suspected arson, and Royal Governor Tryon specifically blamed George Washington. Trevelyan, *The American Revolution*, 309–311; Schecter, *The Battle for New York*; and Johnston, *The Campaign of 1776* around New York and Brooklyn.

18. *Lee Papers*, vol. 1, 134–136, 235, letter to General Washington, January 5, 1776.

19. *Lee Papers*, instructions to Major-General Charles Lee, January 8, 1776, 1:236–237.

20. *Lee Papers*, letter to General Washington, January 16, 1776, 1:240.

21. *Lee Papers*, letter to the Chairman of the New York Committee of Safety, January 23, 1776, 1:256–258; 257.

22. Lee wrote to Washington on February 19, describing his efforts to fortify Long Island and deal with Manhattan: "What to do with the city, I own, puzzles me; it is so encircled with deep navigable water, that whoever commands the sea must command the town. . . . I shall barrier the principal streets, and at least if I cannot make it a continental garrison, it shall be a disputable field of battle" (*Lee Papers*, letter to General Washington, February 19, 1776, 1:308–310; 309).

23. *Lee Papers*, letter from John Adams, February 19, 1776, 1:312.

24. *Lee Papers*, letter from Benjamin Rush, February 19, 1776, 1:313–314; 314.

25. *Lee Papers*, letter to General Washington, February 14, 1776, 1:295–297; 297.

26. Lee wrote to Congress on February 22, 1776, accepting the Canadian position "with the greatest zeal and alacrity" but still professing physical distress: "As I am yet very weak and tender, after my illness, I shall take the liberty to remain here a few days, at least till I am able to walk and ride with a tolerable degree of ease, which, at present, I am incapable of doing" (*Lee Papers*, letter to the President of Congress, February 22, 1776, 1:320–323; 320–321).

27. *Lee Papers*, letter from General Gates, January 22, 1776, 1:251–253; 252; letter to General Washington, January 24, 1776, 1:259–260.

28. *Lee Papers*, letter from John Adams, February 19, 1776, 1:312.

29. *Lee Papers*, letter to Benjamin Rush, February 25, 1776, 1:325–326; 325.

30. *Lee Papers*, letter to Robert Morris, January 27, 1775, 1:168–169; 168. Almost exactly one year later, Lee reaffirmed his call for independence in another letter to Morris, January 30, 1776, 1:266–268.

31. *Lee Papers*, letter to Richard Henry Lee, September 2, 1775, 1:203–204.

32. *Lee Papers*, letter to John Adams, October 5, 1775, 1:208–210; 210.

33. *Lee Papers*, letter to Robert Morris, January 30, 1776, 1:266–268.

34. *Lee Papers*, letter to the President of the Provincial Congress of New York, March 4, 1776, 1:344–345; 345.

35. *Lee Papers*, letter to Isaac Sears, March 5, 1776, 1:345–346; see also the form of the oath in the footnote on 346–347.

36. *Lee Papers*, letter from the Provincial Congress of New York, March 6, 1776, 1:349–350.

37. *Lee Papers*, letter to the Provincial Congress of New York, March 6, 1776, 1:350–352; 352.

38. *Lee Papers*, "Report on the Defence of New York, March 1776," 1:354–57; 357, also printed in the *Journals of the Continental Congress*, March 14, 1776. One might wonder if Lee had been a fan of Jonathan Swift's satire, "A Modest Proposal," which proposed the eating of Irish children as a blessing to society.

39. *Journals of the Continental Congress*, March 9, 1776: "Resolved, That no oath by way of test be imposed upon, exacted, or required of any of the inhabitants of these colonies, by any military officers." The following note accompanies the resolutions in the *Journals*, http://memory.loc.gov/cgi-bin/query/r?ammem/hlaw:@field(DOCID+@lit(jc00461: "This resolve was framed, debated and passed in consequence of a letter of General Charles Lee, dated March 5, received and debated this day." The resolution was printed in the *Pennsylvania Gazette*, March 13, 1776:

> General Lee informed Congress, by letter, that he had imposed a Test upon the inhabitants of our Colony, in order to ascertain their political principles. However salutary such a measure might be, when grounded on a legal and constitutional basis, we were much alarmed that it should owe its authority to any military officer, however distinguished for his zeal, his rank, his accomplishments, and services. We considered it as one of the most solemn and important acts of legislation, and a high encroachment upon your rights as the Representatives of a free people. We could not, therefore, be silent upon so momentous a point, though we were not favoured with your sentiments or instructions, nor informed of what, or whether anything had passed between you and the General respecting the disaffected inhabitants. We took up the subject on general principles. There can be no liberty where the military

is not subordinate to the civil power in everything not immediately connected with their operations. Your House, the natural and proper tribunal for all civil matters within the circle of your own jurisdiction, was assembled, and Congress itself within the General's reach, ready to enforce every reasonable proposition for the publick safety. To one or other he ought to have applied. A similar effort in Rhode Island had passed over unnoticed; reiterated precedents must become dangerous; we therefore conceived it to be our unquestionable duty to assert the independence and superiority of the civil power, and to call the attention of Congress to this unwarrantable invasion of its rights by one of their officers. A resolution passed in consequence, on the 8th [9th] of March, that no oath, by way of test, be imposed upon, exacted, or required of any inhabitant of these Colonies by any military officer; and it was ordered to be immediately published. We flatter ourselves that our conduct on this occasion will meet with your approbation.

(New York Delegates to the New York Committee of Safety, March, 1, 1776. Force, *American Archives*, 4th ser., 5:1392)

40. *Lee Papers*, letter from Richard Henry Lee, April 1, 1776, 1:367–368.

41. *Lee Papers*, letter from Richard Henry Lee, March 25, 1776, 1:362–363; letter to John Hancock, March 21, 1776, 1:360–361; 361.

42. *Lee Papers*, letter from George Washington, March 14, 1776, 1:357–359; 358.

43. See *Lee Papers*, letter to Samuel Purviance, April 6, 1776, 1:381–382, with the order to take troops to Annapolis "to seize the person of Govr Eden—the sin & blame be on my head"; and Lee's apology to the Maryland Committee of Safety, letter to Daniel of St. Thomas Jenifer, May 6, 1776, 1:472–474.

44. Lee makes this recommendation in a letter to the president of the Committee of Safety of Virginia, dated April 8, 1776: "I say Sir, after having considered your strength and weakness, no circumstance appears to me so seriously alarming as the disposition and situation of the Inhabitants of the lower Counties Norfolk and Princess Ann; . . . it will be difficult if not impossible to secure and preserve the Province unless these Inhabitants, thus dangerously disposed, are removed from the very spot where they can do such infinite mischief" (*Lee Papers*, 1:393–394). The Committee of Safety agreed and ordered the removal (see "Proceedings, in the Committee of Safety at Williamsburg, April xth 1776," in *Lee Papers*, 1:406–408).

45. *Lee Papers*, letter to Edmund Pendleton, May 4, 1776, 1:467–469; letter from Pendleton, May 5, 1776, 1:470–471.

46. A reference to Shakespeare's *Richard III* (act 4, scene 4), which Lee repeats in a letter to Richard Henry Lee on the same day.

47. *Lee Papers*, letter to George Washington, April 5, 1776, 1:376–378.

48. Lee proposed "oared boats, mounting a six-pounder at the head of each, . . . whose principle should be boarding" (*Lee Papers*, letter to Richard Henry Lee, April 12, 1776, 2:416–417).

49. *Lee Papers*, President Rutledge to Colonel Moultrie, June 9, 1776, 2:57.

50. See, as an example of command instructions, the "General Orders" issued June 12, 1776: "The town-militia are to receive their orders from Brigadier General Armstrong. The country militia from Brigadier General Howe. The North Carolina forces are to be considered as a corps of reserve; and to be under the immediate command of General Lee" (*Lee Papers*, 2:65). Even greater detail is provided in the General

Orders of June 15 and 16. See, as direction on defense, the detail in a letter to Colonel Horry about the defense of Sullivan Island from Long Island: "As the old field where you are stationed (if I recollect right) affords no natural shelter for Riflemen, I would recommend it to you to intersect it with a number of small trenches, at the distance of sixty or seventy yards, one in the rear of the other. They should be shallow, and the dirt thrown out towards the enemy, as otherways when possessed of, they would serve the enemy as protection, as well as they had done for yourselves" (*Lee Papers*, 2:68).

51. *Lee Papers*, letter to President Rutledge, June 22, 1776, 2:80–81.

52. McCrady, *History of South Carolina in the Revolution*, 146–148

53. *Lee Papers*, letter to George Washington, July 1, 1776, 2:101.

54. *Lee Papers*, letter to the president of the Convention of Virginia, June 29, 1776, 2:93.

CHAPTER 8 — REJOINING WASHINGTON

1. *Lee Papers*, letter to Robert Morris, July 2, 1776, 2:117–119.

2. *Lee Papers*, letter from Richard Henry Lee, May 27, 1766, 2:45–46.

3. See a letter from Benjamin Franklin to John Beckwith, dated May 17, 1779, in *The Papers of Benjamin Franklin*, vol. 29. In this letter, three years later, Franklin deflects an apparent offer from Major General John Beckwith of the Twentieth Foot, to serve in America. Franklin's letter refers to a letter of recommendation in Beckwith's favor from "Prince Ferdinand," as does Richard Henry Lee's letter. Franklin suggests that Beckwith is too late and that the flood of foreign officers had caused significant financial and rank problems for Congress. Ironically, the major general had four sons who served admirably in the service of Great Britain in the following decades. It does not appear that this is the same Beckwith who served with Lee in the Forty-fourth Regiment during the French and Indian War, and who assisted in an attempt on Lee's life at that time (see chapter 2), because this Beckwith was with a different unit in Europe at the time.

4. *Lee Papers*, letter to Richard Henry Lee, July 19, 1776, 2:146–148.

5. *Lee Papers*, letter from the President of Congress, August 8, 1776, 2:205–206.

6. *Lee Papers*, letter to the Board of War and Ordnance, August 27, 1776, 2:241–245; 244.

7. *Lee Papers*, letter to the Governor at Cape François, August 30, 1776, 2:255–258; 255–256.

8. *Lee Papers*, letter to the President of Congress, October 10, 1776, 2:259–260.

9. *Lee Papers*, letter to General Gates, October 14, 1776, 2:261–262.

10. *Lee Papers*, letter to Benjamin Rush, November 2, 1776, 2:262–263.

11. *Lee Papers*, letter to Benjamin Franklin, November 6, 1776, 2:266–267.

12. *Lee Papers*, letter to Colonel Reed, November 16, 1776, 2:283–284; 283.

13. *Lee Papers*, letter to Benjamin Rush, November 20, 1776, 2:288–289; 288.

14. *Lee Papers*, letter to Benjamin Rush, November 20, 1776, 2:288–289.

15. Washington, like most contemporaries, referred to the area we now call New Jersey as "the Jerseys," reflecting its origins as two proprietorships, East Jersey and West Jersey. I will refer to it hereafter simply as "New Jersey."

16. *Lee Papers*, letter from General Washington, November 10, 1776, 2:267–270.

17. *Lee Papers*, letter from General Washington, November 16, 1776, 2:279–280.

18. *Lee Papers*, letter from Colonel Reed, November 16, 1776, 2:284–285.

19. *Lee Papers*, letter to General Washington, November 19, 1776, 2:287–288.

20. *Lee Papers*, letter from William Grayson, November 20, 1776, 2:289–290.

21. *Lee Papers*, letter to General Heath, November 21, 1776, 2:290–291.

22. *Lee Papers*, letter to General Heath, November 26, 1776, 2:313–314.

23. *Lee Papers*, letter from General Washington, December 3, 1776, 2:329.

24. See Lee's letter to the president of the Council of Massachusetts, also dated November 21, 1776, where he declares such a strategy "absolute insanity" (*Lee Papers*, 2:291–292).

25. *Lee Papers*, letter from General Washington, November 21, 1776, 2:294–297.

26. *Lee Papers*, letter from Colonel Reed, November 21, 1776, 2:293–294.

27. *Lee Papers*, letter to Colonel Reed, November 24, 1776, 2:305–306.

28. *Lee Papers*, letter to General Washington, November 24, 1776, 2:307.

29. *Lee Papers*, letter from General Washington, November 24, 1776, 2:309–310; 309.

30. *Lee Papers*, letter to General Washington, November 26, 1776, 2:315–316.

31. *Lee Papers*, letter from General Washington, November 27, 1776, 2:318.

32. *Lee Papers*, letter to General Washington, November 30, 1776, 2:322–323.

33. *Lee Papers*, letter from General Washington, December 1, 1776, 2:326.

34. *Lee Papers*, letter from General Washington, December 3, 1776, 2:329.

35. *Lee Papers*, letter to General Washington, December 4, 1776, 2:329–330.

36. *Lee Papers*, letter to General Washington, December 8, 1776, 2:336–337.

37. *Lee Papers*, letter to General Washington, December 8, 1776, 2:337–338.

38. *Lee Papers*, letters from General Washington, December 10, 1776, 2:341–342; December 11, 1776, 2:343–344; December 14, 1776, 2:349–350.

39. Muenchausen, *At General Howe's Side*; see the entries for December 5, 9, 10, and 11, 1776.

40. *Lee Papers*, letter to General Washington, December 8, 1776, 2:337–338: "I cannot convince myself that Philadelphia is their object at present." Lee had some intelligence that the British troops not in New Jersey were moving eastward and northward.

41. See Lutnick, *The American Revolution and the British Press*, 97–98.

42. Wilkinson, *Memoirs of My Own Times*. In his recounting of the tale, Wilkinson provides cogent reflections on the character of Charles Lee and the tenuous position of George Washington as commander in chief at this point in the war. He thoughts on the outcome of the war had Lee not been captured are also of interest. See appendix A.

43. The several British and American accounts of Lee's capture, including Harcourt's description, differ only in the minor details. A contemporaneous newspaper report appeared in *Freeman's Journal* on December 31, 1776:

> December 13.—This morning, about eleven o'clock, General Lee was taken prisoner at Baskenridge, in New Jersey, by Colonel Harcourt with a party of light horse. The sentry placed at the door of the house at which General Lee was stopping, saw the troopers coming on the run, and at first supposed them to be ours; but soon perceived his mistake by their swords, which are more crooked than ours. His piece not being loaded, he charged; they rose up to him and said, "Don't shoot; if you fire we will blow your brains out." General Lee cries out, "for God's sake, what shall I do?" The lady of the house took him up stairs, in order to hide him between the chimney and the breastwork over the fireplace, but he could not, the place being so small. The enemy at this time firing in at the windows, the captain gave orders to set fire to the

house. The general seeing no way of escaping, sent down he would resign himself. They fired three times at the messenger, but missed him. The general came down without his hat or outside coat, and said, "I hope you will use me as a gentleman; let me get my hat and coat." The captain said, "General Lee, I know you well; I know you are a gentleman; you shall be used as such. I know you too well to suffer you to go for your hat and coat," and ordered him to mount. Upon which they went off, carrying with them the general and a Frenchman, left the baggage, wounded one of the aide-de-camps, and one or two of the guard. There were but thirteen men with the general. He was about four miles from his division, and a mile out of the road. Intelligence of General Lee's unguarded situation was given to the enemy last night by an inhabitant of Baskenridge, personally known to the general, and who had made great pretensions of friendship for the American cause, though at heart the greatest villain that ever existed. This Judas rode all the preceding night to carry the intelligence, and served as a pilot to conduct the enemy, and came personally with them to the house where the general was taken. The enemy showed an ungenerous, nay, boyish triumph, after they had got him secure at Brunswick, by making his horse drunk, while they toasted their king till they were in the same condition. A band or two of music played all night to proclaim their joy for this important acquisition. They say we cannot now stand another campaign. Mistaken fools! To think the fate of America depended on one man. They will find ere long that it has no other effect than to urge us on to a noble revenge.

See also Trevelyan, *The American Revolution*, 65–69; and Evelyn, *Memoirs and Letters of Captain William Granville*, 103–106.

44. *Lee Papers*, letter to Horatio Gates, December 13, 1776, 2:348.

45. In a letter to his brother John Augustine just days later, Washington expressed similar despair at the military and political situation facing the Americans:

I think our Affairs are in a very bad situation; not so much from the apprehension of Genl. Howe's Army, as from the defection of New York, Jerseys, and Pensylvania. In short, the Conduct of the Jerseys has been most Infamous. Instead of turning out to defend their Country and affording aid to our Army, they are making their submissions as fast as they can. If they the Jerseys had given us any support, we might have made a stand at Hackensack and after that at Brunswick, but the few Militia that were in Arms, disbanded themselves . . . and left the poor remains of our Army to make the best we could of it.

I have no doubt but that General Howe will still make an attempt upon Philadelphia this Winter. I see nothing to oppose him a fortnight hence, as the time of all the Troops, except those of Virginia (reduced almost to nothing,) and Smallwood's Regiment of Maryland, (equally as bad) will expire in less than that time. In a word my dear Sir, *if every nerve is not strain'd to recruit the New Army with all possible expedition, I think the game is pretty near up, owing, in a great measure, to the insidious Arts of the Enemy, and disaffection of the Colonies before mentioned,* but principally to the accursed policy of short Inlistments, and placing too great a dependence on the Militia the Evil consequences of which were foretold 15 Months ago with a spirit almost Prophetick. (Fitzpatrick and Matteson, *Writings of George Washington*, letter to John Augustine Washington, December 18, 1776, 6:396–398)

His anguish, however, now included the capture of Lee as well.

46. See Lutnick, *The American Revolution and the British Press*, 97–99. See also Trevelyan, who relates that "there were joy and triumph in London as though a battle had been won," in part because "Lee's showy qualities, and his dramatic history, had caught the imagination of the writing world" (*American Revolution*, 69).

47. Apparently, Lee's tenuous position caused consternation in a number of quarters. A group of Hessian prisoners in Trenton, New Jersey, were closely confined, and British officer Archibald Campbell was placed for four months in a dungeon in Massachusetts by authorities who thought they were retaliating for cruel treatment of Lee. The back-and-forth continued anew in June, when Lee was placed aboard the *Centurion* in New York Harbor. Congress once again expressed its willingness to retaliate, and Howe sought direction from London to get himself out of the middle of this embarrassing and dangerous situation (see Alden, *General Charles Lee*, 181–182).

48. A beautifully written letter addressed to a friend in the British military, Captain Primrose Kennedy, appeared shortly after Lee's capture, expressing the perfect tone of a treasured captive:

> The fortune of war, the activity of Colonel Harcourt, and rascality of my own troops have made me your prisoner. I submit to my fate, and I hope that whatever may be my destiny, I shall meet it with becoming fortitude; but I have the consolation of thinking, amidst all my distresses, that I was engaged in the noblest cause that ever interest mankind. It would seem that Providence has determined that not one freeman should be left upon the earth; and the success of your arms more than foretell one universal system of slavery. Imagine not, however, that I lament my fortunes, or mean to deprecate the malice of my enemies; if any sorrow can at present affect me, it is that of a great continent apparently destined for empire, frustrated in the honest ambition of being free, and enslaved by men, whom unfortunately I call my countrymen.

This letter appears to be a fake, however (see Evelyn, *Memoirs and Letters of Captain William Granville*, 106nh, and Alden, *General Charles Lee*, 334–335n5).

49. Among Lee's guests was Friedrich von Muenchausen, Howe's aide-de-camp, who joined Lee for lunch on April 6. Muenchausen was thrilled that Lee could describe his time in "Hannover and Brunswick" and the people he met there, including Muenchausen's brother, the war-counsellor. Muenchausen described Lee as "a very intelligent man and a pleasant conversationalist," skilled in French, German, and Italian. He also notes that "he did not miss an opportunity to make some casual critical remarks" (Muenchausen, *At General Howe's Side*, entry for April 6, 1777).

50. General Greene to John Adams, March 3, 1777, and John Adams to General Greene, March ——, 1777. See the notes taken by Dr. Benjamin Rush on the debate over Lee's request in the Congress, including the concerns that Lee was being used by General Howe, was imbued with "an unbounded share of Vanity," and that some thought he "threw himself in the way of being taken prisoner" (Rush, "Historical Notes," 140–142).

51. Richard Henry Lee, *Memoir of the Life of Richard Henry Lee*, letter to Charles Lee, February 11, 1777, 180–181; 181.

CHAPTER 9 — CAPTIVITY, BETRAYAL, EXCHANGE

1. See the plan in appendix B.

2. See a thorough discussion of the authenticity of the document in Alden, *General Charles Lee*, 336–337nn49–55. Alden, who sees no treachery in the plan and accepts the

argument that Lee was trying to confuse or trick the British, declares the document "unquestionably authentic" (336–337n49). Note 49 also alludes to an 1860 essay by Charles Carter Lee, the son of Light Horse Harry Lee, disputing its authenticity. The *New York Times*, at that same time, November 12, 1860, accepts the authenticity of the document after considerable review.

3. Patterson, *Knight Errant of Liberty*, 174–179; Alden, *General Charles Lee*, 164–189. The American oath was administered to Lee in June 1778, after his parole.

4. Schaefer, "The Whole Duty of Man," 169.

5. See Boudinot, *Exchange of Major General Charles Lee*. According to Boudinot, Lee told him that his calls for a congressional delegation during his captivity were for the purpose of passing on intelligence that he had gathered about the British strategy in the coming months. Of course, such a discussion would be in violation of the oath he gave to the British upon receiving freedom of movement during his parole, and Boudinot tells the story with some disdain for Lee's lack of concern for this issue of honor. Supposedly, Lee produced several sheets of paper with the information, which Boudinot refused. Boudinot was horrified at Lee's cavalier attitude.

6. Sir William Howe's account of the capture, for one, suggests that Lee begged for his life. See Alden, *General Charles Lee*, 333n23. George Moore, in *The Treason of Charles Lee*, goes out of his way to recount all of the reports of Lee's cowardice upon his capture in Basking Ridge in 1776, 63–64.

7. "I, _____ _____, do acknowledge the United States of America to be free, independent and sovereign states, and declare that the people thereof owe no allegiance or obedience to George the third, King of Great Britain; and I do renounce, refuse and abjure any allegiance or obedience to him; and I do swear (or affirm) that I will to the utmost of my power support, maintain and defend the said United States against the said King George the third, and his heirs, and successors, and his and their abettors, assistants and adherents, and will serve the United States in the office of _____ which I now hold, with fidelity, according to the best of my skill and understanding. So help me God." Biographer John Richard Alden goes on at some length to tell this story and then dismisses its significance by citing Lee's objections to other loyalty oaths he faced but ignoring Lee's insistence on loyalty oaths in Rhode Island and New York City in December 1775 and early 1776. Alden, *General Charles Lee*, 201–202.

8. Apparently, this story was told by the Marquis to biographer Jared Sparks in 1828, according to biographer John Richard Alden, *General Charles Lee*, 340n17. See also Stryker, *Battle of Monmouth*, 13–14.

9. *New York Times*, November 12, 1860.

10. Moore, *Treason of Charles Lee*, 90–94; Patterson, *Knight Errant of Liberty*, 179–181.

11. Alden, *General Charles Lee*, 175.

12. Samuel White Patterson, Lee's other recent biographer, does absolve Lee by accepting (or developing) the argument that Lee's sole purpose in writing the plan was to trick General Howe into a doomed strategy and that Howe bought the ruse hook, line, and sinker.

13. The back-and-forth between Washington and General Howe over Lee's exchange continued throughout 1777, with Congress intervening as well with threats and retributions impacting British captives, especially Hessian officers. Lee's biographer John Richard Alden goes into detail on this subject and suggests that the threat to

the Hessians explains the reluctance of General Howe to return Lee to England and may have also influenced the ministry on the subject of Lee's treatment, in order to avoid losing the dedication of the German mercenaries to the war.

14. Letter dated August 22, 1777, from Charles Lee to Henry Clinton: "Whatever predicament I stand on, and however criminal my conduct may appear in your way of thinking—I am convinced that you wish I should be treated with decency—but I am in my present situation subject to such abominable insults, that I earnestly request you to change the place of my confinement even to the common Prison" (Henry Clinton Collection, Clements Library, University of Michigan; see also Alden, *General Charles Lee*, 184–185).

15. See Patterson, *Knight Errant of Liberty*, 188. See also a detailed contemporaneous account of the capture in the *Pennsylvania Evening Post*, August 7, 1777, and the account of Abel Potter, one of the volunteers, who gave details as part of his pension application, in Dann, *Revolution Remembered*, 22–26.

16. *Lee Papers*, letter to General Washington, December 30, 1777, 2:376–377.

17. Boudinot, *Exchange of Major-General Charles Lee.*

18. Ibid.

19. It has been suggested that Washington's warm welcome for Charles Lee on April 5, 1778, may have been staged to serve his own purposes. Apparently discontent was again rising over Washington's effectiveness as commander in chief and his growing popularity among the troops. Some in Congress were once again looking for an alternative—perhaps Horatio Gates, the hero of Saratoga, or the soon-to-be-exchanged Charles Lee. Washington may have wanted to demonstrate his strength among the rank and file, and Lee's return provided that opportunity. See Alden, *General Charles Lee*, 189–190.

20. *Lee Papers*, letter from Charles Pettit to Col. Thomas Bradford, May 19, 1778, 2:393, making the request to accommodate General Lee at the request of "his Excellency" George Washington.

21. See Boudinot, *Exchange of Major-General Charles Lee.* Samuel Patterson, Lee's fawning biographer, dismisses this story as absurd.

22. *Lee Papers*, letter to General Washington, April 13, 1778, 2:382–383, and enclosed, "A Plan for the Formation of the American Army in the least Expensive Manner possible, and at the same Time for rendering their Manœuvres so little complex that all the Essentials may be learnt, and practiced in a few Weeks," 2:382–389.

23. *Lee Papers*, letter from George Washington, April 22, 1778, 2:390–391.

24. *Lee Papers*, letter to the President of Congress, April 17, 1778, 2:389–390.

25. *Lee Papers*, letter to the President of Congress, May 13, 1778, 2:392–393.

26. *Lee Papers*, "Memorandum," May 1778, 2:394–395.

27. *Lee Papers*, letter to General Washington, June 15, 1778, 2:399–402; 401.

28. *Lee Papers*, letter to Benjamin Rush, June 4, 1778, 2:397–399; 398.

29. See the extended discussion of this correspondence in Alden, *General Charles Lee*, 194, and the postscript to a letter from George Johnson, dated June 17, 1778: "Sir Henry Clinton bids me thank you for your letter, and charges me to enclose one he has received for you, from England" (*Lee Papers*, 2:405–406; 406).

30. Mitchell, *Price of Independence*, 63–64; Van Doren, *Secret History of the American Revolution*, 34–35.

CHAPTER 10 — MONMOUTH

1. Whitlock, *La Fayette*, 1:135–139.

2. See appendix D for the list of officers and men on the field on June 28, 1778, who went on to serve the United States in positions of importance in the years to come.

3. Parmet and Hecht, *Aaron Burr*, 44.

4. *Lee Papers*, letter from Colonel Hamilton to Elias Boudinot, July 5, 1778, 2:467–472; 468. Hamilton suggests that Charles Lee caused the country to lose "the finest opportunity America ever possessed." He states that Lee was "either a driveler in the business of soldiership or something much worse."

5. Stryker attributes this phrase to Lee in his book, *The Battle of Monmouth*, 77, as does Alden, *General Charles Lee*, 208.

6. *Papers of George Washington*, 525–526, http://rotunda.upress.virginia.edu/founders/default.xqy?keys=GEWN-print-03-15-02-0550.

7. *Lee Papers*, letter from Colonel Hamilton to General Washington, June 26, 1778, 2:420–421; 420; and letter from Colonel Hamilton to George Washington, [June 26th, 1778, evening], 424–425; 424.

8. *Lee Papers*, letter to General Washington, June 25, 1778, 2:417–418; 417.

9. *Lee Papers*, General Lafayette to General Washington, June 26, 1778, 2:418–419.

10. Letter from Charles Lee to Henry Clinton, June 4, 1778: "General Lee presents his most sincere and humble respects to Sr Henry Clinton—He wishes him all possible happiness and health and begs whatever the event of the present unfortunate contest that He will believe General Lee to be his most respectable and obliged humble Servant." Henry Clinton Collection, Clements Library, University of Michigan.

11. *Lee Papers*, "Plan of an Army, etc.," 2:383–389; 388.

12. See a full discussion of the persons who witnessed the exchange between Washington and Lee in Scheer and Rankin, *Rebels and Redcoats*, 329–331; see also appendix D.

13. The details of the battle and the movements of the troops come from several sources, including the following: Smith, *The Battle of Monmouth*; Smith, *New Jersey's Revolutionary Experience*; Stryker, *The Battle of Monmouth*; Thayer, *The Making of a Scapegoat*; Bilby and Jenkins, *Monmouth Court House*; Murrin and Waldron, *Conflict at Monmouth Court House*; the official reports of Washington (July 1, 1778) and Sir Henry Clinton (July 5, 1778) in *The Battle of Monmouth, June 28, 1778, as Officially Reported by General George Washington and General Sir Henry Clinton*; and the testimony transcribed at the court-martial of Charles Lee.

14. This is the explanation given by Hamilton during the subsequent court-martial proceedings, but several others suggest that the reason for moving the troops closer was to prevent or forestall a nighttime attack. Hamilton's explanation makes more sense. *Lee Papers*, 3:8.

15. *Proceedings of a General Court Martial*, reprinted in *Lee Papers*, 3:102.

16. General Morgan's troops did not become involved in the fighting on June 28. See the discussion in Smith, *The Battle of Monmouth*, 8–9, that this message may have caused confusion. Smith suspects that Lee's dating the letter the 28th and referring to the action as scheduled for tomorrow may have mislead Morgan to believe that the fight would be the next day, citing a letter by Morgan acknowledging receipt of Lee's message and showing some confusion about the dates.

17. Bilby and Jenkins, *Monmouth Court House*, 186–188. They identify the guide as David Forman, a militia commander in Monmouth County.

18. *Proceedings of a General Court Martial*, reprinted in *Lee Papers*, 3:8.

19. See *Lee Papers* for the testimony of Lieutenant Colonel Meade, 3:62; Colonel Tilghman, 3:79–81; Captain Mercer, 3:112. Lee heard it as, "All this may be very true, Sir, but you ought not to have undertaken it unless you intended to go through with it" (3:192). A number of witnesses also testified that Lee had expressed his opinion throughout the day that he had opposed this engagement in the first place. See the testimony of Doctor Griffiths, 3:82–83 and Colonel Tilghman, 3.81. On both issues, Lieutenant Colonel Brooks testified: "His Excellency shewing considerable warmth, and said, he was sorry that General Lee undertook the command unless he meant to fight the enemy, (or words to that effect.) General Lee observed that it was his private opinion that it was not for the interest of the army, or America, I can't say which, to have a general action brought on, but not withstanding was willing to obey his orders at all times. But in the situation he had been, he thought it by no means warrantable to bring on an action, or words to that effect" (3:147).

20. In his summation at the court-martial, Lee went out of his way to describe this exchange with Hamilton because, as he puts it, "it is even an impeachment of my qualifications as an officer." According to Lee, Hamilton, "flourishing his sword," appeared "most flustered and in a frenzy of valour" in his zeal to defend a hill of only temporary advantage. Apparently Lee was stunned by Hamilton's eagerness to die even before performing the practical task at hand to get Lee's troops in a proper position. Lee was at this point in his court-martial defense attempting to demonstrate that he was in full control of his emotions and in proper military demeanor although some others around him (Alexander Hamilton, for one) were not. *Lee Papers*, 3:200–201.

21. P. Headley, *Life of Lafayette*, 94.

22. See the discussion of the Molly Pitcher story in appendix D. Her heroics may have taken place at Comb's Hill in the afternoon fighting.

23. Reprinted in *The Battle of Monmouth, June 28, 1778, as Officially Reported by General George Washington and General Sir Henry Clinton*, 7.

24. Clinton's official report, dated July 5, 1778, reprinted in *The Battle of Monmouth, June 28, 1778, as Officially Reported by General George Washington and General Sir Henry Clinton*, 8–12; 11.

25. John Trumbull in *McFingal*, as cited in Stryker, *The Battle of Monmouth*, 228n2.

26. See also a fascinating retelling of the Battle of Monmouth on its one hundredth anniversary in the *New York Times*, published June 23, 1878:

For Washington the battle was a moral or political necessity, and all that he did could not have been done better. Lee is not responsible for what occurred in the morning, but a scape-goat was requisite, and *the indulgence of his acrimonious temper afforded an opportunity of throwing the blame upon him*. It was equally a matter of absolute necessity that no doubt should be permitted to get abroad that the Americans had not been unquestionably victorious. (emphasis added)

The New York *Times* article makes no mention of "Mr. Lee's Plan," which had been discovered and reported in the paper twenty years earlier.

27. *Lee Papers*, letter from Generals Wayne and Scott to General Washington, June 30, 1778, 2:438–441.

28. *Lee Papers*, letter to General Washington, July 1 [June 30th], 1778, 2:435–436.

29. *Lee Papers*, letter to General Washington, June 28th [30th], 1778, 2:435–438; 437.

30. *Lee Papers*, letter from General Washington, June 30, 1778, 2:437.

31. *Lee Papers*, letter to General Washington, June 30, 1778, 2:438.

CHAPTER 11 — COURT-MARTIAL

1. *Lee Papers*, letter from Generals Wayne and Scott to General Washington, June 30, 1778, 2:438–440; 440.

2. *The Battle of Monmouth, June 28, 1778, as Officially Reported by General George Washington and General Sir Henry Clinton.*

3. *Proceedings of a General Court Martial*, reprinted in *Lee Papers*, 3:1–208; 2.

4. *Lee Papers*, letter from George Washington to John Augustine Washington, July 4, 1778, 2:459–461; 459.

5. Brigadier Generals Smallwood, Poor, Woodford, and Huntingdon; Colonels Irvine, Shepard, Swift, Wigglesworth, Angel, Clarke, Williams, and Febiger.

6. *Proceedings of a General Court Martial*, reprinted in *Lee Papers*, 3:3.

7. Ibid., 3:4–5.

8. Ibid., 3:182.

9. Ibid., 3:199–200.

10. In *Lee Papers*, vol. 3: Colonel Stewart, "six hundred infantry, besides the horse, which appeared to be pretty numerous" (41); Colonel Richard Butler, "about fifteen hundred foot, and between one hundred and fifty and two hundred horse" (46); Lieutenant Colonel Lawrence, "never appeared to me to consist of more than fifteen hundred infantry and cavalry, or two thousand at the most" (54); Lieutenant Colonel Alexander Hamilton, "did not exceed eight hundred infantry and cavalry, to the best of my judgment, if there were so many" (58); Lieutenant Colonel Fitzgerald, "I think from twelve to fifteen hundred" (70); Baron von Steuben, "the enemy, whose strength I conceived to be 1,500 men of infantry, and about 150 horse" (95); Captain Mercer, "two thousand men," and "altogether, to be about three thousand horse and foot" (116); Colonel Jackson, "at least three thousand men, but as I saw no end to them, I had reason to suppose there were more" (125); Lieutenant Colonel Olney, "to be between four and five thousand" (128); Lieutenant Colonel Oswald, "between two and three thousand" (138); Captain Stewart, at three o'clock, "From eight hundred to one thousand cavalry, and from six to eight thousand infantry, and ten pieces of cannon" (161); Captain Edwards, "Two thousand might have appeared in my sight, but I did not see their rear" (167).

11. *Lee Papers*, 3:206.

12. Ibid., 206–207. And see his earlier comments on the same subject at 190: "And I solemnly protest, that at this instant when I address'd the General, I was totally ignorant that a man of my corps had filed off to his rear, with his particular orders; I was ignorant of it that night, I was ignorant of it next day; nay I protest to God I remained in this ignorance till long after this present Court-Martial was assembled."

13. *Lee Papers*, letter to Benjamin Rush, August 13, 1778, 3:228–229.

14. *Lee Papers*, letter to Richard Henry Lee, September 29, 1778, 3:237–238.

15. *Lee Papers*, letter from Major Evan Edwards, August 30, 1778, 3:229–230; letter from Major John Clark, September 3, 1778, 3:230–232.

16. *Lee Papers*, letter to Col. Aaron Burr, "October 1778," 3:238–239.

17. *Lee Papers*, letter to Benjamin Rush, September 29, 1778, 3:236 237.

18. *Lee Papers*, letter from President Reed to General Greene, November 5, 1778, 3:245–253.

19. *Lee Papers*, "General Lee's Vindication to the Public," December 1778, 3:255–265; 258–259.

20. Ibid., 261.

21. See Alden, *General Charles Lee*, 190–91. See also Boudinot, *Exchange of Major-General Charles Lee*, 6–7.

22. *Lee Papers*, "General Lee's Vindication to the Public," December 1778, 3:261.

23. *Lee Papers*, letter from General Washington to President Reed, December 12, 1778, 3:273–274.

24. Ibid., 3:274.

25. *Lee Papers*, letter from Baron von Steuben, December 2, 1778, 3:253.

26. *Lee Papers*, "Narrative of a Duel between General Lee and Colonel Laurens, December 24, 1778," 3:283–285.

27. *Lee Papers*, letter to General Wayne, January 7, 1779, 3:292–293.

28. *Lee Papers*, letter to General Wayne, August 11, 1779, 3:356–357.

CHAPTER 12 — BITTERNESS, DESPAIR, AND DEATH

1. "Some Queries, Political and Military, Humbly Offered to the Consideration of the Public," published in the *Maryland Journal and Baltimore Advertiser*, July 6, 1779, in *Lee Papers*, 3:341–345.

2. See Neagles, *Summer Soldiers*, chap. 4, for a review of high-level courts-martial during the war.

3. *Lee Papers*, letter to General Horatio Gates, March 29, 1779, 3:318–321; 320.

4. *Lee Papers*, letter from Dr. Browne to Major General Gates, April 6, 1779, 3:331–332.

5. *Lee Papers*, letter from Joseph Nourse to Major General Gates, August 12, 1779, 3:357–359, 358.

6. *Lee Papers*, letter from Major Eustace, August 24, 1779, 3:362–364.

7. *Lee Papers*, letter from Benjamin Rush, October 24, 1779, 3:380–381.

8. See Alden, *General Charles Lee*, 250–254.

9. *Lee Papers*, letter to the President of Congress, undated, but most likely January 1780, 3:405.

10. *Lee Papers*, letter to the President of Congress, January 30, 1780, 3:407–409; 407.

11. See note 20, below.

12. *Lee Papers*, letter to the president of Congress, April 22, 1780, 3:423–426, 425–426.

13. *Lee Papers*, letter to Major General Horatio Gates, March 29, 1779, 3:318–321.

14. *Lee Papers*, letter to Sidney Lee, September 24, 1779, 3:365–368; 366.

15. *Lee Papers*, letter to Benjamin Rush, September 26, 1779, 3:370–375; 374. The reprint of this letter in *Lee Papers* contains this unusual note: "The first part of this letter is copied from the original of which one sheet was found among *The Lee Papers*. The remainder is taken from the draft in one of the letter books in which some words stricken out by the writer are here printed in brackets. The last paragraph above [dealing with acknowledgements to "your most amiable wife" and others] is evidently a second draft of the concluding portion of the letter" (*Lee Papers*, 1:375).

16. *Lee Papers*, "Memorandum," May 1778, 2:394–395.

17. Rather than George Washington, one better choice might be General Horatio Gates, Lee's neighbor in Virginia and friend as early as 1773. Gates's biographer acknowledges that Gates's relationship with Lee cooled sometime after 1778, in part because of Gates's suspicion that Lee had collaborated with the British during his captivity. See Paul Nelson, *General Horatio Gates*, 257. Perhaps Gates learned of "Mr. Lee's Plan" from Lee's own lips and, watching his actions after Monmouth, could not accept the explanation that the plan was a ruse to misguide the British. And another possibility is Lee's financier, Robert Morris, who questioned Lee about his friendly relations with known Tories after Monmouth. See Lee's lengthy response in *Lee Papers*, 455–459; 456, in which he admits that his support for the Declaration of Independence was for its value in bargaining with the British government for greater rights: "I considered that unless America declared herself independent, she had nothing to cede which would not go to her vitals on accommodation."

18. *Lee Papers*, letter to Sidney Lee, September 9, 1779, 3:365–368; 366, 455–459.

19. See also on this subject, *Lee Papers*, letter to Robert Morris, June 16, 1781, 3:455–459; 456.

20. *Lee Papers*, letter to Major General Gates, December 19, 1779, 3:400–402; 400.

21. *Lee Papers*, letter to Benjamin Rush, April 30, 1780, 3:417–418.

22. Charles Lee to James Robertson, May 1778, in the Henry Clinton Collection.

23. *Lee Papers*, letter to Sidney Lee, December 11, 1781, 3:464–465.

24. See Alden, *General Charles Lee*, 285, 290; and *Lee Papers*, letter from John Eustace, December 13, 1779, 3:396–398: 397: "To your friendship Sir, I bid adieu—of every connexion with you—I take leave with a painful kind of pleasure."

25. *Lee Papers*, letter to the President of Congress, October 3, 1780, 3:445–447.

26. *Lee Papers*, letter to the President of Congress, October 8, 1780, 3:447–448.

27. *Lee Papers*, letter to Sidney Lee, June 22, 1782, 4:9–22; 9 and 10.

28. *Lee Papers*, letter to William Goddard, July 21, 1781, 3:459–460; 460.

29. *Lee Papers*, letter to Benjamin Rush, December 19, 1781, 3:467–469; 467.

30. *Lee Papers*, letter to Richard Henry Lee, April 12, 1782, 4:2–4; 3.

31. *Lee Papers*, letter to Robert Morris, August 15, 1782, 4:25–27.

32. Biographer Samuel White Patterson suggests that Lee fought another duel just months prior to his death and that the wound he received at the hand of Major Matthew Clarkson hastened his death. Patterson, *Knight Errant of Liberty*, 278.

33. *Lee Papers*, copy of General Lee's will, September 10, 1782, 4:29–33.

APPENDIX C: WASHINGTON AND LEE'S BATTLEFIELD CONFRONTATION

1. Stryker, *The Battle of Monmouth*, 180–181. This is a secondhand report of an interview that Lafayette gave in 1812, also recounted, without authority, in Alden, *General Charles Lee*, 323n29, generally recalled as part of the lore surrounding this incident.

2. *Lee Papers*, 3:112.

3. *Lee Papers*, 3:81.

4. *Lee Papers*, 3:147.

5. *Lee Papers*, 3:156.

6. Martin, *Private Yankee Doodle*, 127.

7. *Lee Papers*, 3:191–192.

BIBLIOGRAPHY

Alden, John Richard. *General Charles Lee, Traitor or Patriot?* Baton Rouge: Louisiana State University Press, 1951.

Allan, Herbert S. *John Hancock: Patriot in Purple.* New York: Macmillan, 1948.

Anderson, Fred. *Crucible of War: The Seven Years' War and the Fate of Empire in British North America 1754–1766.* New York: Alfred A. Knopf, 2000.

Aptheker, Herbert. *American Negro Slave Revolts.* 6th ed. New York: International, 1993.

The Battle of Monmouth, June 28, 1778, as Officially Reported by General George Washington and General Sir Henry Clinton. Freehold, NJ: Society of the Cincinnati in the State of New Jersey, 1973.

Becker, Carl Lotus, and Arthur M. Schlesinger. *The History of Political Parties in the Province of New York, 1760–1776.* Madison: University of Wisconsin Press, 1960.

Beer, George Louis. *British Colonial Policy, 1754–1765.* New York: Macmillan, 1922.

Berger, Carl. *Broadsides and Bayonets: The Propaganda War of the American Revolution.* Philadelphia: University of Pennsylvania Press, 1961.

Bilby, Joseph B., and Katherine B. Jenkins. *Monmouth Court House: The Battle That Made the American Army.* Yardley, PA: Westholme, 2010.

Bill, Alfred Hoyt. *Valley Forge: The Making of an Army.* New York: Harper & Bros., 1952.

Billias, George Athan, ed. *George Washington's Generals and Opponents: Their Exploits and Leadership.* New York: Da Capo Press, 1994.

Boudinot, Elias. *Exchange of Major-General Charles Lee, from a Manuscript of Elias Boudinot.* Philadelphia, 1891.

Boulton, James T. *The Language of Politics in the Age of Wilkes and Burke.* London: Routledge & Kegan Paul, 1963.

Brooks, Victor. *The Boston Campaign: April 1775–March 1776.* Conshohocken, Pa.: Combined Books, 1999.

Bunbury, Sir Henry, Bart. *Memoir of Charles Lee, Major-General in the Service of the U.S. of America.* London, 1838.

Butterfield, L. H., ed. *Adams Family Correspondence.* Vol. 1. Cambridge, Mass.: Belknap Press, 1963.

————. *Diary and Autobiography of John Adams.* Cambridge, Mass.: Belknap Press, 1961.

————. *Letters of Benjamin Rush.* Vol. 1: *1761–1792.* Princeton, N.J.: American Philosophical Society, 1951.

Butterwick, Richard. *Poland's Last King and English Culture: Stanislaw August Poniatowski, 1732–1798.* Oxford: Oxford University Press, 1998.

Chernow, Ron. *Washington: A Life.* New York: Penguin Press, 2010.

Conway, Moncure Daniel. *The Life of Thomas Paine: With a History of His Literary, Political, and Religious Career in America, France, and England.* Vol. 1. New York: G. P. Putnam's Sons, 1892.

Crabb, Terry. 44th Regiment of Foot. http://44thregiment.itgo.com/links.html.

Cresswell, Donald H. *The American Revolution in Drawings and Prints.* Washington, D.C.: Library of Congress, 1975.

Dabney, William M., and Marion Dargan. *William Henry Drayton & the American Revolution.* Albuquerque: University of New Mexico Press, 1962.

Dann, John C. *The Revolution Remembered: Eyewitness Accounts of the War for Independence.* Chicago: University of Chicago Press, 1980.

Doyle, Joseph B. *Frederick von Steuben and the American Revolution.* Steubenville, Ohio: H. C. Cook Co., 1913.

Dupuy, R. Ernest, and Trevor N. Dupuy. *Military Heritage of America.* New York: McGraw-Hill, 1956.

Eddlem, Thomas R. "Father of Our Country: George Washington Sacrificed for His Country's Well-Being and Never Sought Personal Gain. With His Leadership and Moral Character, He Embodied the True Spirit of America (History: Greatness of the Founders)." *New American* 7 (April 2003): 35ff.

Evelyn, William Granville. *Memoirs and Letters of Captain William Granville.* Bedford, Wash.: Applewood Books, 1879.

Fischer, David Hackett. *Washington's Crossing.* New York: Oxford University Press, 2004.

Fisher, Sydney George. *The Struggle for American Independence.* Vol. 1. Freeport, N.Y.: Books for Libraries, 1971.

————. *The True History of the American Revolution.* Philadelphia: J. B. Lippincott, 1902.

Fiske, John. *The American Revolution.* 4th ed. 2 vols. Boston: Houghton Mifflin, 1891.

————. "Charles Lee, Soldier of Fortune," in *Essays, Literary Scenes and Characters in American History, Part 1,* 53–98. New York: Macmillan, 1902.

Fleming, Thomas. "The Military 'Grimes' of Charles Lee." *American Heritage* (Fall 1968).

————. *1776, Year of Illusions.* New York: W. W. Norton, 1975.

Flexner, James Thomas. *George Washington: The Forge of Experience, 1732–1775.* Boston: Little, Brown, 1965.

Force, Peter. *American Archives.* 4th series. Washington, D.C., 1837–1853.

Franklin, Benjamin. *The Papers of Benjamin Franklin.* Digital edition, sponsored by the American Philosophical Society of Yale University. http://franklinpapers.org/franklin.

Gelb, Norman. "Winter of Discontent." *Smithsonian Magazine* 34, no. 2 (May 2003).

Gottschalk, Louis. *Lafayette Comes to America.* Chicago: University of Chicago Press, 1935.

Grant, Anne. *Memoirs of an American Lady.* Albany, N.Y.: J. Munsell, 1876.

Greene, Francis Vinton. *The Revolutionary War and the Military Policy of the United States.* New York: Charles Scribner's Sons, 1911.

Greene, George Washington. *The German Element in the War of American Independence.* New York: Hurd & Houghton, 1876.

Gregg, Gary L. II, and Matthew Spalding, eds. *Patriot Sage: George Washington and the American Political Tradition.* Wilmington, Del.: ISI, 1999.

Hale, Edward Everett. *The Life of George Washington: Studied Anew.* New York: G. P. Putnam's Sons, 1889.

Harvey, Richard J., Jr. *General John Burgoyne.* Newark: University of Delaware Press, 1963.

Hatch, Louis Clinton. *The Administration of the American Revolutionary Army.* New York: Longmans Green and Co., 1904.

Headley, Joel Tyler. *Washington and His Generals.* Vol. 1. Philadelphia: Carey & Hart, 1847.

———. *Washington and His Generals.* Vol. 2. New York: Baker & Scribner, 1848.

Headley, Phineas Camp. *Life of Lafayette.* Auburn, N.Y.: Derby & Miller, 1851.

Hibbert, Christopher. *George III: A Personal History.* New York: Basic Books, 1998.

———. *Redcoats and Rebels: The American Revolution through British Eyes.* New York: W. W. Norton, 1990.

Higginbotham, Don. *The War of American Independence.* Bloomington: Indiana University Press, 1977.

Hosmer, James K. *Samuel Adams.* 7th ed. Boston: Houghton Mifflin, 1888.

Howard, George Elliott. *Preliminaries of the Revolution, 1763–1775.* New York: AMS, 1905.

Hoyt, Albert Harrison. *Sketch of the Life of the Rev. Thomas Bradbury Chandler, D.D., Rector of St. John's Church, Elizabethtown, New Jersey, 1751–1790.* Boston: D. Clapp & Son, 1873.

Humphrey, Carol Sue. *The Revolutionary Era: Primary Documents on Events from 1776 to 1800.* Westport, Conn.: Greenwood, 2003.

Hyman, Harold M. *To Try Men's Souls: Loyalty Tests in American History.* Berkeley: University of California Press, 1959.

Jacobs, James Ripley. *Tarnished Warrior: Major-General James Wilkinson.* New York: Macmillan, 1938.

Johnston, Henry Phelps. *The Campaign of 1776 around New York and Brooklyn.* New York: Da Capo Press, 1971.

Journals of the Continental Congress, 1774–1789. http://memory.loc.gov/ammem/amlaw/lwjclink.html.

Junius [pseud.]. *Letters of Junius (Selected).* Edited by Hannaford Bennett. London: John Long, 1907.

Knollenberg, Bernhard. *Washington and the Revolution, a Reappraisal: Gates, Conway, and the Continental Congress.* New York: Macmillan, 1940.

Kurtz, Stephen G., and James H. Hutson, eds. *Essays on the American Revolution.* Chapel Hill: University of North Carolina Press, 1973.

Kwasny, Mark V. *Washington's Partisan War, 1775–1783*. Kent, Ohio: Kent State University Press, 1996.

Langworthy, Edward, ed. *The Memoirs of Major General Lee*. London, 1792.

Lecky, William Edward Hartpole. *The American Revolution, 1763–1783*. Edited by James Albert Woodburn. New York: D. Appleton, 1898.

Lee, Charles. *The Lee Papers*. 4 vols. New York: New-York Historical Society, 1871–1874.

———. Charles Lee to Henry Clinton, letters dated January 28, 1763; August 22, 1777; May 3, 1778 (addressed to James Robinson); and June 4, 1778. In the Henry Clinton Collection, Clements Library, University of Michigan.

[Lee, Charles?]. *The Importance of Canada Considered: In Two Letters to a Noble Lord*. London: R. & J. Dodsley, 1761.

Lee, Richard Henry. *Memoir of the Life of Richard Henry Lee*. Philadelphia: C. Carey & I. Lea, 1825.

Little, Shelby. *George Washington*. New York: Minton, Balch & Co., 1929.

Lock, F. P. *Edmund Burke*. Vol. 1. Oxford: Clarendon, 1998.

Lodge, Henry Cabot. *George Washington*. 2 vols. Boston: Houghton Mifflin, 1898–1917.

Loth, David. *Alexander Hamilton: Portrait of a Prodigy*. New York: Carrick & Evans, 1939.

Lutnick, Solomon, *The American Revolution and the British Press*. Columbia: University of Missouri Press, 1967.

Maccoby, S. *English Radicalism 1762–1785*. London: George Allen and Unwin, 1955.

Macmillan, Margaret Burnham. *The War Governors in the American Revolution*. New York: Columbia University Press, 1943.

Martin, Joseph Plumb. *Private Yankee Doodle, Being a Narrative of Some of the Adventures of a Revolutionary Soldier*. Boston: Little, Brown, 1962.

Martyn, Charles. *The Life of Artemas Ward: The First Commander-In-Chief of the American Revolution*. Port Washington, N.Y.: A. Ward, 1921.

Matloff, Maurice, ed. *American Military History: 1775–1902*. Conshohocken, Pa.: Combined Books, 1996.

Maurois, André. *Adrienne: The Life of the Marquise De La Fayette*. New York: McGraw-Hill, 1961.

Mayo, Bernard. *Myths and Men: Patrick Henry, George Washington, Thomas Jefferson*. Athens: University of Georgia Press, 1959.

McCrady, Edward. *The History of South Carolina in the Revolution, 1775–1780*. New York: Russell & Russell, 1969.

McDonald, Forrest. *Alexander Hamilton: A Biography*. New York: W. W. Norton, 1979.

Middlekauff, Robert. *The Glorious Cause: The American Revolution, 1763–1789*. New York: Oxford University Press, 1985.

Miller, John C. *Origins of the American Revolution*. Boston: Little, Brown, 1943.

Mitchell, Broadus. *The Price of Independence: A Realistic View of the American Revolution*. New York: Oxford University Press, 1974.

Moore, Frank. *Diary of the American Revolution: From Newspapers and Original Documents*. Vol. 2. New York: Charles Scribner, 1860.

Moore, George H. *The Treason of Charles Lee*. New York: Charles Scribner, 1860.

Muenchausen, Friedrich von. *At General Howe's Side 1776–1778: The Diary of Captain Friedrich von Muenchausen.* Monmouth Beach, N.J.: Philip Freneau Press, 1974.

Murrin, Mary R., and Richard Waldron, eds. *Conflict at Monmouth Court House: Proceedings of a Symposium Commemorating the Two-Hundredth Anniversary of the Battle of Monmouth.* Trenton, NJ: New Jersey Historical Commission, 1978.

Neagles, James C. *Summer Soldiers: A Survey & Index of Revolutionary War Courts-Martial.* Salt Lake City, Utah: Ancestry Incorporated, 1986.

Nelson, Paul David. *Anthony Wayne, Soldier of the Early Republic.* Bloomington: Indiana University Press, 1985.

———. *General Horatio Gates: A Biography.* Baton Rouge: Louisiana State University Press, 1976.

———. *William Tryon and the Course of Empire: A Life in British Imperial Service.* Chapel Hill: University of North Carolina Press, 1990.

Nelson, Peter. *The American Revolution in New York: Its Political, Social and Economic Significance. For General Use as Part of the Program of the Executive Committee on the One Hundred and Fiftieth Anniversary of the American Revolution.* Albany, N.Y.: State University of New York Press, 1926.

Nelson, William H. *The American Tory.* Oxford: Clarendon, 1961.

Nester, William R. *The First Global War: Britain, France, and the Fate of North America, 1756–1775.* Westport, Conn.: Praeger, 2000.

Nickerson, Hoffman. *The Turning Point of the Revolution; or, Burgoyne in America.* Boston: Houghton Mifflin, 1928.

O'Conor, Norreys Jephson. *A Servant of the Crown in England and in North America, 1756–1761, Based upon the Papers of John Appy, Secretary and Judge Advocate of His Majesty's Forces.* New York: D. Appleton–Century, 1938.

Palmer, John McAuley, and Calvin Chapin Memorial Publication Fund. *General Von Steuben.* New Haven, Conn.: Yale University Press, 1937.

Parkman, Francis. *Pioneers of France in the New World.* Lincoln: University of Nebraska Press, 1996.

Parmet, Herbert S., and Marie B. Hecht. *Aaron Burr: Portrait of an Ambitious Man.* New York: Macmillan, 1967.

Patterson, Samuel White. *Horatio Gates: Defender of American Liberties.* New York: Columbia University Press, 1941.

———. *Knight Errant of Liberty: The Triumph and Tragedy of General Charles Lee.* New York: Lantern Press, 1958.

Phillips, Kevin. *The Cousins' Wars: Religion, Politics, and the Triumph of Anglo-America.* New York: Basic Books, 1999.

Pole, J. R. *Political Representation in England and the Origins of the American Republic.* London: Macmillan, 1966.

Pound, Arthur, and Richard E. Day. *Johnson of the Mohawks: A Biography of Sir William Johnson, Irish Immigrant, Mohawk War Chief, American Soldier, Empire Builder.* New York: Macmillan, 1930.

Roche, John F. *Joseph Reed.* New York: Columbia University Press, 1957.

Rocker, Rudolf. *Pioneers of American Freedom: Origin of Liberal and Radical Thought in America.* Translated by Arthur E. Briggs. Los Angeles: Rocker Publications Committee, 1949.

Rogers, Nicholas. *Crowds, Culture, and Politics in Georgian Britain.* Oxford: Clarendon, 1998.

Rossie, Jonathan G. *The Politics of Command in the American Revolution.* Syracuse, N.Y.: Syracuse University Press, 1975.

Rush, Benjamin. "Historical Notes of Dr. Benjamin Rush, 1777." *Pennsylvania Magazine of History and Biography* 27, no. 2 (1903): 129–150.

Russell, Preston. "The Conway Cabal." *American Heritage* 46, no. 1 (February–March 1995): 84+.

Saffell, W.T.R. *Records of the Revolutionary War: Containing the Military and Financial Correspondence of Distinguished Officers.* New York: Pudney & Russell, 1858.

Sawyer, Joseph Dillaway. *Washington.* Vol. 1. New York: Macmillan, 1927.

Schachner, Nathan. *Aaron Burr: A Biography.* New York: A. S. Barnes, 1961.

Schaefer, James J. "The Whole Duty of Man: Charles Lee and the Politics of Reputation, Masculinity and Identity during the Revolutionary Era, 1755–1783." Ph.D. diss., University of Toledo, 2006.

Schecter, Barnet. *The Battle for New York.* New York: Walker & Co., 2002.

Scheer, George F., and Hugh F. Rankin. *Rebels and Redcoats: The American Revolution through the Eyes of Those Who Fought and Lived It.* Cleveland, Ohio: Da Capo Press, 1957.

Searcy, Martha Condray. *The Georgia-Florida Contest in the American Revolution, 1776–1778.* Tuscaloosa: University of Alabama Press, 1985.

Shy, John W. "Charles Lee: The Soldier as Radical." In *George Washington's Generals and Opponents: Their Exploits and Leadership,* edited by George Athan Billias. New York: Da Capo Press, 1994.

Smith, Frank. *Thomas Paine: Liberator.* New York: Frederick A. Stokes, 1938.

Smith, J. Spear. "Memoir of the Baron de Kalb." Read at a meeting of the Maryland Historical Society (January 7, 1858). Baltimore, 1858.

Smith, Samuel Steele. *The Battle of Monmouth.* Monmouth Beach, N.J.: Philip Freneau Press, 1964.

———. *New Jersey's Revolutionary Experience: The Battle of Monmouth.* Red Bank, N.J.: New Jersey Historical Commission, 1975.

Sparks, Jared. *Life of Charles Lee.* In *The Library of American Biography,* 2nd ser., vol. 8. Boston: Charles C. Little and James Brown, 1846. Reprinted in *The Lee Papers,* 4:197–334.

Starkey, Armstrong. *European and Native American Warfare, 1675–1815.* London: University College London, 1998.

Stryker, William S. *The Battle of Monmouth.* 1899. Reprint, Princeton, N.J.: Princeton University Press, 1927.

Symonds, Craig L., and William J. Clipson. *A Battlefield Atlas of the American Revolution.* Annapolis, Md.: Nautical & Aviation Publishing Co., 1986.

Syrett, Harold C., ed. *The Papers of Alexander Hamilton.* Vol. 1: *1768–1778.* New York: Columbia University Press, 1961.

Tatum, Edward H., and Ambrose Serle. *The American Journal of Ambrose Serle, Secretary to Lord Howe, 1776–1778.* San Marino, Calif.: Huntington Library, 1940.

Taylor, Robert J., ed. *Papers of John Adams.* Cambridge, Mass.: Belknap Press, 1979.

Thayer, Theodore. *The Making of a Scapegoat: Washington and Lee at Monmouth.* Port Washington, N.Y.: Kennikat Press, 1976.

————. *Nathanael Greene: Strategist of the American Revolution*. New York: Twayne, 1960.

Tiedemann, Joseph S. *Reluctant Revolutionaries: New York City and the Road to Independence, 1763–1776*. Ithaca, N.Y.: Cornell University Press, 1997.

Tower, Charlemagne, Jr. *The Marquis De Lafayette in the American Revolution: With Some Account of the Attitude of France toward the War of Independence*. Vol. 1. Philadelphia: J. B. Lippincott, 1895.

Trevelyan, George Otto, Bart. *The American Revolution.* London: Longmans, Green & Co., 1907.

————. *George the Third and Charles Fox: The Concluding Part of the American Revolution*. 2 vols. London: Longmans, Green & Co., 1912.

Tyler, Moses Coit. *The Literary History of the American Revolution, 1763–1783*. Vol. 1. New York: G. P. Putnam's Sons, 1897.

Unger, Harlow Giles. *John Hancock: Merchant King and American Patriot*. New York: John Wiley & Sons, 2000.

————. *Lafayette*. New York: John Wiley & Sons, 2002.

Valentine, Alan. *Lord Stirling*. New York: Oxford University Press, 1969.

Van Doren, Carl. *Secret History of the American Revolution*. New York: Viking Press, 1943.

Van Tyne, Claude H. *England & America: Rivals in the American Revolution*. Cambridge: Cambridge University Press, 1927.

————. *The Loyalists in the American Revolution*. New York: Peter Smith, 1929.

Wahlke, John C., ed. *The Causes of the American Revolution*. Rev. ed. Boston: D. C. Heath, 1962.

Ward, Harry M. *The War for Independence and the Transformation of American Society*. London: University College London, 1999.

Washington, George. *The Papers of George Washington Digital Edition*. Edited by Theodore J. Crackel. Charlottesville: University of Virginia Press, Rotunda, 2008. http://gwpapers.virginia.edu/digitaledition.html.

————. *The Writings of George Washington from the Original Manuscript Sources, 1745–1799*. Edited by John C. Fitzpatrick and David Maydole Matteson. 39 vols. Washington, D.C.: U.S. Government Printing Office, 1931–1944.

Whitlock, Brand. *La Fayette*. Vol. 1. New York: D. Appleton, 1929.

Whittemore, Charles P. *A General of the Revolution: John Sullivan of New Hampshire*. New York: Columbia University Press, 1961.

Wickwire, Mary, and Franklin Wickwire. *Cornwallis: The Imperial Years*. Chapel Hill: University of North Carolina Press, 1980.

Wilkinson, James. *Memoirs of My Own Times*. Philadelphia: Abraham Small, 1816.

Willcox, William B. *Portrait of a General: Sir Henry Clinton in the War of Independence*. New York: Alfred A. Knopf, 1964.

Wood, W. J. *Battles of the Revolutionary War, 1775–1781*. Chapel Hill, N.C.: Algonquin Books, 1990.

Woodward, W. E. *Lafayette*. New York: Farrar & Rinehart, 1938.

————. *Tom Paine: America's Godfather, 1737–1809*. New York: E. P. Dutton, 1945.

Wrong, George M. *Washington and His Comrades in Arms: A Chronicle of the War of Independence*. New Haven, Conn.: Yale University Press, 1921.

Young, Eleanor. *Forgotten Patriot: Robert Morris*. New York: Macmillan, 1950.

INDEX

Louisbourg, Canada, 93

Loyalists, 6, 74–75, 78, 105, 111, 134–135, 203, 209. *See also* Tories

loyalty oaths: form of, 245n7; in New York, 111–112, 200, 239n39, 245n7; in Rhode Island, 105, 245n7; at Valley Forge, 142, 145

Lyons, France, 36

Macaroni club, 44

Macchiavelli, Nicolò, 150

Macleane, Lauglin, 53

Malta, 36

Manalapan, N.J., 167

Manhattan, N.Y., 98, 108, 123–127, 147, 155, 137, 180, 210, 214, 230n11

Manwarring, Mrs., 35, 60

marriage, 16, 22, 59–60, 180, 232n20

Martinique, 90, 93, 236n4, 237n4

Maryland, xi, 15, 39, 66, 68, 70, 113, 140, 144, 195, 198, 218–220, 227; Maryland Committee of Safety, 240n43; Maryland militia, 236n26

Maryland Journal and Baltimore Advertiser, 192, 250n1

Mason, George, 68

Massachusetts, 2–3, 11–12, 72–73, 101, 103, 106, 195, 244n47; Massachusetts Committee of Safety, 4; Massachusetts militia, 3, 19; Massachusetts Provincial Congress, 103

Maxwell, General William, 155, 159, 167–168, 170, 172

McDougall, Alexander, 105, 238n16

McFingal (Trumbull), 248n25

McHenry, Doctor, 187

McHenry, James, 227

Meade, Lieutenant Colonel, 248n19

members of Continental Congress, 1–2, 4–5, 61, 68, 70, 80, 138, 189, 194, 196, 226, 236n26

"Memorandum" (Lee), 150, 198, 246n26, 251n16

Mercer, Brigadier General Hugh, 12, 89, 94–96

Mercer, Captain John Francis, 164, 221, 227, 248n19, 249n10

Messasagas, 28

Middle Colonies, 150–151, 157, 198

military colony, 38, 46, 233n17, 233n19

militia, 12, 46, 94–95, 236n25, 243nn25–26; in the French and Indian War, 79, 248; in the Revolutionary War, 80, 121, 127, 170, 211, 214, 243n45

Minghini, Giuseppe, 55, 58, 137, 148, 204, 206, 234n36

Mingo warriors, 15

Minorca, 36

Mississippi River, 10, 28, 57, 234n1

Mohawks/Mohocks, 13, 16, 21, 54, 58, 230n7, 231n16

Moldavia, 36, 45

Molly Pitcher, 225–226, 248n22

Monckton, Henry, 156, 231n6

money issues. *See* finances and financial difficulties

Monmouth battlefield, 48, 185. *See also* Battle of Monmouth

Monmouth County, N.J., 248n17

Monmouth Courthouse, N.J., 152, 163, 168, 228, 247n13

Monongahela River, 18, 15, 18, 88, 70, 90, 91, 94, 230n3

Monroe, James, 226

Montcalm, Marquis de, 18, 108

Montgomery, Brigadier General Richard, 79, 89–90, 92–96, 108, 229n6

Montreal, Canada, 10, 22, 27, 93

Moore, George, x, 145–147, 210, 245n6

morasses, at Monmouth, 160, 163, 167–168, 170–175, 184, 188–189, 221–222, 225–226

Morgan, Colonel Daniel, 90, 155, 159, 163–165, 170, 181, 227–228, 247n16

Morocco, 193

Morris, Gouvernour, 206

Morris, Robert: correspondence with, 56, 101, 105, 108, 110, 206, 234nn35 36, 235n39, 237n1, 237n3, 238n6, 239n30, 239n33, 241n1, 251n19, 251n31; as financier, 58, 83, 137, 204; as friend and supporter, 55, 111, 251n16

Morristown, N.J., 131, 133, 154

mother. *See* Lee, Isabella

Moultrie, Colonel William, 116–119

Mount Vernon (Washington's estate), 70, 91

Mount Washington. *See* Fort Washington

"Mr. Lee's Plan." *See* Lee's Plan

"my Country," 197

Native Americans, 10, 11, 13, 15–19, 21–24, 28, 60, 66, 67, 93–94, 229n2. *See also specific tribes*

Native American wife. *See* American Indian wife

Newark, N.J., 131

New Brunswick, N.J., 131, 133, 180–181, 243n45

New England, 2, 71–72, 78, 111, 126, 140, 148, 205

New Hampshire, 73, 227

ABOUT THE AUTHOR

Dominick Mazzagetti is the author of *"True Jersey Blues": The Civil War Correspondence of Lucien A. Voorhees and William Mackenzie Thompson.* He wrote a history column for the *Hunterdon County Democrat* for five years, detailing the stories of Hunterdon County and the lives of its people from the earliest settlements to the present day. He comes to this avocation with a background in law and banking and a deep love and respect for history.

Mazzagetti graduated from Rutgers University in 1969 and Cornell Law School in 1972. He clerked for the Chief Justice of the New Jersey Supreme Court and practiced law for many years in the state. In 1982, he joined the administration of Governor Thomas Kean as deputy commissioner of banking and most recently served as president of RomAsia Bank. He served for several years on the Hunterdon County Cultural and Heritage Commission and has spoken before historical societies throughout the state on the role of the New Jersey Fifteenth Regiment in the Civil War.